BEDOUIN POETS OF THE NAFŪD DESERT

LETTER FROM THE GENERAL EDITOR

The Library of Arabic Literature makes available Arabic editions and English translations of significant works of Arabic literature, with an emphasis on the seventh to nineteenth centuries. The Library of Arabic Literature thus includes texts from the pre-Islamic era to the  cusp of the modern period, and encompasses a wide range of genres, including poetry, poetics, fiction, religion, philosophy, law, science, travel writing, history, and historiography.

Books in the series are edited and translated by internationally recognized scholars. They are published in parallel-text and English-only editions in both print and electronic formats. PDFs of Arabic editions are available for free download. The Library of Arabic Literature also publishes distinct scholarly editions with critical apparatus.

The Library encourages scholars to produce authoritative Arabic editions, accompanied by modern, lucid English translations, with the ultimate goal of introducing Arabic's rich literary heritage to a general audience of readers as well as to scholars and students.

The publications of the Library of Arabic Literature are generously supported by Tamkeen under the NYU Abu Dhabi Research Institute Award G1003 and are published by NYU Press.

Philip F. Kennedy
General Editor, Library of Arabic Literature

Bedouin Poets of the Nafūd Desert

BY

Khalaf Abū Zwayyid,
ʿAdwān al-Hirbīd, and
ʿAjlān ibn Rmāl

TRANSLATED BY
Marcel Kurpershoek

FOREWORD BY
Rocío Quispe Agnoli

VOLUME EDITOR
Philip F. Kennedy

NEW YORK UNIVERSITY PRESS
New York

NEW YORK UNIVERSITY PRESS
New York

Library of Congress Cataloging-in-Publication Data

Names: Abū Zūwayd, Khalf, 1844-1942, author. | Hirbīd, ʿAdwān, –1896, author. |
    Ibn Rmāl, ʿAjlān, author. | Kurpershoek, P. M., editor, translator.
Title: Bedouin poets of the Nafūd desert / Khalaf Abū Zwayyid, ʿAdwān al-Hirbīd,
    and ʿAjlān ibn Rmāl ; edited and translated by Marcel Kupershoek, volume editor
    Phillip F. Kennedy.
Other titles: Library of Arabic literature.
Description: New York City : New York University Press, 2025. | Series: Library of
    Arabic literature | Includes bibliographical references and index.
Identifiers: LCCN 2024052771 (print) | LCCN 2024052772 (ebook) | ISBN 9781479840656
    (paperback) | ISBN 9781479840663 (ebook) | ISBN 9781479840670 (ebook)
Subjects: LCSH: Dialect poetry, Arabic—Saudi Arabia—Translations into English. |
    Arabic poetry—Bedouin authors—Translations into English. | Arabic poetry—19th
    century—Translations into English. | Arabic poetry—20th century—Translations into
    English. | LCGFT: Poetry.
Classification: LCC PJ8005.65.E54 B43 2025 (print) | LCC PJ8005.65.E54 (ebook) |
    DDC 892.7/150895382—dc23/eng/20250531
LC record available at https://lccn.loc.gov/2024052771
LC ebook record available at https://lccn.loc.gov/2024052772

This book is printed on acid-free paper, and its binding materials are chosen for strength
and durability. We strive to use environmentally responsible suppliers and materials to
the greatest extent possible in publishing our books.

The manufacturer's authorized representative in the EU for product safety is Mare
Nostrum Group B.V., Mauritskade 21D, 1091 GC Amsterdam, The Netherlands.
Email: gpsr@mare-nostrum.co.uk.

Series design and composition by Nicole Hayward.

Typeset in Adobe Text

Manufactured in the United States of America

10 9 8 7 6 5 4 3 2 1

To my brothers, Ernest Kurpershoek and Eric Kurpershoek

Contents

ʿAJLĀN IBN RMĀL / 189

ABBREVIATIONS

CA	classical Arabic
cf.	compare
f. pl.	feminine plural
HA*	Hess Archive
lit.	literally
n.	noun
pl.	plural
sg.	singular
v., vv.	verse(s) (a single line of Arabic, translated as a couplet)

Foreword

ROCÍO QUISPE AGNOLI

In the early twentieth century, a blind man in Ḥā'il, Saudi Arabia, asked to be brought before Prince ʿAbd al-ʿAzīz ibn Musāʿid. The prince was attending a study session with a group of men of the Ikhwān, a strict religious vanguard for the House of Saud, discussing the words and teachings of Prophet Muḥammad, and did not wish to be interrupted. However, the old blind man insisted on lauding the prince with the best he could offer from his art: some verses he had composed to honor him. The prince argued that the time for verses had passed and that in this more puritanical era, he and his men had more important matters to attend to. Nevertheless, the old man insisted on being heard and responded: "It is poetry, not just verses." (§1.4) The prince let him recite. When the bard had finished, there were no words of praise, only silence. The silence was, however, a prelude to acknowledgment. A few minutes later, the prince ordered his men to give the poet a strong camel, one that could fetch water for his grove. In this way, even in a new social and political environment that frowned on some traditions as frivolous or even irreligious, the prince acknowledged the poetic skills of Khalaf Abū Zwayyid, one of three Bedouin poets whose lyric voices and rhythmic prose are featured in this volume.

This episode exemplifies the life of the Bedouin poet through the lens of his craft and provides insights into Bedouin poetry of the late nineteenth and early twentieth centuries. It would be difficult not to see the links between the works of these poets and those of artists of the spoken word in other literary traditions. In medieval Spain, for example, traveling minstrels or jongleurs (*juglares*) shared their songs in public squares and inns in exchange for a few cents, wine, food, or other rewards. The Spanish word "juglar" comes from the Latin "jocularis, joculator," which refers to a person who makes jokes. Their service was to entertain their audience by reciting popular tales. At the same time, they contributed to the dissemination of oral traditions about popular heroes and anti-heroes. One of the best-known examples of the jongleurs' craft or minstrelsy (*mester de juglaría*) is *Poema de Mío Cid*, an anonymous epic poem composed between 1140 and 1207. It tells the story of Rodrigo Díaz de Vivar (d. 1099), known as *El Cid*, a Castilian hero who, despite being banished by the king, loyally served him during the period of conflict between Castile and the *Taifas* (Muslim principalities and kingdoms) of Al-Andalus in the Iberian Peninsula. An exiled nobleman and warrior, Rodrigo regains royal favor with his valiant acts. In the oral art of Spanish minstrelsy, music, performance, and poetry converge to form a cohesive whole. As in the works of the traveling minstrels of medieval Spain, in the oral art of Bedouin poets Khalaf Abū Zwayyid (d. 1942), ʿAdwān al-Hirbīd (d. 1896), and ʿAjlān ibn Rmāl (fl. early 20th century), narratives and verses converge to provide solace, teaching, praise, reflections on life in the desert, and expressions of love.

These poets used their creative words to honor rulers, shaykhs, and beautiful women, among other characters of the Nafūd Desert. Their performances and recitations were usually met with praise and reward, the most desirable of which was a camel. In the exchange between Abū Zwayyid and the prince mentioned above, the poetic performance is not met with the usual praise but instead with silence. This situation surprises the bard and sheds light on the changing times for the genre, its characters, its artists, and its listeners. On one side are the men who accompany the prince, the Ikhwān, who tried to make the Bedouins settle around the sedentary populations of the Peninsula, and who do not tolerate the poet and his craft. On the other side, however, is the poet, who is ultimately rewarded for his art.

In the twentieth century, social change seemed inevitable, but links to the past could not be ignored and poetry, a necessity for the soul, had to perdure; as Abū Zwayyid later says, it is a vital feature of human nature: "such verse is sweeter than a cool cascade of water." The choice of the word *shakhālīl* ("cascade"), pleasantly sweet and refreshing, and signaling a life well-lived, invites the English reader to ponder the crucial role of poetry in the desert akin to the continuous flow of an element, water, fundamental for human life. Many twentieth-century Latin American poets regard "cascada" as one of the most beautiful words of the Spanish language. Its beauty relies on its sonority (an onomatopoeic sound that imitates the waterfall) and its connotations of flowing energy, birth, and the beginning of life. Similarly, in his praise of Saʿūd Abū Khashm, Abū Zwayyid writes that much-expected rainfall comes from "God of life-bringing clouds." (§12.1) Water is the medium from which life began on the planet billions of years ago, when Earth's surface was covered with oceans that were the wellspring for all life. One cannot help but think of the verse of the Bedouin poets as a cascade of fresh water that instills life.

In the works of these Bedouin poets, one can also read a criticism of those who question the nomadic way of life and who would prefer that longstanding oral performance be transformed into "modern" genres, eventually to be converted to ink on paper. This critique reveals the fear that oral poetry, which is inseparable from the Bedouins' journeys through the desert, will lose its value with the imposition of modern ways of making literature.

These wordsmiths, artists of the recited word, also share a concern for preserving moral integrity. ʿAjlān ibn Rmāl, for example, denounces the ravages of modernity on traditional Bedouin society. For this poet, who escapes with his family to what many consider an empty and barren space, the Nafūd Desert is a safe place, a refuge. In ʿAdwān al-Hirbīd's verses, the lamentation in the face of multiple adversities—the death of his brothers, an arduous journey through the desert to a settlement that turns out to be abandoned and empty—is characterized by a painful plea reminiscent of the indigenous chronicler Guamán Poma de Ayala in early seventeenth century colonial Peru. In a world exposed to cultural transformation, to a point they see as devastating, the lament for a world now lost is a recurring motif. Traditional social distinctions begin to disintegrate, and the world is turned upside down (*mundo al revés*) as Guamán Poma also noted when describing the displacement and lot of the Indigenous peoples under Spanish rule. In the face of desolation and loss, both authors, ʿAdwān al-Hirbīd and Guamán Poma, lament loudly their situation, raising their prayers and pleas to God.

On the other hand, both Abū Zwayyid and ʿAdwān al-Hirbīd address their children in their poetry to educate and advise them. Zwayyid tries to teach patience to his son, while al-Hirbīd speaks of an ungrateful and selfish child. These poets' parental admonishments bring to mind the magical realist writings of Mexican author Juan Rulfo (1917-86), in which he addresses the theme of the indifferent, ungrateful, and selfish son as a resistance or challenge to the father's authority, with dire consequences. For example, in Rulfo's story "No oyes ladrar a los perros" ("Do You Hear the Dogs Barking?"), a father crosses the countryside at night carrying his wounded son on his back on his way to the nearest village to seek the assistance of a doctor. He repeatedly asks his son, who has been shot in a fight, if he can hear the dogs barking—a sign that the village is near. Confronted by his father's painful memories, the young man weeps quietly. When the sound of barking dogs finally emerges, the father discovers that his son is dead, his body gone limp. His final lament mourns the son's death but also his failure to sustain the father's faint hope that could have saved him. The end of Rulfo's story contrasts with al-Hirbīd's lyric, in which adversities become a source of strength despite his son's ingratitude.

Apart from dealing with painful themes in poetry, such as ungrateful children and the loss of traditions in the face of the inevitable arrival of modernity, all three poets aspired to entertain through poetic dialogues and friendly oral duels. Abū Zwayyid approaches heroic characters with picaresque tones; ʿAdwān al-Hirbīd celebrates moments of joy and God's creation; ʿAjlān ibn Rmāl converses with his interlocutors while entertaining them with the delivery of his verses.

The poetry of all three praises and critiques, comforts and/or gives advice, reflects philosophically about life, and draws portraits of loved ones. Abū Zwayyid tests his wit when criticizing Muḥammad ibn Rashīd, ruler of the Rashīdī kingdom in northern Arabia, the most powerful prince in his time. But he also praises a shaykh's strength and his effective handling of camels when the poet calls him "rider of a fast, rugged desert crosser." (§12.1) Love and admiration for camels are ever present in Bedouin poetry. So is admiration and praise of the woman who becomes the center of attention and desire.

In the works of all three poets, we read how Bedouin women expressed their desire to be celebrated through lyric recitation and songs. As the translator, Marcel Kurpershoek, notes, Bedouin women in these poems do not remain anonymous: they are identified by name—Khaznah al-Fiḍīl, daughter of Ibn Rmāl; Mkīdah, daughter of Jamʿān al-Ghēthī; Tarfah, daughter of Falāḥ ibn Fāliḥ al-Shlāgī; Mnīrah, daughter of Zēdān ibn Bshayyir; Khansā, daughter of al-Jimʿī, among others—and are active subjects who demand to be delivered poetry of praise. In turn, they are willing to offer rewards to the poets, even love and a life with them. Such lauding of women's beauty and character converges with what is called "portrait poetry" in Spanish American Baroque literature, in which the poetic voice exalts the physical qualities and noble character of the female subject depicted in the poem. She is thus an ideal individual to be admired and with whom the poet falls in love.

The Bedouin poets' lyrical representation of the Nafūd as a space of intersections and crossroads, a refuge with its own social and economic codes that experiences conflict in the face of an encroaching modernity, transcends a stereotypical view of the desert as an empty and barren place. It is a space in which oral poetry and storytelling flourish, delivering advice, musing on love, admiring camels, and lamenting loss and change. It is a reader's privilege to look into this universe through the gaze of its poets.

Rocío Quispe Agnoli
Michigan State University

Acknowledgments

The fieldwork and research that went into this edition and translation would not have been possible without a Humanities Research Fellowship offered by the New York University Abu Dhabi Institute. I am deeply grateful for the imaginative commitment shown by the institute's leadership of Dr. Reindert Falkenburg and Dr. Martin Klimke, and the program's associate director, Alexandra Sandu.

Dr. Saad Sowayan is not only the foremost authority on Arabian culture, but also a dear friend and a source of inspiration and guidance. As the collector, editor, and interpreter of a vast amount of oral Bedouin heritage, including this volume's Arabic text, he has unfailingly and with enviable patience answered my countless questions regarding interpretation. His scholarly presence has enabled my efforts to come to fruition. During my years of research in 2015–22, I was overwhelmed by the famous hospitality and ready interest shown to visitors by the people of the Nafūd Desert. This edition would not have been possible without the learned help of my principal informant, Ibrāhīm ibn Suʿayyid al-Hamazānī of the Aslam division of Shammar. We have been close friends since a visit to Ḥāʾil in 1988, when his father, the renowned poet and transmitter Suʿayyid ibn Fuhayd al-Dūkhī al-Hamazānī, asked me to explain a poem with a particularly difficult rhyme, composed for the occasion to test my seriousness of purpose. I always found a warm welcome in the majlis of Nazzāl ibn Muḥammad ibn Suʿayyid al-Shammarī and his friend Aḥmad ʿAbdallah Khalaf al-Shaghdalī, who in their turn enlisted the assistance of other aficionados through Twitter. I am also grateful to Dr. Khalif al-Shammarī of Ḥā'il University for sharing his expertise in modern history and taking me to visit one of the last surviving sources of Sowayan's recordings, the Bedouin poet and transmitter Riḍā ibn Ṭārif al-Shammarī at the ancient wells of Līnah, before he passed away in 2016.

Through these years, I was fortunate to find in the King Faisal Center for Research and Islamic Studies in Riyadh a home away from home, and I formed an abiding attachment to this deeply humanist scholarly institution.

Introduction

Ensconced behind vast deserts and the granite barrier of the Ajā mountain range, the town of Ḥāʾil in northern Arabia, the capital of the Ibn Rashīd dynasty (1834–1921), was a magnet for visitors of every kind.[1] A hub of long-distance desert transportation, the province's core area of Jabal Shammar (Shammar Mountain) offered safety and a spirit of tolerance and civility. Its strategic location and influence attracted caravans of traders and pilgrims, tribal shaykhs, lords of Najdī oasis towns, European travelers and scholars, illiterate Bedouin poets, and learned Arabs. Marvelously attuned to the customs and way of life of the Bedouin, the majlis of the princely court, described with excitement by European explorers, was an arena of choice for poets vying for preeminence and favor with the rulers. Poetic excellence was rewarded, and performing for a discriminating and critical audience stirred competitors to give it their all. Many of the Ibn Rashīd princes were poets in their own right and some are counted among Arabia's greatest bards, their verses cited with admiration by aficionados until today. For these reasons, the court's culture radiated over many hundreds of miles, and the role of the Ibn Rashīd in the domain of Arabian tribal and Bedouin culture was similar to that of the court of al-Ḥīrah for poetry in pre-Islamic times.

Over the centuries, tribes have come and gone, merged, and transformed. Critically, though, the ecosystem; pastoral and oasis economy; means of cultivation, irrigation, and transportation;

and traditions and customs embodied in the so-called desert code have in their essentials continued as before. In the nineteenth century, much of the fighting was still done with matchlocks and cold weapons. Storytellers dwell on quaint habits such as the poet Abū Zwayyid walking about armed with a sword. Toward the end of the century, the pace of change picked up markedly. The three Bedouin poets whose verse and lore are presented in this volume lived to see, or at least hear of, modernity's accelerating encroachment. Deadly firearms made raiding less entertaining as a chivalrous sport.[2] Muḥammad ibn Rashīd, in whose time the principality expanded to include the dominions of the House of Saud in Riyadh and the Bedouin culture of the north, had seen how a telegraph machine functioned in Baghdad.[3] The text makes mention of the extension of the Ottoman railway from Damascus to Medina in Hejaz Province and the possession of automobiles by some shaykhs in Syria and Mesopotamia in the run-up to the First World War. New anxieties crept in, and more than ever the sands of the Nafūd Desert seemed a refuge from unwelcome events beyond, summed up in the poet ʿAjlān ibn Rmāl's nostalgic sigh (§52.6, v. 1):

My home, sanctuary from telegraph and rail:
I am not cut out to be a maker of bombs.[4]

Even more profound was the impact of another development that shook Bedouin society, and its poets in particular. The Ikhwān, "the Brothers," the religiously motivated armed vanguard that laid the ground for the restoration of Saudi supremacy, created deep fissures in tribal society, pitting clans and even family members against one another.[5] The easygoing old ways of the Bedouin were frowned upon and adherence to the strict tenets of puritanical Wahhabism were harshly enforced. Tobacco, men's long tresses, music, poetry, and a certain tolerance for more informal religious practices fell by the wayside. Traditional social distinctions and respect for inherited or conventionally acquired prestige were scoffed at and spurned.[6] ʿAjlān's despair at being witness to this cultural devastation is echoed by transmitters decades later in nostalgic offhand remarks about "times when truthfulness still counted for something" (§2.3).[7] In poetry, the hallowed motif of a world gone topsy-turvy gained a new poignancy (§49.8, v. 2):

> Ibn Saʿūd has curbed warhorses and chiefs;
>> nobles became servants; bastards went on a spree.

Unable to conceal his disgust, ʿAjlān burst out (§52.6, vv. 4–5):

> Escaping riffraff, shirt hems smeared with shit,
>> blockheads wrapped about with pompous turbans,
> I put ten days of riding between me and them,
>> marching at a grueling pace deep into the night.

And in derision of a purportedly religious thuggery that trampled over the old Bedouin virtues, he added: "Ugh, God help you, conflicted by double ancestry" (§52.6, v. 8)—that is, the generous-spirited ancestors of the bloodline and those who inculcated the new doctrine and "seek Paradise by slaughtering their relatives" (§52.7, v. 9).[8] Like many in the Arabian north, who were close to areas that remained outside the Saudi reach and were already in the habit of migrating and traveling there, ʿAjlān took his family first to the Nafūd sands ("lofty dunes, our hideout from those fanatics"), and from there toward the Syrian desert (§52.5, v. 3).

ʿAjlān, the third poet in this volume, whose oeuvre is slighter than those of his two fellow poets, has left us with the most explicit denunciations and descriptions of the havoc wreaked on traditional Bedouin society, an imposition of homegrown modernity more fatal than any other blow it received since the pre-Islamic Kingdom of al-Ḥīrah. Yet, in the end, he grudgingly makes his peace and pays obeisance to the new governor of Ḥāʾil, a member of the House of Saud, as had Abū Zwayyid. Implicit in their conversations with the new ruler is the notion that Ibn Saud has the final word. Also, given the fact that the House of Saud had a broader understanding of society and dictated how far the Ikhwān were allowed to go, these poets and others recognized that its princes might offer some protection against excesses deemed harmful to social harmony. It is impossible to tell whether the measure of forbearance shown by the Saudi governor is a gloss put on events by transmitters of the lore, or whether it was truly experienced by the poets at the time.[9] In any case, it chimes with a widespread opinion in Saudi Arabia concerning the existence of an unwritten compact between rulers and society. Differences with the Ikhwān came to a head in the Saudi showdown with their most hardline elements, who rebelled against the limits imposed on them in 1929.

ʿADWĀN AL-HIRBĪD

The poet ʿAdwān al-Hirbīd cuts a very different figure from Abū Zwayyid and ʿAjlān, hewing closer to the poets of the "Romantic School," grouped around Ibn Sbayyil in the small town of Nifī and other parts of ʿĀliyat Najd (the High Najd), south of Ḥāʾil, beyond al-Qasīm Province. More modest in attitude and ambition than his two fellow poets, yet more subtle and intricate in his verse, al-Hirbīd demands to be seen as an ordinary person, someone who has no business ingratiating himself with the high and mighty. On one occasion, he was chided by the members of his tribe for turning a deaf ear to an invitation by Muḥammad ibn Rashīd. The excuse he gave was that answering the call might not go down well with the ruler at the time, Bandar ibn Ṭalāl.[10]

Yet al-Hirbīd shows no trace of timidity when slugging it out in verbal matches with other poets. In such duels, he invariably comes out as the hardest hitter, whose final punch flattens his opponent with a knockout. The pièce de résistance is a section that starts with his ire at a poem mocking how he treated his palm trees. His detractor speaks scathingly of him for giving his palms female names. A concatenation of events leads to a climax that gives birth to one of the most famous poems in northern Arabia, which goes by the name of al-Shēkhah, "Lady Shaykh" (§49). It opens with a furious outburst against two camel nomads of his clan, one of them the poet who had impersonated his disconsolate palm trees. They accuse him of cowardice because he, as a sheepherder whose animals have little tolerance for water deprivation, urges the shaykh to lead the tribe and herds home from the spring pastures in the Nafūd at the onset of the hot season. Adding insult to injury, they call him out for being a tobacco addict who hankers after a smoke at home, and a poet who, like all poets, is only talk and no action, conveniently forgetting that they are poets themselves. Al-Shēkhah is especially significant and unique for including a kind of *fihrist* of Arabian oral culture: a catalog of famous poets who were also respected men of action, be they early classical or Nabaṭī poets, Bedouin or oasis dwellers (§49.19, vv. 16–31).[11]

Apart from the gripping histrionics of dueling poets, the narrative leaves no doubt that the episode stems from a pastoral divide that runs through much of the lore connected with al-Hirbīd and others. In the class-conscious society of Arabian Bedouin, camel nomads are regarded as superior to herders of sheep and goats.[12] Al-Hirbīd is pictured as belonging to the latter category. It is at the root of all his troubles: in the transmitters' masterful telling, whenever he joins the true Bedouin on a migration to a pastoral idyll of desert meadows, carpeted with herbage after plentiful rains, his rhapsodic elation gives way to melancholy. It bursts into crisis, then ends in sobering catharsis and poise regained: his powerful artistic and intellectual voice overcomes his lower status in the group. In the lead-up to al-Shēkhah and another episode of migration to spring pastures, he and his adopted son Jrēs keep falling behind, unnerved and exhausted, while his camel-owning fellow tribesmen cover the distance in a breeze, are having a good time and doing some falcon hunting as the women set up camp in late afternoon, easily making do with camels' milk in the absence of water. At the same time, al-Hirbīd seems particularly attached to his groves of date palms, and he has been loaned sheep by his better-off kinsmen. The pros and cons of raising camels versus small cattle and of Bedouin mobility versus the settled existence of palm cultivation are spun out in detail in his poems and lore.

In the oral tradition, such differences in lifestyle make for never-ending exchanges of poetry comparing one to the other and discussing their respective merits and disadvantages. In this case, one also suspects that al-Hirbīd's camel-versus-sheep predicament has been emphasized as part of his poetic persona: a struggling, hard-pressed underdog who against all odds employs his acumen, imaginative art, and psychological insight to emerge victorious—or at least with his aura of deeply felt humanism enhanced. For these poets, preserving one's moral integrity is an overriding concern.[13] Al-Hirbīd's skinny sheep are part of a running gag, including his orphan child's disdain for taking care of the lowly animals and al-Hirbīd's lines of verse with an impersonation of his adoptive son's point of view.

The setting for the sheep motif is thrown into sharp relief in his opening selections. Having married the sole surviving wife of his murdered brothers from a sense of duty, the poet takes it upon himself to care for and educate her child, Jrēs. His efforts come to naught. When Jrēs is old enough to herd the sheep given on loan by fellow clansmen, he is taunted by boys pasturing camels—sheep and goats are traditionally tended by girls—and as a result refuses to carry out this chore. Obdurate and thickheaded, he asks for the impossible—camels—and from that moment on leaves it to his uncle to drive the sheep out in the morning. The poet, seeing his careful child-rearing and character-building efforts in shambles, pours his heart out. As in other instances of initially failed parenting in Nabaṭī poetry, the son will later emerge as his father's pillar of strength on a journey with camel nomads in the Nafūd Desert, as mentioned above. In al-Hirbīd's humorous impersonation of poetic dialogue, Jrēs turns the tables on his stepfather, whom he mocks for his fruitless amorous pursuit of much younger girls.

As a lyrical poet, al-Hirbīd is held in special esteem for his ghazals, or love poetry, with many original touches inspired by the desert and oasis environment. His style is noteworthy for its shorter versions of the extended simile, or "submerged similes," in which the subject underlying the comparison is not even mentioned: the poet counts on the audience recognizing it from the imagery of the comparison (for example, §17.5, v. 6). One poem, §41, is composed in a unique long meter. The poet shows a philosophical bent in his contemplation of Creation when, an avid hunter, he opens the belly of a bustard and finds other creatures, each smaller than the previous one, like a set of matryoshka dolls: the Lord has made "eat or be eaten" the rule of His universe (§43).

As the narrative progresses, the poet fights his gloom regarding his project to educate his son, and shows a combative side. Jrēs soon comes in for biting sarcasm and scathing remarks. More serious skirmishes ensue when the poet locks horns with his equals, tearing into poetic opponents with rebuttals that leave their reputations in shreds—figuratively speaking, because the verbal rough-and-tumble might be in jest. From the picture given by the storytellers, al-Hirbīd emerges as a complex, multifaceted artistic personality. No dashing raider, he appears genuinely, and sometimes jokingly, introspective, and self-critical to an extent rarely seen in Arabian poetry. In a modest way, he cuts a fatherly figure. Though generally unassuming, he jealously guards his pride and self-esteem, yet he is also pleasure-loving and intensely social. Romantically inclined, he sensually and delicately warbles of his love when he is at ease. In a pensive mood, he gives free rein to his wandering thoughts. In his dialogues, he engages in tongue-in-cheek and lighthearted banter, punctuated with melodramatic touches. When slighted or made the butt of flippant remarks, he is capable of devilish outbursts of fury. His lyrical verse keeps historical events at bay and is free from Abū Zwayyid's penchant for name-dropping. Faced with the dilemmas common to all humanity, the likable al-Hirbīd finds his way, whether cheerful or saddened, always forging ahead with unfailing psychological insight, and guided by his art.

Khalaf Abū Zwayyid

Khalaf Abū Zwayyid is the most famous of the three poets in the volume. Some of his poetry has been preserved in manuscript, whereas the works of the other two poets have survived exclusively in oral tradition.[14] His artistic persona stands in stark contrast to the portrayal of al-Hirbīd. Throughout his career, Abū Zwayyid consorted with the highest aristocracy of tribal shaykhs and frequented their majlises. He gained notoriety for his barbs aimed at the most powerful prince of Arabia in his time, Muḥammad ibn Rashīd. The insults were prickly because of his unabashed flattery of Ibn Shaʿlān, head of the clan of chiefs of the Rwalah tribe (who, according to the narrative, murdered al-Hirbīd's brothers and their families).[15] As a relative of the Ibn Rakhīṣ shaykhs of Shammar, who had played a pivotal role in establishing the rule of Ibn Rashīd, moving in the corridors of power came naturally to Abū Zwayyid. Though not himself one of the clan's shaykhs, belonging to the Ibn Rakhīṣ was sufficient claim to desert nobility.

In Abū Zwayyid's poems, set within the narratives, history unfolds, from the pinnacle of political grandeur and flourishing of Bedouin culture during Muḥammad ibn Rashīd's reign to the sordid, cruel, and at times tragicomical spectacle of prolonged decline, and finally to the House of Ibn Rashīd's demise without a whimper at the hands of Ibn Saud. Abū Zwayyid is shown sparring and jesting with the great on familiar terms. The circles in which he moves include not only Ibn Rashīd, but some of the brightest luminaries in the Bedouin universe: the shaykhs of the ʿAnazah confederation, Ibn Shaʿlān of the Rwalah and Ibn Hadhdhāl of the ʿAmārāt; he also eulogizes the Jarbā shaykhs of Shammar in Iraq. Embedded in his ode to Ibn Shaʿlān is a reference to his "uselessness" to women craving real men, a none-too-subtle allusion to Muḥammad ibn Rashīd's infertility. This broadside was especially injurious as it came in the context of gushing praise for his host, Ibn Shaʿlān, a "stud," dreamt of by beauties (§4.1, v. 12), and for Ibn Mhēd, the shaykh of the Fidʿān of ʿAnazah, the father of Ibn Shaʿlān's wife Turkiyyah. For this reason, the poem earned him an outpouring of scorn from his opponents, all well-known poets, who rushed to the defense of Ibn Rashīd.[16] But when Abū Zwayyid was staying with Ibn Hadhdhāl, and Ibn Shaʿlān came on a visit, he told them that he rated Ibn Hadhdhāl's hospitality higher than that of the visitor. On his return from Ibn Hadhdhāl, and through the good offices of Ibn Rakhīṣ, he made his entry into the courtyard of the Barzān castle, dressed in a white shroud, to the astonishment of the crowds of visitors.[17] Once Ibn Rashīd and his brutal cousin Ḥmūd became aware of the weird visitor's identity, they flew into a rage. Ḥmūd demanded his execution on the spot, wishing to "taste [his] blood" (§10.3).[18] But Abū Zwayyid pleaded that his key verse had been distorted and made offensive by his enemies. As proof, he produced the correct wording of the verse that extolled the virtues of Ibn Rashīd beyond even those of Ibn Shaʿlān.[19] A slave cut off his forelock and Ibn Rashīd dismissed him.[20]

Again and again, Abū Zwayyid is shown pushing his luck and displaying a fondness for verbal brinkmanship. The narrators portray him as a gambler who is tempted to see how far he can go, relying on his quick wit and powers of repartee. It is not necessarily the case that he had such an irreverent attitude toward shaykhs generally held in awe. Rather, as can often be seen in the anecdotes of the tenth-century *Book of Songs* (*Kitāb al-Aghānī*), his effrontery has become a trademark of his poetic persona, as has his ugliness, which seemed to have made him even more attractive to many Bedouin women of high birth. As a poet, he has the knack of using women's fascination with him to advantage—and women are shown by the transmitters as being better at perceiving truth behind outward appearances than men.[21] Both Ibn Shaʿlān and Ibn Hadhdhāl call on him to persuade their runaway wives, who are sisters, to return to them and their children and accept a reconciliation (§§6–7). He is richly rewarded by both women for his adulation of their beauty and, especially, for his paeans to their father, whose name is synonymous with boundless generosity in the desert interior of Arabia, Syria, and Iraq. Abū Zwayyid's powers of persuasion and extensive knowledge of precedent also make him an invincible opponent in cases brought before tribal judges who give opinions in accordance with Bedouin customary law. While at Ibn Shaʿlān's camp, he was called upon as a legal expert in his own right to solve a case that threatened to descend into an armed brawl between sons of Ibn Shaʿlān (§5).

As in the chain of events leading to the composition of al-Hirbīd's al-Shēkhah poem, an unintentional slight, here prompted by Abū Zwayyid's repellent physiognomy, sets in motion a sequence of poems and attracts female attention until his future wife comes in search of him. At her suggestion, she and the poet are given permission by her father to marry and spend three nights together in a small wedding tent on condition that the marriage will be dissolved if she is not pregnant after their days of seclusion. She becomes the mother of his son Dikhīl, who causes as much disappointment to his father as Jrēs to al-Hirbīd. The counsel and exhortations in Abū Zwayyid's verses to Dikhīl do not bear fruit. The son brings shame to his father by losing a case in a court of customary law, whereas Abū Zwayyid had always won his legal battles. Again, none of this is to be taken literally. Like Māniʿ, the son of the early-eighteenth-century poet Ḥmēdān al-Shwēʿir, the characters of Jrēs and Dikhīl serve as foils that allow their makers to present verses of wisdom and spew their anger at the world's iniquities.[22]

Abū Zwayyid's poetry often brings material gain, though that is rarely stated as the principal aim. For example, he is showered with costly presents for his successful practice of marriage counseling. In the general tableau sketched by the transmitters, it is a by-product of his struggle to make ends meet. Following a severe spell of drought in which his camels perished, he and his family are rescued by a friend with whom he goes raiding. Rewarded for the dangerous job of scouting for enemy herds, he is gifted with the most beautiful she-camel and sings the animal's and his friend's praises in verse (§21).[23]

Abū Zwayyid is regarded as the foremost master of camel description—a genre hardly touched by al-Hirbīd, just as Abū Zwayyid has very few pure ghazals to his name. Often looked upon as the most boring part of Arabian poetry, the camel sections of Abū Zwayyid come alive in vibrant scenes. They are not catalogs of animal parts, as in the best-known pre-Islamic examples. For those familiar with the animal as a mount, his camel sections are instantly recognizable: the animal's behavior and movements under all kinds of conditions are sharply observed. Real-life experience and riding enthusiasm combine with sympathetic insight and artistic mastery to produce exhilarating scenes. For that reason, Abū Zwayyid's red-hued she-camel, his messenger's fiery mount for swift delivery of a poem to the addressee, has become a trademark of his poetry.[24]

Abū Zwayyid and al-Hirbīd, arguably the greatest north Arabian Bedouin poets, draw on the same vast repository of motifs, imagery, and literary conventions accumulated over more than a thousand years in the Arabian ecosystem of deserts, arid lands, and oases. However, they differ markedly when it comes to their approach to chiaroscuro, the pervasive and stark binary oppositions in Bedouin poetry. Al-Hirbīd draws his contrasts to enhance his lyricism; Abū Zwayyid does so to boost his bravado. If one goes by the narrative lore, such aspects of style often come down to personal characteristics and philosophy of life. Intensely competitive, Abū Zwayyid delights in confounding opponents and friends with saucy remarks and bold feints to come out on top, in spite of an initial perceived disadvantage. The third poet, ʿAjlān, the owner of famed herds of white camels, seems much better off than the hard-bitten Abū Zwayyid. But in a tight situation, as happens on their approach to Ibn Shaʿlān's camp, ʿAjlān panics, whereas Abū Zwayyid keeps his cool and deftly handles the situation. ʿAjlān fumbles for excuses to dodge Ibn Shaʿlān's request to go and mollify his estranged wife;

Abū Zwayyid, on the other hand, lambasts Ibn Shaʿlān for his mistakes and clumsiness, then waits for the right moment to flatter his wife, who against her husband's will rewards him with a coffer full of riches she had received as the price of her reconciliation. ʿAjlān is left empty-handed, reduced to begging Abū Zwayyid for part of his haul.

Turnarounds and upsets against all expectations, crafted to make the underdogs come out on top thanks to their savviness and temerity, are standard fare in oral narrative entertainment. In the guise of realism and historicity, a wondrous tale is served up in the anecdotal style of the classical *Book of Songs*. Abū Zwayyid is presented as a picaresque poet-hero by storytellers and transmitters, who find in him a connection to their own forebears, either through tribal lineage or because of his praise of their ancestors. From its place of origin, the lore moves into the overall domain of Arabian literary taste: once an audience is rooting for the poet-hero, it will naturally fall into the time-hallowed pattern of sympathy for the lesser party who, in defiance of the odds, stages a surprise victory. Therefore, such tales should not be taken literally but rather as organic outgrowths of the interplay of individual talent and personality, literary and cultural convention, and networks of audiences with common interests and backgrounds.

These narratives-cum-poetry are of relatively recent date. Bedouin poetry, as preserved in oral tradition, probably had its heyday in the second half or last quarter of the nineteenth century. Around 1982, this lore was recorded from storytellers who were born not long after that time, some of whom were close to the dramatis personae. Grafted onto events that took place within the purview of modern history, these traditions already show manifold signs of transformation from more or less factual reports into legend. In contrast to even earlier periods, however, there are many more reasonably reliable accounts against which facts can be checked: northern Arabia features in numerous nineteenth-century descriptions of travelers, while Saudi historians and ethnographers have compiled even better-informed studies, though without some of the vivid color and detail added by visitors from outside the area.[25]

'Ajlān ibn Rmāl

Like Abū Zwayyid, 'Ajlān is the winner who comes from behind. From this perspective, 'Ajlān and Abū Zwayyid have more in common with each other than either does with al-Hirbīd. Both belong to the upper ranks of Bedouin society. For them, love of camels is bred in the bone. They consort with the most venerated tribal leaders. Wherever they appear, they are in high demand for their wit, their amusing tales that walk the fine line between acceptable and outrageous, and their beautiful poetry on issues of abiding interest to the audience. Their vast knowledge of desert lore is appreciated both for its educational value and for its utility in identifying relevant precedent for issues that fall within the remit of customary law and the ethics of the desert code. There has always been a connection between customary law and poetry. Abū Zwayyid is an example of those Bedouin poets who distinguish themselves "in the defense of their tribal rights in law courts when pleadings and counter pleadings are exchanged back and forth between intense, resolute adversaries."[26] When asked for an opinion on a case, his role approaches that of a tribal judge.[27] With respect to a story in the genre of narratives-cum-poetry, verses of poetry are compared to witnesses giving evidence in customary law proceedings; the section on 'Ajlān demonstrates that poetry may also literally serve as evidence in such cases.[28]

'Ajlān ibn Rmāl belongs to the tribe of al-Rmāl (which means "the sands"), whose main base is the village and oasis of Jubbah, situated at the southern edge of the Great Nafūd Desert, Arabia's second-greatest sea of sand after the Empty Quarter in the south, bordering Oman and Yemen. Jubbah, despite its minuscule size, is one of the most fabled locations in the Arabian desert. For generations of European travelers, heading to the court of Ibn Rashīd armed with letters of recommendation from his notional sovereign,

the Ottoman sultan in distant Istanbul, Jubbah would be the first
vista of greenery and human habitation after five days on camelback
from al-Jawf oasis. Without exception, they describe in their travel-
ogues their jubilation at the delightful contrast upon their arrival.

More practical than these romantically inclined travelers, the
tribespeople of al-Rmāl looked to the sands, and their rich growth
of perennials and cover of plants after spring rains, as a source of
firewood and fodder for their animals, as a barrier against raiders,
and as a safe refuge when pressed by their enemies.[29] Therefore, it
comes as no surprise that the Nafūd, and in particular its strategic
and political importance, looms larger in ʿAjlān's oral traditions than
in the lore of the other two poets. The exception are episodes that
show al-Hirbīd acceding to the request of the Rmāl clans to accom-
pany them on their spring migration into the desert in order to have
the benefit of his entertainment around their campfires in the eve-
ning.[30] To procure themselves that pleasure, they went as far as to
offer baskets suspended over the humps of their camels as transport
for his sheep when they were too fatigued to walk.

Al-Hirbīd plays no role in the lore of ʿAjlān and Abū Zwayyid.
On the other hand, the latter pitched in with a composition of his
own in the exchanges between ʿAjlān and the famous desert knight
Khalaf al-Idhn, a member of the Ibn Shaʿlān clan of the Rwalah
tribe. The story illustrates how, in the pantheon of tribal luminaries,
everyone was caught in the web of drama and soap opera. Khalaf
al-Idhn is the poet–knight who in close combat killed the chivalrous
chief Ibn Mhēd, the warlike father-in-law of Saṭṭām bin Shaʿlān, on
both of whom Abū Zwayyid heaped praise in a poem that aroused
the ire of Ibn Rashīd and made him swear to shed the poet's blood.
Abū Zwayyid and ʿAjlān seem to have regularly run into one another
at the tents of Bedouin shaykhs, who were so grand that they were
called princes by the European visitors. Perhaps their sparring and
teasing buffoonery worked to the advantage of both, as it did for
poets who slugged it out for wowed crowds in the days of early clas-
sical poetry. In the telling of the transmitters, they were therefore

probably friendly competitors, in a camaraderie of peers, who occasionally met on the trail of gatherings, attracted by hospitality provided at the tents of desert lords.

Not long after the capture of Ḥāʾil by the Ikhwān, ʿAjlān and Abū Zwayyid were separately received—somewhat condescendingly, but not in an unfriendly way—by the Saudi governor, Ibn Musāʿid. Though the poets adopted a contrite tone, they did not hide from him that faced with a fait accompli, and for lack of an alternative, they had felt compelled to make their peace and offer allegiance to the new masters. While careful to exhibit a demeanor of proper deference, and an awareness of being at the new ruler's mercy, they kept their dignity and even showed flashes of their trademark wit. Similarly, Ibn Musāʿid's words hint at a wry understanding of the old men's plight and former station, and possibly even a glimmer of nostalgia at the spectacle of obeisance paid, albeit reluctantly, by such unassuming, humanist, and cultured representatives of the ancien régime. Though other reports suggest that the scene may have been spiced up by the narrators, it may well be a fair rendering of what happened at the transfer of political loyalty and the atmospherics surrounding it.[31]

Though advanced in age by the time of Ḥāʾil's fall, ʿAjlān and Abū Zwayyid had remained involved in desert politics almost to the very end. Abū Zwayyid's longest poem, a masterpiece of panegyric, ended with a request to Sʿūd ibn ʿAbd al-ʿAzīz, nicknamed Abū Khashm ("Father of the Nose"; that is, "Big Nose"), who had ascended the Rashīdī throne at the age of twelve, to pay off the debts he owed to one of the ruler's slaves.[32] He was prompted to do so when he discerned an opportunity at the Rashīdī capture of rich spoils in the battle of al-Jawf in 1920. He might have already been blind by that time.

Following the example of many Shammar clans, ʿAjlān fled north, beyond the reach of the Ikhwān. There he attached himself to one of the most influential shaykhs, Fahd ibn Hadhdhāl, a leader of astounding political longevity (see §53.1). Addicted to the poet's art of conversation, the shaykh did everything possible to keep ʿAjlān in his company. At that time, Ibn Hadhdhāl and the Jarbā shaykhs of Shammar in Mesopotamia quarreled about their respective rights to levy protection money from the ʿAnazah and Shammar tribes. When matters came to a head, they were called to the Ottoman-Turkish authorities in Baghdad to argue their case. Both parties agreed on ʿAjlān as their arbiter. ʿAjlān had not been informed and, unaware of what was happening, was brought to Baghdad by Ibn Hadhdhāl's son, driving across the Syrian desert in one of the first automobiles to appear there. Initially reluctant to become embroiled in a tribal hornet's nest, ʿAjlān laid down his conditions. The parties accepted and duly signed an Ottoman document to that effect. With that security, ʿAjlān decided the case by reference to an earlier poem on fights for territory between ʿAnazah and Shammar. No one contested the verses' authenticity and ʿAjlān's ruling was adopted without demur. Ibn Hadhdhāl's son had expected otherwise, but the evidence presented by ʿAjlān showed that the claims of his host, Ibn Hadhdhāl himself, were ill-founded.[33]

Having followed his conscience, ʿAjlān decided, notwithstanding the old shaykh's desperate pleas, that it was time to pack up. Home was in or near the Nafūd. In Ḥāʾil, he asked the Saudi prince, "Grant me protection against those who pretend to be devout, whereas in fact they are not true men of religion in any sense. And by now the gates of poetry have been slammed shut" (§54.4). Likewise, Ibn Musāʿid informed Abū Zwayyid on his arrival: "Look, Abū Zwayyid, we are in a session devoted to the study of the Prophet's sayings. This nonsense of verses is over" (§1.4).

It is not known if al-Hirbīd was still there to witness the dawn of the new age. If so, he must have kept silent, as did a like-minded ghazal poet, Ibn Sbayyil, though the latter lived into the 1930s.[34] By and large, this style of playful, tongue-in-cheek poetry that is both tender and boisterous—the hallmark of inner Arabia's largely secular culture—went underground. But in private the embers were kept alive until the flames were fanned again and leapt up as things gradually eased some decades later.

Tolerance and Freedom in Rashīdī Ḥā'il

The late-eighteenth- and early-nineteenth-century dynasties of Ibn Rashīd and their predecessors, known as Ibn ʿAlī, had their origins in appointments as governors by the Ibn Saud rulers, known as imams, in the first Wahhabi capital of al-Dirʿiyyah. Following the Wahhabi campaigns and violent excesses in the holy cities of the Hejaz, Mecca and Medina, and the destruction of Shiʿi shrines in Iraq, al-Dirʿiyyah was razed in 1819 by troops at the orders of the Egyptian ruler Muḥammad ʿAlī, thus ending the first Saudi state. Restored in the new capital of Riyadh in 1824, Saudi power was much diminished. Thanks to his closeness to the Saudi imam, Fayṣal, ʿAbdallah ibn Rashīd was appointed the Saudi governor in Ḥā'il in 1835, with a short interruption when the Ibn ʿAlī family was reinstated. With the help of the Ibn Rakhīṣ chief, ʿAbdallah returned as Ḥā'il's ruler, an episode that was spun into a romantic legend, fueled by his own verses. When Abū Zwayyid took the risk of setting the record straight with Muḥammad ibn Rashīd, who had sworn to have him killed—no idle threat from someone who had murdered scores of his relatives on accession to power—he subtly reminded him of this assistance by his Ibn Rakhīṣ relatives. ʿAbdallah ibn Rashīd was particularly gifted in the art of poetry, and was the first of many Ibn Rashīd poets. At the Rashīdī court, poetry was held in as high esteem as skill in warfare and statecraft.

ʿAbdallah's brother ʿUbayd (ʿBēd) sealed the fate of Ibn ʿAlī by force of arms. He achieved recognition for his brother's rule by convincing the Ottoman-Egyptian commander in the Hejaz that Ibn Rashīd would be more useful to him than the ousted governors, in particular by providing baggage camels from Shammar and other tribes in their orbit. ʿAbdallah and ʿUbayd made a compact according to which ʿAbdallah's descendants would succeed him as emir of the fledgling state, while the descendants of ʿUbayd would be the commanders-in-chief of the armed forces.[35] ʿAbdallah and ʿUbayd, though of very different character, were inseparable, and so were Muḥammad ibn Rashīd and ʿUbayd's son Ḥmūd, under whose stewardship the dynasty reached its apogee. ʿUbayd and Ḥmūd were the most prolific poets of the House of Ibn Rashīd, and some of ʿUbayd's verses remain popular today.[36] Their numerous battles were celebrated in their compositions and their panache vaunted. No event of political note passed without being recorded in verse. Tireless in their public relations, they were in regular correspondence with numerous tribal poets and shaykhs. Thus, they acted as the prince's ministers of propaganda and information, of defense, and of home affairs.

In addition, the Ibn Rashīd rulers maintained a legion of poets who followed them on the campaign trail and who were in attendance at the court to brag about their masters' achievements. The three poets in this volume did not belong to this group of eulogists: they were true artists who valued their independence above anything else, though they did freely interact and joust with colleagues in the rulers' retinue.[37] Practically state functionaries, the court poets were no mere hacks; some were even of considerable note. As a result, a significant part of the military and political fortunes of the Rashīdī state was reflected in poetry. And despite the obvious bias, these compositions tell us much about the inner workings of the system and the general outlook at a court that became the measure of things in large swaths of Arabia.

ʿUbayd and his son Ḥmūd were more closely aligned with the dynasty's Wahhabi roots. But even such displays of devoutness were diluted by Ḥāʾil's proximity to the more diverse areas north of the Nafūd and by the town's significance as a station on the east-to-west pilgrim and trade routes. Though austerity was not a façade, neither was it imposed or considered an incontrovertible standard of behavior.[38] Politically, this was useful in relations with Riyadh and in keeping the more fervent believers among the population from becoming too uncomfortable with the regime. 'Abdallah's successor, Ṭalāl, inherited an established dominion that left him free to concentrate on peaceful pursuits such as the expansion of trade and attending to the general welfare. In connection with the latter, he allowed Shi'i merchants from Iraq and Persia to set up shop. Though despised even more than Christians by many, they flourished economically and, thanks to the protection they received, were not bothered. General safety was one of the most valued features of Rashīdī rule. The Finnish traveler Georg August Wallin wrote: "There is a common saying among the present inhabitants, that one may go from one end of their land to another, bearing his gold on his head without being troubled with any questions."[39] No wonder Ḥā'il became a magnet for European visitors attracted to Arabia.

European Eyewitness Accounts and the Nafūd Poets

With the xenophobic Wahhabi capital Riyadh mostly out of bounds to travelers, nineteenth-century explorers of Arabia headed in increasing numbers to the Hejaz, and also to Ḥā'il, a capital in the Arabian desert. Most wrote observant, detailed, learned, and highly readable accounts of their impressions, such as Charles M. Doughty's two-volume *Travels in Arabia Deserta*, a source of inspiration for T. E. Lawrence (Lawrence of Arabia) and his *The Seven Pillars of Wisdom*.[40]

Religion as such, other than commonly practiced rituals, hardly features in the lore and poetry of Abū Zwayyid and al-Hirbīd. This undoubtedly reflects the general situation in northern tribal circles. Abū Zwayyid takes an inclusive view of the Lord's compassion (§25.5, v. 2):

> Creator of the Shi'ah, of Unbelievers and Islam,
>> all equally desirous of noble conduct's rewards,

and of his fellow tribesmen's international linguistic orientation: "Eloquent in Arabic and proficient in Turkish" (§25.2, v. 21). From travelers' reports we know that these are no vain boasts. Doughty writes that Muḥammad ibn Rashīd knew Turkish, "and he knew [. . .] Persian; Mohammed, formerly conductor of the pilgrimage, can also speak in that language."[41] In 1883, the prince enjoyed a reading from al-Qasṭallānī's *Life of Muhammad*, brought by Julius Euting from Cairo, and selections from the pre-Islamic *Muʿallaqāt* poems, "recited in an impermissible singsong manner."[42] In another session, the prince gave Euting a manuscript of the *Muʿallaqāt* and "a beautiful manuscript with poems and commentary of al-Mutanabbī."[43] Clearly, classical secular literary culture and native Nabaṭī tradition were much in vogue at the Rashīdī court. Among the population at large, however, classical poetry was practically unknown and the oral tradition reigned supreme. In this domain, interest in literate circles remained overwhelmingly confined to religious writings.

The parallels between the lore of the three Nafūd poets and the sizable travel literature concerning the Rashīdī court and northern Arabia would need a separate study. Reports from both sides, foreign and indigenous, are hardly ever contradictory, but perspectives and emphases naturally differ depending on the culture of the observers. Sometimes they share an uncanny resemblance, even in minute details. One extraordinary example is the description of Doughty's efforts to bring about a reconciliation between a chief of the Fugarā tribe of ʿAnazah and his young runaway wife, who was the daughter of a shaykh.[44] The manner in which the chief makes his request to Doughty; his speech and the telltale signs of his deep depression; the scene of the young woman with her relatives in a tent, surrounded by a big circle of sympathizing gossips; the artful means of persuasion employed; her eventual quasi-reluctant return; and the elation and gratitude of her husband are a choreographed performance, each step reflected in the stories of Abū Zwayyid's role as marriage counselor to the preeminent Bedouin shaykhs of the Arabian north, Ibn Shaʿlān and Ibn Hadhdhāl. The principal wife of

Saṭṭām ibn Shaʿlān, Turkiyyah, daughter of Ibn Mhēd, and her love marriage to Saṭṭām, feature realistically and romantically in Alois Musil's study of the Rwalah tribe, in which he takes Bedouin poetry as his point of departure (see §6.1 and §7.1). While in the service of the Austrian-Hungarian government, Musil made the most of his time as a reconnaissance agent to study the customs and poetry of these Bedouin. An important source for the oral Bedouin poetry noted by Musil, including a charming poem by al-Hirbīd, was Ṭrād, one of the sons of Saṭṭām. His mother belonged to the Sirḥān tribe, and she instructed Ṭrād in committing to memory a vast cache of oral Bedouin poetry. Ṭrād features in the chapter of Abū Zwayyid as one of two sons of Saṭṭām who had mobilized their armed followings to battle it out over the rights of their respective clients, one a camel trader of the ʿUqayl (ʿGēl), a commercial guild mainly based in al-Qasīm, the other a Bedouin of the tribe of the Shararāt, famous for breeding premium riding camels.[45] When matters threatened to spiral out of control, Abū Zwayyid saved the situation with a solution that set a precedent under tribal law among Shammar.

Gender Relations in the Arabian North

Women are ubiquitous in the lore relating to all three poets. In poetry, they are mostly portrayed in line with (male) convention, in the sense that they are the object of male admiration of their beauty. The poets enumerate their physical features and exult at the stunning sum total of their parts, much as in the traditional camel description. This volume includes some unusual, and occasionally astonishingly candid, scenes of physical and spiritual give-and-take between Bedouin poet and female companion (see, for instance, §18.3). As with other aspects of the orally transmitted texts, it is difficult to determine with any degree of precision where convention ends and lived experience begins.

Convention dates back to the beginnings of Arabic poetry, which even in the early Islamic era is to a considerable degree an extension of poetry originating in the Arabian Peninsula. The closest stylistic parallel to the lore in this volume, the narratives-cum-poetry of *The Book of Songs*, provides many early examples of a pervasive feature in the Abū Zwayyid and al-Hirbīd material: the all-consuming eagerness of Bedouin women to have their praises sung by renowned bards. Poets pursue women and women pursue poets. *The Book of Songs* describes, for example, how Nuṣayb, on a visit to the Holy Mosque in Mecca, overheard a circle of high-born, literarily inclined women reciting verses of their favorite composers of love poetry, himself one of them, and how he was avidly questioned when he revealed his identity.[46] Abū Zwayyid and al-Hirbīd were similarly sought after.

Sometimes women ask for more, as a matter of pride. Laylā, the mother of ʿAbd al-ʿAzīz ibn Marwān, the Umayyad governor of Egypt, stood in the way of Nuṣayb's recompense until he mentioned her by name in his verses.[47] A girl called Mnīrah refused to accept a poem of al-Hirbīd because he only extolled her charms in the final verses and had not devoted the entire poem to her (see §35.1). Renowned poets are charmed and cajoled into singing women's praises, or persuaded to do so by niceties, a means of spreading word of their ravishing looks, thereby attracting suitors. Having requested a drink of water from a servant girl, Nuṣayb is asked to glorify her good looks in verse. He asks her to tell him her name (Hind) and the name of a nearby mountainous outcrop (Qanā), and on the spot rhapsodizes in verse that he would forever love the Qanā outcrop because of a girl named Hind living at its foot. The verses spread like wildfire. The girl's wishes were fulfilled and she was offered a suitable marriage prospect.[48] In the same fashion, a recently divorced woman contrived to have al-Hirbīd all to herself, away from other women, by dolling herself up and expertly packing and loading the dates for which he had come. Like Hind, she was rewarded with charming verses (see §36.1).

Women who interact with the Nafūd poets are mentioned by name, and often with the name of their father, in marked contrast to the anonymous and more stereotyped women one encounters in the verses of ghazal poets in the Najdī oasis towns. Though the latter pretend to be at the mercy of ladies who enjoy nothing more than toying with their delicate souls, they seem mostly oblivious to any kind of real-life personality behind a woman's bewitching shape. Abū Zwayyid, by contrast, engages in lively discussions with female members of households. And he seems mightily pleased when Bedouin women take the initiative and act as if in command of the situation. Al-Hirbīd is shown making detours simply for the pleasure of chatting with a shepherdess who loves conversation and anecdotes.[49] Sowayan explains that "Bedouin ghazal is about real love stories because Bedouin society, unlike the settled communities, does not lock up women and does not regard love as blameworthy," and Musil notes that it was not rare for Bedouin to have love marriages.[50]

In some narrative sections, the teller of the story makes no secret of his distaste for the restrictive norms introduced in the post-Rashīd era and laments the pervasive social distrust regarding gender relations. The text is interspersed with comments such as: "This was in the olden days, before Bedouin girls began to cover up and act bashfully, when they still consorted freely with men and spent time in their company [...]. The nice olden ways, free of whispers and base gossip" (§17.5). Or: "Yes, in those days the girls had their role to play" (§33.1). Indeed, the female members of the House of Ibn Rashīd were taught to read and write, and were instructed in the Qurʾan.[51] And from 1908 until the collapse of the Rashīdī state, real power in Ḥāʾil rested with Fāṭimah, the daughter of Zāmil al-Sibhān, from a family that had intermarried with the Ibn Rashīd rulers.[52]

The Three Poets in Society

While the impression of each poet's station in society and appearance varies depending on the narrator, the details mostly match. The stories about ʿAjlān are limited to his deeds and his tactics. The sources of his income are not mentioned, but as the owner of sizable herds of the famous white camels of the Rmāl tribe, he must have been fairly well-to-do. Al-Hirbīd and Abū Zwayyid, on the other hand, are repeatedly portrayed as hard-pressed to make ends meet, and occasionally as destitute—that is, until their poetic skills result in a sudden windfall. Al-Hirbīd, after the misfortune that befell his family, scrapes together a living by keeping sheep loaned to him by fellow tribesmen, but his distaste for playing nice and cozying up to the rich and powerful worked against him. Somewhat incongruous with these portrayals are stories and poetry of the prominent part played by his productive groves of date palms in the open spaces between the granite rocks of Ajā Mountain.[53]

Abū Zwayyid is the closest to being seen as a poet wedded to his vocation, someone who "made a living from his tongue. He composed poems as he followed the trail of shaykhs who gave him presents" (§10.1).[54] Likewise, al-Hirbīd "entertained people with his stories and accompanied his recitations with tunes from his rebab" (§32.1). ʿAjlān was "a conversationalist in the majlis, someone whom shaykhs liked to have around them, and a poet who also entertained at his own tent" (§50.1). Conversation is key, especially narratives-cum-poetry, the *giṣṣah w-giṣīdah* genre in Najd.[55]

Occasionally, Abū Zwayyid is shown supplementing his income by taking part in the Bedouin for-profit sport of raiding other tribes for their camels. The expression for going on a raid used in these texts is "to try one's luck in stocking up with God-given booty" (*ytarazzag allāh*, CA *rizq*: "subsistence granted by God"). Interestingly, the poet participates both in private expeditions of plunder and in the "official" large-scale robbing tours yearly launched by Muḥammad ibn Rashīd.[56] By joining the latter, the poet took part in a state-sponsored activity that contributed significantly to the budget and thus kept the wheels of finance and the local economy turning. A unique example of a state based mainly on one Bedouin tribe, Shammar, the Ibn Rashīd principality maintained its position and popularity through daily lavish hospitality to all comers.[57] Every day, hundreds were fed a substantial meal in the courtyard of the Barzān palace.[58] Some loot from successful raids, such as thoroughbred horses from the House's fabled stables, was given to visitors of importance, tribal shaykhs and headmen of towns, and sent to solidify friendship with the Saudi princes in Riyadh, the Great Sharif in Mecca, the Ottoman-Turkish sultan and the Ottoman representatives in the Hejaz, and other neighboring powers.

Income was principally generated from zakat levied on the subjects of Ibn Rashīd, from trade and transport, and from the pilgrim caravans from Iraq that passed through Rashīdī territory to the Hejaz and back. Tribes around the periphery of the Shammar territory were liable to attack and despoilment of their herds if they refused to pay taxes similar to those levied in the core area of Jabal Shammar. The tribes roaming the desert areas from northern Syria and Iraq to Najrān in the south, bordering Yemen, remained by and large outside the writ of town-based political centers. By that excuse, they were considered legitimate targets for plunder, the more so because the attackers did not have to fear reprisals. During the nineteenth century, the scope for this Rashīdī practice was considerably expanded thanks to the destructive infighting within the House of Saud and to the sharp erosion of its reach, even in its native Najd. Muḥammad ibn Rashīd is said to have led more than forty raiding expeditions against the confederation of ʿUtaybah tribes alone.[59] The Shammar Bedouin were not able to hide their wealth from the Rashīdī tax collectors. One ruse employed to mislead the tax collectors through the intervention of al-Hirbīd on behalf of his fellow tribesmen is included in this volume (see §44.2).

In addition to his frequently straitened circumstances, Abū Zwayyid labored under the disadvantage of his unappealing appearance. Hyperbole used in description of his face became proverbial. He was walleyed and his eyes were said to be bulbous and positioned toward the side of his face, like the eyes of a locust (see §10.3 and §18.5). His self-descriptions include "the wolf-faced bane of his pursuers, a mangy camel in a pen made of thorny bushes where those infected with smallpox are quarantined" (§17.2).[60] However, the combination of hideous looks, artistic renown, unshakable composure, pluck, and savviness proved irresistible to the ladies of Shammar and beyond. He was tracked down by his future wife, who had sworn to kiss him if she found him after hearing his poem about a beautiful woman. What she saw, as she came splashing toward him through the shallow water of a desert pond of rainwater, was "the snout of a hyena and watery eyes that made for poor vision. He stood there squinting and straining his eyes to have a good look at the girl as she hurried toward him, with her skirt lifted from the surface of the water and her shiny legs like lamps illuminated from below" (§18.3).

Al-Hirbīd's deadly invective poetry described the repulsive appearance of rival poets (§48.5, v. 2 and §48.9, vv. 19–20). In his comments, the transmitter adds that one of these opponents "had suffered the loss of his eyelashes" and another "had rheumy eyes, messy with white discharge," and "was capable of wolfing down two trays of food and still have appetite for more" (§48.7).

Judging the Poetry

If much poetry was composed with a specific purpose and subject in mind, such practicality was not judged off-putting by the audience. On the contrary, one transmitter of this oral poetry lauds Abū Zwayyid's poetry precisely because "every verse is spot on: it hits the target and pierces through its target." Contrasting it with much modern Arabic poetry, he opines that his "poems are about matters that are very recognizable. Every single word is to the point and deals with a real subject" (§5.1).

Hitting the mark was what early classical poets like al-Farazdaq strove to achieve in fashioning their verses. The Bedouin poet thinks like Ibn Mayyādah, who, when criticized for some metrical flaws, said, "Listen, Ibn Jundab, poetry is like an arrow in your quiver, made to hit the target, rising and falling, straying and on target."[61] It is assumed that in pre-Islamic times, some poets specialized in invective poetry and that their audience regarded this as an effective instrument in real-world contests. These poets had powers associated with sorcerers.[62] In al-Hirbīd's poetry, however, one detects signs that the original animist belief in poetry's power as a curse may have retained a measure of credibility. In one instance, the poet, aggravated by the departure of his beloved, considers that he does not want to hurt her father, who is a decent man, and instead might cripple her camel, forcing her return. In another instance, following an exchange of invective, his competitor's palm grove, near to his own, inexplicably burns down. By the late nineteenth century, poetic conventions and practices dating back to pre-Islamic times, even if not used in all seriousness, were recognized by the audience for what they were.

Style, Imagery, Technique

The poets' individual characters as portrayed in the narratives also come through in their poetry. Often, certain details in lines of verse have been woven into the narrative thread simply as a matter of fact, sometimes with the purpose of elucidating an allusion or an elliptical remark. But stories and poems are not always evenly matched. On the way back from a failed raid, Abū Zwayyid and other camel riders indulge in pranks and race their mounts at a gallop. Counter to expectation, his poem about their lighthearted capers starts out in a grave and somber tone, bemoaning that the "era has saddled us with woeful leaders" (§13.2, v. 8) and that all traditional values and virtues have been upended. The opening verses reflect the poet's distress at the anarchy and rot that rapidly eroded the Rashīdī edifice of government when Muḥammad ibn Rashīd passed away. Nine verses later, without transition, the poet celebrates the wild ride on "the mount of [his] dreams" (§13.2, v. 10) and the lightning-fast successful capture of booty.[63]

The great majority of Abū Zwayyid's poems open with a messenger dispatched on a spirited, at times impetuous she-camel. This trademark red-hued beast, kept in check by a skilled and daring rider, might be taken as a metaphor for the poet's pugnacious and fiery temper. Up to the end of his life, Abū Zwayyid appears as an enterprising, cheeky Bedouin hero. Even old, blind, and frail, when he is led to the vaguely menacing presence of the new ruler, a prince of the House of Saud, he gently and half teasingly succeeds in drawing him out. He may well have been the only poet to leave the new court and its grim circle of turbaned Ikhwān with the gift of a camel for use as a draft animal.[64] Here, style and content match to perfection.

Almost none of the poems by al-Hirbīd feature a camel prelude. The wistful, slightly elegiac tone of his chapter's first poems, lamenting the loss of his brothers and their families at the hands of Ibn Shaʿlān Bedouin raiders, draws on the imagery of the early classical poet's laments at an abandoned campsite. Al-Hirbīd's poetry hits the mark too, but in a subtler manner, by exploring the twisted pathways and unexpected detours of sentiment and wandering thoughts. Tribal pride is celebrated, but the dominant impression is one of personal feeling, from joyful passion to raging anger and sad resignation.

Devoted to his sheep, which are half-mockingly contrasted with camel herding, and to his palm groves, al-Hirbīd comes across as tribal but only partially Bedouin, even as he treks and consorts with the camel nomads. Abū Zwayyid, for instance, hardly mentions date palms in his poetry, whereas al-Hirbīd weaves the details of the tree's efflorescence intricately into his ghazal (see §34.2, vv. 12–14).[65] If he speaks about Bedouin life, he often does so in a mode of self-deprecation, comparable to Ibn Sbayyil lowering himself to the position of a villager as he looks up to the towering Bedouin. Ibn Sbayyil's "I am just a villager—they, redoubtable Bedouin"[66] is mirrored in al-Hirbīd's "Breathless, we pant after camels and horsemen / who raid for sport..." (§32.10, v. 5). And yet, even he cannot escape camel imagery for the similes and metaphors of his ghazal. The lore of the Nafūd poets aptly underscores Doughty's observation that "camels, the only substance of the nomads, are the occasion of all their contending."[67] From the beginning, the camel was a metaphor used to describe certain aspects of poetry itself. The seventh-century Dhū l-Rummah, for instance, tells one of his poem's addressees that he will soon receive rhymes like a beautifully adorned, broken-in camel, to be followed by likewise tamed and well-trained poetry.[68] In Bedouin poetry, the metaphor is taken further: the camel stands for the poem itself, as in the standard expression "I mounted and dispatched a poem" (*arkabt lī giṣīdah*). The next step in the development of the metaphor is to do away entirely with the object of comparison and speak of a camel in lieu of a poem.[69] On his marriage-saving excursion to the estranged wife of Ibn Hadhdhāl, al-Hirbīd tells her about the fast camel he has readied for her. "Let me hear it," she says, and in the poem she is likened to a nicely caparisoned white she-camel. Among the presents she gives him as a reward for his camel/poem are a real camel loaded with goods and an even more valuable mare (§7).

The most egregious and comical example of full identification of poem and camel occurs in a conversation between Abū Zwayyid, who is accompanied by a Rwēlī companion,[70] and Muḥammad ibn Rashīd during a raiding expedition. Abū Zwayyid lodges a complaint with the prince about his Rwēlī friend, accusing him of acting like a stupid, undiscriminating young male camel trying to cover a pregnant female; that is, of plagiarizing one of his poems. He goes on to say that he found one of his camels with his Rwēlī mate, while all of his camels (that is, poems) are truly his own. The prince, himself a poet steeped in desert lore, at once deciphers the code language: the verses have been composed by Abū Zwayyid but he did his Rwēlī friend a favor by allowing him to claim the lines as his own. "Let's have it, then!" he says with a straight face (§15.1). The Rwēlī recites it and the prince asks if it is a stand-alone composition or has any "sisters"—a group of pedigree riding camels of the same color and strain are called "sisters." On being informed that these lines are all there is, the prince orders his servants to let the Rwēlī pick one of the camels. To the astonishment of the attendants, the ugliest beast in the herd is chosen: walleyed like the poet, a long navel cord dangling from its belly, chewing on a bone.[71] Like the ugly poet, it is an example of a recurring motif in oral lore: smart heroes who deceive but are not deceived by appearances. The Rwēlī, a crack cameleer, knows what he is doing. With his training, the beast metamorphoses into a champion long-distance desert cruiser.[72] He thanks Abū Zwayyid for helping him with the ruse in verses that this time might be his own.

The text presumes an audience steeped in this oral poetry's conventions. Just as the audience knows that a "camel" may stand for a poem, mention of certain objects evokes associations of the thing to which it refers, and that need not be explicitly identified. From the context, it should be obvious that the sparkle of a sword's blade is the finely chiseled straight nose of the woman haunting the poet (§17.5, v. 6). The nose does not need to be mentioned; its omission introduces an element of speed, excitement, and enjoyment at being able to decipher these small riddles delivered staccato-like, in rapid succession. Virtually all the features of this oral poetry are designed to enhance the addictive pleasures of conversation and verbal entertainment in the majlis.

Abū Zwayyid's camel-shaped, marriage-saving poem (§7) that persuaded Nūrah to give Shaykh Ibn Hadhdhāl another chance is a masterpiece of deft turns and twists. Scenes switch in rapid succession to create an exhilarating impression of speed and daring. The camel itself, "towering on giraffe-like legs," is "God's favored racer." Its pace seamlessly transitions to the exploits of Nūrah's father. Some men of the "shaykh's raiding group" are welcomed at home by an unattractive mate who "yells and shouts with abandon," and the more fortunate, people like the shaykh, are welcomed by sweet smiles. The daughter of this "shaykh of shaykhs," the most alluring of camels, "Insouciant, she strides in scented fur dyed yellow." With a final flourish, Nūrah is crowned as the equal of Ibn Shaʿlān:

> Never did I see Nūrah's like among kin or friends,
>> or ever hear of her equal from anyone.[73]

In a further example, warned in a dream by the daughter of the chief of the Rmāl, al-Hijhūj, he extols her father, sends his verse with "a skittish camel that hates getting hit," praises him, and then seemingly deviates into scenes of camel robbery and hot pursuit. Next comes an imagined dialogue of a young man who announces his intention to raid, expecting his tribal elders to caution him against it. However, he is encouraged to prove his mettle—a backhanded way of paying a compliment to his sweetheart's father, al-Hijhūj.[74] Surprisingly, the poem ends with a diatribe against a pastoralist who is ridiculed for "fattening his sheep and churning butter," an inveterate miser, the opposite of camel nomads born to be noble and generous (§17.6).[75] Stripped of its plumage, the piece's aim is simply to praise al-Hijhūj as a champion among his tribal competitors: chief of tribesmen who habitually and without a care send their sons on the warpath. Valuing prestige above all else, they pour scorn on a life of profit-making for its own sake. For the poet, achieving similar success for himself not only depends on the praised shaykh's real-life status, but also on artful delivery. He endeavors to stand out from the crowd of poets and dazzle the audience with amazing swerves and dashes—a technique at which Abū Zwayyid excels. Similarly, al-Hirbīd's ghazal depicts a buxom girl who helps a cousin and promised future husband to hoist water from a well. Rope in hand, she is distracted by the appearance of the poet, and the future husband punishes her with a hard pull on the rope that makes her fall to the ground. Al-Hirbīd's poem curses the jealous fiancé, then without further explanation transforms the girl into a tender young she-camel forced to join a raiding expedition and keep pace with "pitiless, hard-bitten mounts / ridden by boisterous, hookah-smoking toughs" (§39.3).

For the uninitiated, such abrupt transitions might be disorienting. The technique's building blocks are miniature set pieces, borrowed from convention and molded into the poet's personal style to be turned into short and dense vignettes. Related to similes and extended similes, these are not merely figures of speech: pried loose from the poem's frame, they can run to several verses and can be quasi-independent units. Delivered in a spirited performance, the recitation assumes the presence of an audience so steeped in the lore that they can effortlessly grasp the meaning and scope. Preservation in oral transmission is testimony to the collective experience and intimate knowledge of the environment that underlies this kind of highly stylized speech. In this way, all observers, indigenous and foreign, reckon poetry itself to be an inextricable part of Arabian desert life. This poetry summarizes and puts a slant on events and thought in this arid land, at once fertilized and brought forth by it, and at times exercising considerable influence on developments in its habitat.

This may explain one of the most remarkable features of the poetry: the systematic reduction of matters to values and imagery characterized by stark, binary opposition. A warrior comes home to "a wife like a hissing snake" (§7.2, v. 9) and another to the "sweet smiles of a dazzling beauty" (§7.2, v. 13); some camels "stagger across wastes like invalids" (§7.2, v. 4); for others, "uphill stretches serve to make her run faster still" (§7.2, v. 7); and so on (see also §18.8, v. 1 and §19.5, v. 2). Routine use of hyperbole in Bedouin and early classical poetry are part of the poet's aspiration to sharpen such oppositions to the utmost. But if poet and transmitter stretch credulity, they do so in accordance with the taste of an audience rooting for the poem's subject to overcome all odds and countervailing forces. Ultimately, the tendency toward binary opposition can be traced to the poetry's harsh natural setting. In a vast wilderness crisscrossed by a patchwork of tribal hostility, one might be faced at any moment with life-or-death situations, severe droughts, and other blows of Fate; or be given sudden relief by rain or good fortune. Like the desert itself, such an environment is inhospitable to softer tones and nuanced speculation. Either/or situations and the lack of forewarning require quick decisions, carried out with unwavering determination. Born in the desert, the three poets are among the last representatives of nineteenth- and early-twentieth-century Bedouin life.

Having inherited verbal art and imagery from the earliest classical poetry of Arabia, their spirited performances illuminate the circumstances in which the tradition is rooted in pre-Islamic times, and indeed, their poetry and technique are best understood against that historical background.

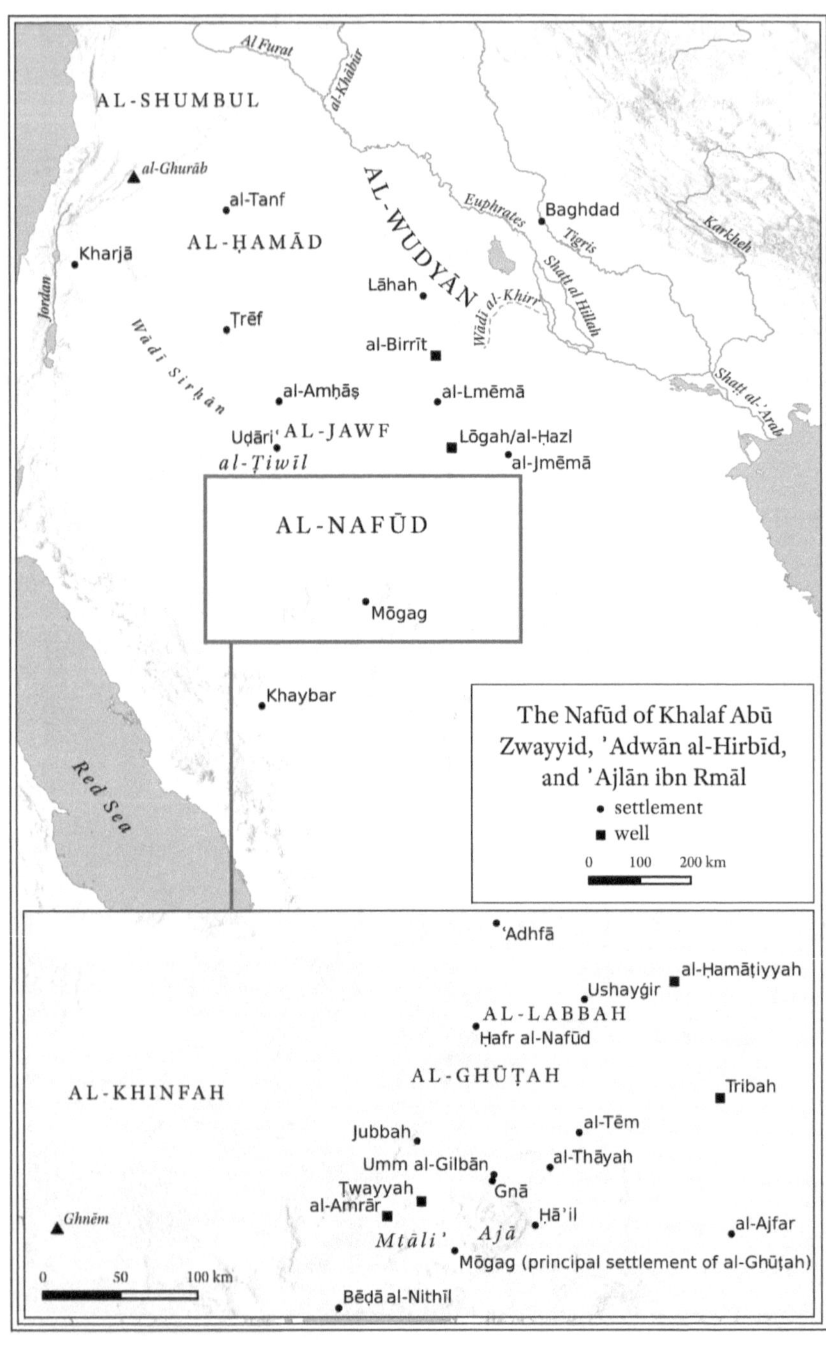

Al Furat
AL-SHUMBUL
al-Khabur
AL-WUDYĀN
al-Ghurāb
al-Tanf
AL-ḤAMĀD
Euphrates
Baghdad
Tigris
Karkheh
Kharjā
Jordan
Lāhah
Wādī al-Khirr
Shaṭṭ al Hillah
Trēf
Wādi Sirḥān
al-Birrīt
al-Amḥāṣ
al-Lmēmā
Shaṭṭ al-'Arab
Uḍāri' AL-JAWF
al-Ṭiwīl
Lōgah/al-Ḥazl
al-Jmēmā
AL-NAFŪD
Mōgag
Khaybar
Red Sea
The Nafūd of Khalaf Abū
Zwayyid, 'Adwān al-Hirbīd,
and 'Ajlān ibn Rmāl
• settlement
■ well
0   100   200 km
'Adhfā
al-Ḥamāṭiyyah
Ushayġir
AL-LABBAH
Ḥafr al-Nafūd
AL-GHŪṬAH
Tribah
AL-KHINFAH
al-Tēm
Jubbah
al-Thāyah
Umm al-Gilbān
Ṭwayyah
Gnā
al-Amrār
Ghnēm
Mtāli'   Ajā   Hā'il
al-Ajfar
Mōgag (principal settlement of al-Ghūṭah)
0   50   100 km
Bēḍā al-Nithīl

Note on the Translation

None of this volume's poems and stories have appeared in English translation, with the exception of one poem by al-Hirbīd (§35.3) in Musil, *The Manners and Customs of the Rwala Bedouins*, 321–23.

Not all courtesy expressions used by the transmitters in addressing the audience are included in the translation. Sometimes the transmitter or narrator departs from the narrative thread and directly addresses his audience or interpolates observations of his own. These moments should be easily recognizable in the translation and serve as a reminder of the text's origin in oral performance.

Because the oeuvre of the three poets is in the idiom of Najdī vernacular poetry, called Nabaṭī poetry, their names and those of others are transliterated in a way that more closely reflects the pronunciation of this predominantly oral poetry (recited on social occasions), and accepted among specialists. Names like ʿAbdallah (ʿAbd Allāh) and Ḍēfallah (Ḍayf Allāh) are written as they are spoken and in accordance with meter. Najdī Nabaṭī poetry has its own idiom, much of it borrowed from conventions that date back to the pre-Islamic beginnings of Arabic poetry.

The classical spelling of a name is used where this is more convenient or recognizable for readers. In this Introduction and elsewhere, some personal names, names of towns, and other geographical features mentioned in the poetry are transliterated according to the standard classical Arabic spelling or according to common spelling in English. For instance, Wahhabi, not Wahhābī, and Saud, as in the House of Saud. If names are commonly spelled in a certain way in English—for example, Ibn Rashīd, Ibn Rakhīṣ, Turkī, and Turkiyyah—that spelling is followed, rather than the vernacular Ibn Rishīd, Ibn Rikhīṣ, Tirkī, and Tirkiyyah. This applies to tribal names, which are also often spelled in a great variety of ways: ʿUtaybah, ʿAnazah, and Muṭayr, and not, as in the vernacular, ʿTēbah, ʿNizah, and Mṭēr. Occasionally, as appropriate, names and words that occur in the vernacular text may be given in the Introduction and the endnotes (for example, if they occur in book titles or as official family names) according to the classical Arabic transliteration. For instance, the name Ibn Musāʿid, which is Ibn Msāʿid according to the vernacular, is written throughout in accordance with the classical spelling. In transliteration of vernacular text and notes to the text, the assimilation of the sun letters in pronunciation is shown.

In the Arabic text, names of sections of tribes—for instance, "al-Hirbīd's clan"—are referred to with the English definite article in lieu of the Arabic article "al-": "the Swēd" rather than "al-Swēd." Tribal names such as Shammar are not used with the Arabic definite article, and thus do not appear with "the" in English. "Shammar" is also used as a collective for the entire tribal confederation or a group of tribespeople. Furthermore, it occurs as an adjective, such as Shammar division, Shammar troops; the word "Shammarī" refers to an individual from the tribe. In "Shammar made a run for it," the reference is not to the entire tribe, but to a group or small number of individuals of the tribe. In case of the indefinite "Shammar," the translation may add "tribespeople" or similar so as not to make it appear as the name of an individual.

Riding camels, frequently described in a poem's opening verses as part of the messenger motif, are always female, and a single riding camel will be referred to as "she;" the same applies to date palms.

The transliteration in these parts of the volume will hew closer to the classical Arabic practice in other respects and details: the *nisbah* of Shammar will be written as Shammarī, with a macron on the final vowel, and not as Shammari, as is common in the transliteration of the vernacular where all final vowels are long by definition, thus obviating the need for a macron. In the notes, transliterated verses in the Najdī vernacular show the affricated *g* (CA *qāf*) and *k* as, respectively, *g′* and *č*. In this domain, it is not possible in a script developed to represent classical Arabic to render features such as the merging of the phonemes *ẓ* and *ḍ*: in this edition, the distinction between the two is made according to the classical Arabic root.

Notes to the Introduction

1   Ḥā'il is the spelling in classical Arabic (hereafter CA). In the spoken language, it is pronounced Ḥāyil, which is the spelling adopted in this volume.

2   The ʿUtaybah chief Mnāḥī al-Hēḍal lamented that firearms did away with chivalry, making "silly nobodies and good noblemen equals" (Sowayan, *al-Ṣaḥrā' al-ʿarabiyyah*, 469).

3   As Muḥammad ibn Rashīd told Doughty (*Arabia Deserta*, 1:651).

4   The waterless Great Nafūd sand desert, forbidding in the hot season, is also rhapsodized as a paradise following rains of spring.

5   The Ikhwān, "Brothers," not to be confused with the later Society of the Muslim Brothers (*Jamāʿat al-Ikhwān al-Muslimīn*), was shorthand for *Ikhwān man ṭāʿa Allāh*, "Brothers of Those Obedient to God." This was the name given to the religiously inspired troops, mostly composed of recently settled Bedouin, that played a crucial role in the conquests of the later king ʿAbd al-ʿAzīz (or Ibn Saud) in laying the foundations for the creation of the Kingdom of Saudi Arabia.

6   As another contemporary put it: "The Ikhwān took a very different course and were hostile to our time-honored, hallowed norms (*salm*, pl. *slum*)" (Sowayan, *Ayyām al-ʿarab al-awākhir*, 510). By 1918, "almost one-fourth of the Shammar had become *Ikhwan* and allied themselves with Ibn Saud" (Al-Rasheed, *Politics in an Arabian Oasis: The Rashidi Tribal Dynasty*, 225).

7   This seems to have been the general opinion among transmitters in the area: "It is said that a captured raider at that time never lied,

always told the truth" (Sowayan, *The Arabian Oral Historical Narrative*, 111).

8   "The Wahhabi call had managed to split tribal coalitions and many loyal sections entered the battle against their own tribesmen," an aggravation of the divided loyalty between tribe and state (al-Fahad, "The *ʿImama* vs. the *ʿIqal*: Hadari-Bedouin Conflict and the Formation of the Saudi State," 74, nn114, 118). ʿAjlān mentions some examples of such religiously inspired killings (§52.6 and §52.7). Initially, old tribal feuds spilled over into the new age in a new guise (e.g., Sowayan, *al-Ṣaḥrāʾ al-ʿarabiyyah*, 546; Von Oppenheim, *Die Beduinen*, 1:107–8).

9   The long rule of Ibn Musāʿid in Ḥāʾil, a member of the Jluwī branch of the House of Saud, known for its severity, lasted with some interruptions until his death in 1970.

10 The birth and death dates of the three poets are unknown. From this detail, it might be surmised that al-Hirbīd flourished slightly earlier than the other two poets, whose texts make no mention of a ruler before Muḥammad ibn Rashīd (r. 1873–97). However, Abū Zwayyid composed a poem on ʿAbd al-Karīm al-Jarbā, who was executed by the Ottoman Turks in 1871, and therefore this poem must date from before the short rule of Bandar ibn Ṭalāl (r. 1869–73). Unlike Abū Zwayyid and ʿAjlān, al-Hirbīd is not shown as having witnessed the transition from Rashīdī to Saudi rule in Ḥāʾil in 1921.

11 The expression "knight and poet" (*fāris wa-shāʿir*) corresponds to the pre-Islamic notion of "the perfect man" (*al-kāmil*, pl. *al-kamalah*); i.e., a poet who is also remarkable for bravery. Dhū l-Iṣbaʿ is similarly named "knight and poet, someone who frequently went raiding and took part in famous battles" (al-Isfahānī, *al-Aghānī*, 3:25, 89). ʿAbdallah, the first Rashīdī ruler, and his brother ʿUbayd are among the poets listed in al-Hirbīd's al-Shēkhah poem.

12 "Both camel nomads and cultivators of date palm groves look down their noses at herders of sheep and goats" (Sowayan, *al-Ṣaḥrāʾ al-ʿarabiyyah*, 380).

13 Likewise, the main issue for ʿAjlān is not to act against his conscience, thereby keeping his honor and integrity.

14 Steeped in oral tradition, these illiterate poets were acutely aware of the view posterity would take of them and are shown keeping an eye on their legacy. Al-Hirbīd, who listed the immortal names in his al-Shēkhah poem, casually said of his compositions: "verses sown and waiting for future generations" (§48.9, v. 7). A century or so later, this elicited the transmitter's admiring comment: "Where is ʿAdwān now? And we are still reciting his poetry!" Poetry is more valuable than possessions such as camels, clothes, and money because "praise sung in poetry remains and paeans go from mouth to mouth" (al-Iṣfahānī, *al-Aghānī*, 1:343).

15 When the poet Rāshid al-Hijlī praised Saṭṭām ibn Shaʿlān, Muḥammad ibn Rashīd threatened to kill him and had him thrown in jail until he apologized in a poem (al-Suwaydāʾ, *Manṭiqat Ḥāʾil ʿabra al-tārīkh*, 425–27). ʿAbd al-ʿAzīz ibn Rashīd ordered the assassination of the poet Shāyish al-Ṣalj for having declined an invitation to pay allegiance and for his response to his earlier persecution (Musil, *Northern Neǧd*, 136–37).

16 See also Sowayan, "Studying Nabaṭi Poetry," on this passage.

17 The poet had put on a white shroud in preparation for his burial, signaling that he was ready to face his execution (and, one suspects, in the hope that it would soften the heart of the irate ruler).

18 The expression "I only want a mouthful of your blood," as Sowayan explains, does not need to be taken literally, though it points to an intention to kill, but it did happen that a warrior would drink the warm blood of a felled opponent if he was slain for revenge (*The Arabian Oral Historical Narrative*, 145, 316).

19 For similar ruses employed by early classical poets, see n. 74 of the translation.

20 In pre-Islamic times, it was customary to cut off the forelock of a released prisoner and keep it as a souvenir; see Jacob, *Altarabisches Beduinenleben*, 137.

21 Similarly, the poet Ibn Ẓāhir, "an old man dressed in rags and carrying a bundle of firewood [. . .] knows how to hide his identity while roaming his lands like a king on an incognito inspection tour" (Kurpershoek,

Love, Death, Fame: Poetry and Lore from the Emirati Oral Tradition; Al-Māyidī ibn Ẓāhir, xxxiv).

22 See Kurpershoek, *Arabian Satire: Poetry from 18th Century Najd: Ḥmēdān al-Shwēʿir*, xxi–xxii. This is made explicit in the verses where al-Hirbīd impersonates the verses of Jrēs (§37.3).

23 For instance, in 1884 the Saudi ruler ʿAbdallah ibn Fayṣal sent thirty-five riders to reconnoiter. They were all surrounded and killed by Ibn Rashīd (Musil, *Northern Neğd*, 277).

24 The great majority of Abū Zwayyid's poems open with a camel description embedded in the messenger motif, the poet's words addressed to the conveyor of his verses to their destination, *yā-rāćib illī*: "O rider of (a camel of such-and-such description)"; see n. 17 of the translation.

25 Al-Suwaydāʾ, *The Region of Ḥāʾil in History (Manṭiqat Ḥāʾil ʿabra al-tārīkh)*, is especially informative and, despite its general title, is principally a detailed account of all aspects of life during the rule of Ibn Rashīd.

26 Sowayan, "Customary Law in Arabia: An Ethnohistorical Perspective." Blunt observed that "disputants bring their cases to the Emir, who settles them in open court, not on the basis of Islamic law, but rather Arabian custom, an authority far older than the Mussulman code" (*A Pilgrimage to Nejd*, 266). Similarly, Sowayan: "Poetry in tribal society practically takes the place of Quran and *ḥadīth* in urban society." In tribal societies, legal and poetic functions overlap and can be complementary (Sowayan, "Tonight My Gun Is Loaded: Poetic Dueling in Arabia.").

27 See §5 on how to deal with a conflict between a neighbor and a guest if both are under the same family's protection.

28 See also Sowayan, *The Arabian Oral Historical Narrative*, 25, and "Customary Law in Arabia."

29 Expert surveys of all aspects of the Nafūd and its ecosystem are given in Watts and Al-Nafie, *Vegetation and Biogeography of the Sand Seas of Saudi Arabia*, and James Mandaville, *Bedouin Ethnobotany*.

30 Whereas Rmāl is a section of the Ghfēlah branch of the Sinjārah division of Shammar, al-Hirbīd belongs to the Swēd branch of the

same division, and they "are considered the closest to each other" (Sowayan, *The Arabian Oral Historical Narrative*, 15). This explains al-Hirbīd's sojourns with the Rmāl. In his poem on the camel nomads of the Ghfēlah (and, by implication, the Rmāl), he vaunts their superiority compared to a miserable shepherd like himself (§32.10, v. 10).

31 A similar, but politically more consequential, pledge of loyalty is given to Ibn Musāʿid by the shaykh and raid leader (*ʿagîd*) of the Rmāl tribe, Ghaḍbān ibn Rmāl, implausibly with the condition that it should not be at the expense of his loyalty to Shammar (Sowayan, *Ayyām al-ʿarab*, 338).

32 A time-honored gesture of Arab rulers. For example, in the Umayyad period, ʿAbd al-Malik ibn Bishr paid off debts accumulated by the poet al-Ḥakam ibn ʿAbdal, and ʿAbd al-ʿAzīz ibn Marwān paid those of Nuṣayb (al-Iṣfahānī, *al-Aghānī*, 2:425, 1:376).

33 In pre-Islamic times, essentially the same procedure was followed to negotiate an end to the war between the tribes of Aws and Khazraj. The aggrieved party agreed on the choice of an arbiter, who stipulated that the parties should give solemn pledges and commitments in writing, stating that they would abide by the outcome of his ruling, whether it was agreeable to them or not (al-Iṣfahānī, *al-Aghānī*, 3: 25–26, 40–41).

34 See Kurpershoek, *Arabian Romantic: Poems on Bedouin Life and Love*; *ʿAbdallāh ibn Sbayyil*, xvi.

35 This division of responsibilities corresponds to the one followed by many Bedouin tribes: armed expeditions were led by a commander regarded as successful (mostly phrased by the Bedouin as "lucky") in capturing rich spoils. The same division existed in pre-Islamic Arabia: a tribe's leader (*sayyid*) would leave leadership in armed conflict to a commander, corresponding to the *ʿagîd* at the time of this edition's poets (Jacob, *Altarabisches Beduinenleben*, 224–25). One poet said of an *ʿagîd*: "Fortune favored him, and he was numbered among the brave men" (Musil, *Rwala*, 606).

36 Doughty calls ʿUbayd "a martial man [. . .], a master of Arabian warfare [. . .], an excellent kassād [poet], he indited of all his desert warfare; his boastful rimes, known wide in the wilderness, were ofttimes sung for me, in the nomad booths" (*Arabia Deserta*, 2:41–42).

37 The retinue included known families of poets: al-Tbēnāwī, al-Jhēlī, Khḍēr ibn Ṣ'ēlīć (see §28 for his riposte to Abū Zwayyid), and many others (al-Suwaydā', *Manṭiqat Ḥā'il*, 487–88). According to one opinion, the five preeminent poets of Shammar are Mbērīć al-Tbēnāwī, 'Adwān al-Hirbīd, Khalaf Abū Zwayyid, 'Ajlān ibn Rmāl, and Khḍēr ibn Ṣ'ēlīć (al-Ẓafīrī, *Dīwān al-shā'ir Abū Zuwayyid, ḥakīm Shammar wa-shā'irūhā*, 19).

38 Ṭalāl ibn Rashīd, for instance, though married to one of the Saudi imam Fayṣal's daughters, was "liberal even to profusion," and was "rumoured to indulge in the heretical pleasure of tobacco, to wear silk, and to be very seldom seen in the mosque." His uncle 'Ubayd balanced matters by being "so devout, so far from the abominations" as to "almost atone for and cover the scandals given by his nephew" (Palgrave, *Narrative of a Year's Journey through Central and Eastern Arabia*, 93–95, 121).

39 Wallin, *Travels in Arabia*, 158.

40 "It is inconceivable for a Najdī *Hadari* (non-Bedouin, settled) to name his son after a Christian. For a Bedouin, so long as such person possessed the requisite 'manliness' (*marjilah*), religion was of no importance; thus, the chiefly family of the Ruwala tribe named their son Orans, after the famous Lawrence of Arabia, who had died only recently" (Al-Fahad, "The '*Imama* vs. the '*Iqal*," 75).

41 Doughty, *Arabia Deserta*, 2:26–27. Eduard Nolde was surprised to learn that Ibn Rashīd was well-informed about Alsace and French-German tensions. Nolde noted that the emir received "a mass of Arabic and Turkish newspapers from Egypt, Syria and Istanbul and keeps up an extensive correspondence. During my presence, every day at least one camel messenger, and sometimes two or three, arrived in the camp from various regions" (Nolde, *Reise nach Innerarabien, Kurdistan und Armenien, 1892*, 44, 89).

42 The poem was possibly rendered in the Nabaṭī meter *al-mashūb*.

43 Julius Euting, *Tagebuch einer Reise in Inner-Arabien*, 2:58, 24. The reference must be to the Cairene Shāfi'ī scholar Abū al-'Abbās al-Qasṭallānī (1448–1517) and his popular history of the Prophet, *al-Mawāhib al-laduniyyah fī al-minaḥ al-Muḥammadiyyah* (published in 1474 and

reprinted in Cairo in 1864–65, not long before Euting's visit). According to Steinberg, "Ecology, Knowledge, and Trade in Central Arabia (Najd) during the Nineteenth and Early Twentieth Centuries," 97, the second half of the nineteenth century saw "the first massive influx of printed books into Central Arabia."

44   Doughty understood "that this is the guest's honourable office"; i.e., to urge an aggrieved Bedouin woman to return to her husband. He adds that there are "nearly none who continue in their first husband's household" (*Arabia Deserta*, 1:276–78). See §6.4 and §7.1 and n. 42 of the translation for the passages in question.

45   On 'Uqayl, see Sowayan, "al-'Uqaylāt" in *al-Ṣaḥrāʾ al-ʿarabiyyah*, 367–72; Musil, *Rwala*, 278–81; and the Glossary.

46   Al-Isfahānī, *al-Aghānī*, 1:377.

47   Al-Isfahānī, *al-Aghānī*, 1:340.

48   Al-Isfahānī, *al-Aghānī*, 1:353.

49   "Bedouin women are renowned for their sweet conversation" (Sowayan, *al-Ṣaḥrāʾ al-ʿarabiyyah*, 442).

50   Sowayan, *al-Ṣaḥrāʾ al-ʿarabiyyah*, 433; Musil, *Northern Neǧd*, 112–13.

51   Al-Suwaydāʾ, *Manṭiqat Ḥāʾil*, 530.

52   Al-Suwaydāʾ, *Manṭiqat Ḥāʾil*, 717.

53   At the time, these groves inside the rock formations of Jabal Shammar were numerous and represented an important source of income (al-Suwaydāʾ, *Manṭiqat Ḥāʾil*, 537, 553).

54   Burckhardt emphasizes the importance of the art of conversation for the Bedouin, and his own enchantment with it (e.g., *Notes on the Bedouins and Wahabys*, 366–67). See also Doughty, *Arabia Deserta*, 1:305–7.

55   For instance, al-Isfahānī, *al-Aghānī*, 2: 313, 327.

56   The entire area between Jabal Shammar and Urfa, today in southeastern Turkey, was subject to raids by 'Anazah and Shammar (Von Oppenheim, *Die Beduinen*, 1:71). Abū Zwayyid sends a poem to Muḥammad ibn Rashīd from the Khābūr River, a northern tributary of the Euphrates (§10.4, v. 7). The ruler's good fortune showed in the long period of plentiful rains during his reign (al-Suwaydāʾ, *Manṭiqat Ḥāʾil*, 599, 607).

Under his successor, years of drought followed, and "the power of the Shamar emir, Eben Rashīd, had collapsed in 1906" (Musil, *Rwala*, 517).

57 "Until recently, the Shammar of Najd were not only a Bedouin tribe, but also the mainstay of a state, the Shammar dominions of Ḥāʾil" (Von Oppenheim, *Die Beduinen*, 3:37).

58 Unanimously described with awe by European visitors (Wallin, Palgrave, Doughty, Blunt, Huber, Euting) and Arabic sources (in particular, the details in al-Suwaydāʾ, *Manṭiqat Ḥāʾil*); see also ʿAjlān's lament, "where the staffs tapping on laden royal trays, loud invitations to paupers waiting for food" (§52.1, v. 3).

59 Palgrave mentions that ʿUbayd ibn Rashīd took to the field with his troops forty times (*Narrative*, 92), and al-Suwaydāʾ quotes Muḥammad ibn Rashīd boasting that he had raided the ʿUtaybah tribe forty-seven times (*Manṭiqat Ḥāʾil*, 399–400).

60 Al-Suwaydāʾ, *al-Amthāl al-shaʾbiyyah fī manṭiqat Ḥāʾil*, 474, 434. The expression is part of the poets' predilection for super-hyperbole, making the incredibly bad even worse or taking the magnificent to even greater heights (e.g., Abu Zwayyid §§6:13, 13, 16:3–4, 48:41, 49:9, 49:13; al-Hirbīd §21:3, 25:4).

61 Al-Isfahānī, *al-Aghānī*, 2:269.

62 Goldziher, *Abhandlungen zur Arabischen Philologie*, section "Über die Vorgeschichte der Hijâʾ-Poesie," 13.

63 There is a strong possibility, of course, that the order of verses changed in the course of transmission and that verses went missing.

64 This is the only episode in which Abū Zwayyid is mentioned as an owner of palm trees.

65 On original touches not found in classical poetry, see al-Suwaydāʾ, *al-Nakhlah al-ʿarabiyyah adabiyyan wa-ʿilmiyyan wa-iqtiṣādiyyan*, 86, 88, and Sowayan, *al-Ṣaḥrāʾ al-ʿarabiyyah*, 379. In two of the three brief references to palm trees in Abū Zwayyid's poetry, two are part of a camel description and one occurs as a simile for a girl's beauty (§5.5, v. 13, §25.8, v. 6).

66 Kurpershoek, *Arabian Romantic*, 117.

67 Doughty, *Arabia Deserta*, 1:261.

68 Dhū l-Rummah, *Dīwān*, 2:715–16.

69 Also, "he dispatched a *giʿūd* (male camel) to so-and-so" (i.e., a poem), and *ʿād jāhum giʿūd abūhum*, "they received a poem from their father." When Shaykh al-ʿAwājī called on ʿAnazah to mobilize against Shammar, and Shammar heard his poem, the latter said, "Listen, folk! Which of you is going to send a camel (*giʿūd*) that overtakes and catches the camel of al-ʿAwājī?" (Sowayan, *al-Ṣaḥrāʾ al-ʿarabiyyah*, 236–37).

70 A Rwēlī is a member of the Rwalah tribe.

71 If camels have a salt deficit, generally because they have not been grazing on saltbushes for an extended period, "they become weak and thin and have a tendency to eat bones and carrion" (Mandaville, *Bedouin Ethnobotany*, 87).

72 The story resembles the poet Ibn Ẓāhir's choice of a young, not very good-looking camel as wages for his service as a camel herd, but the beast grows into an unrivaled racer (Kurpershoek, *Love, Death, Fame*, 153).

73 The line parallels the verse quoted by Ibn Rashīd that almost cost Abū Zwayyid his life. It is a common cliché used for flattery. Musil was honored with almost the same expression in verse: "To another like him no chaste beauty ever gave birth; and of all Bedouin chiefs none equals him" (Musil, *Rwala*, 291).

74 "When a son attains maturity, his father generally gives him a mare or a camel, that he may try his fortune in plundering excursions" (Burckhardt, *Notes*, 114).

75 The verses are a replica of a story about the sixth-century poet ʿUrwah ibn al-Ward (al-Isfahānī, *al-Aghānī*, 3:81–83).

Khalaf Abū Zwayyid

His Life

His full name is Khalaf ibn Dikhīl ibn Khalaf ibn Fāris ibn Zwayyid   1.1
ibn Khalaf ibn Rakhīṣ. His grandfather was a brother of Ḍēfallah and
Ṣāliḥ al-Rakhīṣ, the shaykhs of the Nabhān of the Zmēl of Shammar.
I heard that his grandfather Khalaf went to see Ibn Saʿūd with verses
he had composed in his honor. I only know these two lines:

> I am the oldest of seven brothers: 1.2
> > they ate my eyelids, lashes dropped.
> If not a gift, I crave then for a pledge,
> > as a farmhand awaits a promised meal.[1]

I vaguely remember having seen him, God show him mercy,   1.3
when I was a little kid: a frail and blind old man being led by the
hand. Yet he was known as a bold, gritty, and outstanding indi-
vidual. His sons were Dikhīl, ʿĀmish, and Faḍl. ʿĀmish had a son,
who currently lives in al-Rakhīṣiyyah with his children. Dikhīl and
Faḍl died in the battle of al-ʿĀmiriyyah between the Shaʿlān and the
Nabhān. When Abū Zwayyid passed away, he was over a hundred
years old. He died in the year 1361 [1942], long after the Saudi con-
quest of Ḥāyil [1921]. I was told that he composed poems in praise of
Prince ʿAbd al-ʿAzīz ibn Musāʿid. At the time of the Saudi conquest
of Ḥāyil, he was eighty-six years old.[2]

He went to call on ʿAbd al-ʿAzīz ibn Musāʿid in Ḥāʾil and was   1.4
brought to him by some of his relatives. He found the prince in

the company of the Ikhwān,[3] turbans wrapped around their heads, gnashing their teeth at the sight of this new entrant. They could not stand Abū Zwayyid and his poems.

Abū Zwayyid greeted the prince and said, "With your permission, may you live long, I would like to recite some verses I have composed in your honor."

The prince said, "Look, Abū Zwayyid, we are in a session devoted to the study of the Prophet's sayings. This nonsense of verses is over."

"Poetry, prince! It is poetry, not just some verses."

The prince said, "Well, if it is poetry, then go ahead!"

When Abū Zwayyid had finished his recitation, Ibn Musā'id remained silent. He did not utter a word. Abū Zwayyid had never experienced such a thing before. He was accustomed to praise and encouragement from an audience that showed its appreciation at the end of a poetry recital with the words "Well spoken!"[4] But these people uttered not a single word! And he was blind. He did not see the expression on the faces of the men gathered there. The ominous silence made him feel uneasy.

1.5 Abū Zwayyid said, "I wish God would grant me sight, Prince, since He made it impossible for me to see your face."

"Tell me, what would you do if you could see my face?"

"I would like to see for myself if you are of those who on being praised lift their eyebrows and twist the ends of their mustache or of those who lower their chin and scratch the hairs on their nape."

The prince said, "As sure as I am Abū 'Abdallah! I belong to those who lift their eyebrows and twist their mustache."

"By God, you are truly deserving, son of Turkī!" he said, and added, "Let me just mention that my camel for drawing water from the well has died. My palm trees are thirsting and may turn into dead wood. For their sake, I need another camel as a replacement."

The prince issued orders to one of his servants: "Go, go at once, 'Alī! Give him a camel strong enough to draw water from his well to irrigate his grove!"

His men took a camel from the courtyard where the draft camels were kept, a dark-gray beast with huge knee joints. It was God's will to provide for him. Ibn Musā'id made an exception for him, as he was not in the habit of giving anyone presents.

His Son Dikhīl

Dikhīl, Abū Zwayyid's son, joined a group of raiders who rode out with the aim of despoiling one of the other tribes. They were a small bunch, twenty or at most thirty riders. He took part in a few such robbing expeditions. One of those who also joined belonged to the tribe of Ḥarb, the Bīḍān section. His old father said, "Dikhīl, my boy, I impress on you to keep an eye on your companion and take good care of him." For emphasis, he repeated his advice in a poem. They returned home with their booty and Dikhīl took his share of the robbed camels. Before the booty was divided among his fellow raiders, he put aside two she-camels, beautiful white ones. He explained, "These are reserved for my dear companion, the one my father entrusted to my care." So, over and above those he allotted to every raider, he set aside two more she-camels for his Ḥarbī ward. A little later, Ibn Rakhīṣ came to inspect the booty and supervise the division of the spoils.[5] He said, "Listen, you Ḥarbī! I want to take these camels of yours for myself." Dikhīl protested: "Dear Uncle, he is a companion entrusted to my care." Ibn Rakhīṣ said, "When you have grown up to become a real raid leader, who knows, then you may grant such favors to your friend." He took the camels from the Ḥarbī, leaving Dikhīl to stew in his anger. On that occasion, Abū Zwayyid composed the following verses:

2.2   Dikhīl, listen closely to your father's counsel:
        it takes a man of sound mind to grasp its thrust.

Be considerate with a friend, stay away from dirt!
　　Don't forget that gentlemen treasure companions!
If you find him down and out, in dire straits,
　　lift a load off his back, help him carry it.
Do not let the cords of noble striving slacken!
　　Beware of hurting others, be firm with violators!
With your left, heave mightily at the ropes　　　　　　　　5
　　lest others smash the bucket against the casing.
Always keep a hardy mount close at hand,
　　a reddish camel to cut through simmering air:
Hooves spinning like unhinged pulley wheels
　　hurtle across fearsome desert wastes.
Let it whisk you off into lonely plains:
　　better than to stay, your nose rubbed in dust.
Be first to volunteer at calls to heavy lifting,
　　or risk being counted a mere shred of cloth.
Sluggards hanging back have it coming:　　　　　　　　10
　　may their wives send them packing.
Sparrows find sustenance for their brood;
　　humans must overcome greater hurdles.
Hey! One session seated in a seat of honor
　　equals a bastard's life spent in humiliation.

In court cases, Abū Zwayyid always came out the winner.[6] Now, 2.3
one time his son Dikhīl quarreled unfairly with another raider
about a captured she-camel. The man who had seized the camel and
could rightfully claim its ownership was not Dikhīl, the son of Abū
Zwayyid. Plenty of witnesses had seen that the other man touched
the animal first with his staff. Therefore, his right to the booty was
not in question.[7] Dikhīl protested and argued, but the other merely
said, "Well, do as you wish, but be aware that your only gain will be
the trouble of driving the camel across this stretch of desert." These
were the words of the man who had first touched the she-camel. On
their return, witnesses from among the other raiders had testified

that they had seen the other man making the she-camel his own.
As a result, he took the animal back from Dikhīl. Abū Zwayyid was
disconcerted by this verdict. He resented it as a personal defeat. It
came as a blow to him since he had never lost a case in court. He had
a solid reputation for being someone who spoke the truth and noth-
ing but the truth. Those were times when truthfulness still counted
for something. Dikhīl took it badly too. In response, he went off in a
huff to stay with the ʿLayyān, and married the daughter of Ibn Ghāzī.
That was Dikhīl's response. Thereupon, his father advised him:

2.4

My troubled heart pours forth its verses—
    not a whining dullard's petty complaints.
A dimwit is a stranger to tempestuous feeling:
    clueless, his mind is at a loss to understand.
Dikhīl, if you care to weigh my words, take them:
    they will guide you through midday's blistering heat;
This counsel, dear boy, I entrust to your care
    with an appeal: "Stay faithful to its message!"
5
Never forget, my boy, to requite good with good:
    what use is a right hand forsaken by its left?
I beseech you, apple of my eye, do no harm,
    and let no one get away with wrongful deeds!
In empty deserts you depend on your friend:
    overlook his misstep if he has offended you!
Beware of befriending gutless poltroons:
    They are a rotten breed, profligate in evil ways.
Friends have been bequeathed to you:
    your ancestors' friends from olden days.
10
Ignore what people say—insidious gossip;
    adjust old friends' loads if they go askew.
Be smart, expect no benefit from other folks,
    my boy, except from kinsmen: stout defenders
Against wily enemies lying in wait for ages,
    waggling tongues to entice with honeyed words.

Put yourself out for a noble horse—it pays:
    a stud to beget fillies from pedigree mares.
Bear up! Fortitude fills your kin with awe;
    patient endurance staves off ignominy.
Patience is the key to reputation and salvation: 15
    let foolish dimwits flounder in ignorance!

In the following verses, Abū Zwayyid addresses Dikhīl: 2.5

Once heedless, I looked closer at the world,   1
    a plethora of springs, water holes, and wells:
Eighty pulleys empty buckets into basins;
    from each basin the water runs into a gully.
May big spenders' valleys turn green first,
    carpeted with grass for generous entertainers,
Unflagging servers of coffee kept on the boil,
    deliciously scented in four long-beaked pots;
Peals from beans pounded in brass mortars ring   5
    all night long, like terrifying anguished shrieks.
Fellow seeker, I tell you, fraternizing means
    you're despised for doing a bad turn to a friend.
Laudable deeds should be rewarded with praise:
    reputations shine if glory is won by sword.[8]

—By sword, he means noble acts.

If wise counsel was as much applied as sought,
    other men would not be needed to save the day.[9]
If you open your mind to a dependable man,
    be confident he proffers advice solid as rock;
Never entrust your inner thoughts to wretches: 10
    consort with rogues and you end up maimed.
Dikhīl, my dearest son, my ancestors' scion,
    don't get chummy with foxes playing games!

Hanging with foxes will bring you down;
    fennecs aren't on par with young wolves.[10]
In hunting season choose a peregrine,
    talons dripping with blood from a strike.
Keep company with stalwart braves—
    friends like ropes fit to haul from deepest wells—
15 If things get dicey, they're crafty and cunning;
    if all is fine, honest and upright as preachers.
Befriend robust defenders of the common good,
    prompt in action at their tribesmen's call.
Steer him straight; if he strays, stray with him,
    as if his doing wrong were the right way to go.
Stay clear from rotten apples in your clan:
    their cravenness will never improve.
He'll hide behind a hospitable man's dwelling:
    a cur that blanches at the approach of guests;
20 He invites no one to lounge in his tent,
    but is ever first to snatch up dinner invitations.
Slouched against the side, though sound of limb,[11]
    coming at a crawl in the hour of need.
Eye warily a world brimful of lurking danger,
    ready to pounce and catch you unprepared.
Fortunate the man with clear conscience:
    he is the darling when God's angels call.

Verses in Praise of
ʿAbd al-Karīm al-Jarbā

ʿAbd al-Karīm is God's favorite among men;   3.1
    at his pinnacle, he basks in matchless glory.
He strides robed in power at the Lord's behest,
    gifted to him at the pleasure of the Compassionate.
From the times when Eve and Adam first met,
    his likeness has not been seen in creation.
With his fabled feats comes unrivaled generosity;
    his liberal hands have the magic touch in policy.
He plunges headlong into heaving seas of death   5
    without a care, an intrepid death-defying diver.
His motto, "Take it!," puts his name above all:[12]
    he is like Moses, who talked to God,
As said before me by the stalwart in battle,
    Fajḥān who blocks the way of avengers,

—Fajḥān al-Farāwī.

Whose fast camel mount never tires,
    king of the melee, thwarter of foes' schemes.
ʿAbd al-Karīm, whose gifts gush forth profusion,
    endless streams of camels and spirited mares.
Rulers and Turks recognize his power   10
    of protection paired with acumen and sagacity.

3.2   The story goes that Abū Zwayyid called on al-Hādī al-Jarbā and recited a panegyric poem in which these verses appear:[13]

> These verses were recited in the shaykh's presence:
>   I fondly desired to see your countenance, Ibn Sarrāḥ.[14]
> Mighty chief, your renown's spread far and wide!
>   Indestructible shard of metal, you're invulnerable!
> Over a wadi's red-hot stones, camels are spurred
>   by a falcon unafraid to attack fierce warriors.[15]

—He means big groups of fighters.

> […][16]
>   In the market of death, you hold dear life cheap.

—Proof the clan of Sarrāh are kin to the Jarbā.

His Poems on Saṭṭām ibn Shaʿlān

Rider of a red-brown camel trotting like a wolf,   4.1
 reddish-brown, never having suckled a calf.[17]
A thick-haired tail lashes curved hocks,
 reddish-brown, the tail reaches the heels.
Red-brown camel fit to cross endless plains,
 reddish-brown, fresh, first eyeteeth showing.
Red-brown, bulging thighs stretch the girths:
 speedy, she makes faraway wells an easy ride.
Red-brown, she shatters saddle's wood   5
 at full gallop, stretching her flanks in and out.
We came riding from Najd on camelback
 toward a shaykh—I have no care for others.
We came to Saṭṭām, terror of enemy tribes,
 a friend if other friends turn against you.
If the public awards the trophy of chivalry,
 his feats of arms win widest acclaim by far.
Adored by a wife who sent suitors packing:
 until you came, she scorned all the Bedouin;
Daughter of a legend lionized in assemblies, 10
 he sounds calls to dinner from atop a hill;[18]
His blood-smeared axes felled huge camels
 without a thought for people's need of milk.
Splendid beauties dream of him, a stud:
 what use do they have for a defective organ?[19]

They never gave birth, nor will they ever,

    to the equal of Ṣaṭṭām in the entire world.[20]

In retreat, his horses go limping as if lame,

    then turn and attack at breathtaking speed.

15   Hazzāʿ begot a panther, a lion, and a wolf,

    snake venom spewed by a rabid monster.[21]

Rwalah, the pure, without a foreign strain.

    Hail to their war cry, "The Sublime!"[22]

In verses I do not ramble and flounder:

    Pfui! Let some ears get mad on hearing them.

He does not care even about Ibn Rashīd, who did not impregnate any of the pretty girls. Muḥammad ibn Rashīd was sterile. He remained without offspring.

4.2   Another poet, al-Kwēkibī,[23] responded to these verses and asked Ibn Rashīd for a reward, saying, "For myself and my kinsmen to the fifth degree I ask the right to pasture our camels on the lands of Shammar without risk of getting despoiled of our animals."[24]

1   Abū Zwayyid, weakling unable to climb a lookout,

    wolf-faced dog, busy lapping up curdled milk.

Your camel, Abū Zwayyid, isn't free of blemishes,

    A noble racer spurred on to bring you in a hurry.

You heap praise on Ibn Shaʿlān, born of a rabid bitch,

    feeding on his own kin, too clumsy for worthy prey.

Why not speak of al-Ḍēghamī, virtue's fountainhead:[25]

    unconcerned, he lingers on in battle's wake.

5   His camel troops race like spinning pulley wheels,

    at night through wastes where no enemy treads.

4.3   In a farewell to his host, Abū Zwayyid composed these verses on Ṣaṭṭām ibn Shaʿlān:

Merciless rider urging on a gaunt, sinewy camel: *1*
    under its hooves, plains roll up like carpets.
If riders draw too close, the sturdy beast shies:
    scared, it hurtles forward, running flat out.
Compact on top, haunches broadly spaced,
    it throws its legs with studied nonchalance.
Camels dry out on forced desert marches—
    she breaks a sweat that oils her belly girths.
Camels left in shreds, worn out and limping   *5*
    from deserts crossed, she runs at a crazy pace.
Her battered hooves can do without patches:
    she's built to traverse vast and waterless plains.
Head for Abū Mamdūḥ, may he remain safe;
    my eyes miss being comforted by seeing him.

—Abū Mamdūḥ is Ṣaṭṭām ibn Shaʿlān.

Generosity's every way and byway are his:
    the opposite of bumblers who lack vision.
Stalker of quarry, lion, king of the jungle!
    you spurn all but the mightiest trophies.
His charge's trail teems with bounty hunters: *10*
    camels, cattle galore, trays of food handed out.
Proverbially, the world corrupts through greed.
    Take me! A goat digging up its slaughter knife![26]
Dumbest thing I did was to depart from you,
    yet credit is due when good deeds are done.

He Solves a Dispute between Sons of Ṣaṭṭām ibn Shaʿlān Concerning a Guest and a Neighbor

5.1 If you take a closer look at the poetry of Abū Zwayyid, you find that every verse is spot on: it hits the target and pierces through its target. Is any of it faulty? No more than empty words devoid of meaning? No, absolutely not, there are no such verses! Some of today's poetry is prolix, and may sound pleasant, but perhaps no more than a quarter or a third of it has anything to do with real-life situations.[27] With the exception of a few verses, perhaps. That kind of poetry is sound as far as meter and rhyme are concerned, but it bears no discernible relation to reality as we know it. By contrast, Abū Zwayyid's poems are about matters that are very recognizable. Every word is to the point and deals with a real subject.

5.2 One of his poems deals with a dispute between members of the Shaʿlān clan. It features the verse:

> If your guest quarrels with your neighbor,
>> by God, seek to escape, your reputation intact!

Before this verse, people didn't know what to do in such a situation. If a guest and a neighbor under your protection became embroiled in a dispute, you'd find yourself in a quandary. Impossible to decide whose side you were supposed to be on. In his poem, Abū Zwayyid laid down the law for such cases, which was adopted by Shammar. That is, if you find yourself responsible for a neighbor and a guest in your protective embrace and they start to fight one another, abstain from interfering by any means. The only permissible involvement is an offer of good offices to assist them in achieving reconciliation. You may say things like "Turn to God for help!" and express the hope that nothing untoward will happen to either of them. In such a situation, one should refrain from taking a position about the issue at stake or about which of the two is in the right. Do not tell one of them that he is in the right and the other that his arguments do not hold water. Only use expressions conducive to calming tempers, and use encouragements such as "May God give you recompense!" Provide them with moral guidance. It is not your task to show more respect to one or the other.

It happened, may God bless your days, to the Shaʿlān family: a case that involved two sons of Saṭṭām ibn Shaʿlān, Khālid and Ṭrād. One of them hosted a guest, a traveler, a Sharārī, a member of the tribe of al-Sharārāt. The other had extended protection to a neighbor who came to stay for a certain period, an ʿGēlī trader.[28] The ʿGēlī stayed in his own tent and spent his days bargaining with Bedouin over the price of camels he had come to buy, as ʿGēlī tradesmen used to do back then. The Sharārī had sold a male camel to the ʿGēlī for twenty guineas, the currency of the time. The ʿGēlī took the animal to pasture with the other camels he had bought. When the ʿGēlī wrapped up his business and was about to depart, the Sharārī felt remorse at having sold his camel. "Oh my God," he moaned, "this is the stud I need for my she-camels. Why did I wrong myself in this manner? How could I sell it, knowing that my she-camels will lack a stud?" He said, "My dear little brother, ʿGēlī, here is your money. I hand it back to you." The ʿGēlī said, "It is no longer yours. You've sold your camel to me. It has gone to pasture already. I have branded it with my branding iron, and the money is in your pocket. Impossible! I bought it with legal tender and I am not going to return it to you." The ʿGēlī stubbornly refused to go along and the Sharārī writhed with self-loathing and regret: "Oh my, oh my, poor me! Woe to me, my stud camel!" The Sharārī's host and protector felt pity for him and took his side. He told the ʿGēlī, "You must return the camel to the Sharārī whether you like it or not! The man wants his camel back." But the patron of the ʿGēlī replied for him, "No, he is not going to give up anything against his will!"

5.4   Matters descended into futile altercations, then escalated into a tense standoff between the two sides.[29] All of the Shaʿlān rallied to their respective client's cause. A tug-of-war ensued between Khālid and Ṭrād. They threatened to come to blows and cut each other down. Then some of the Shaʿlān tried to cool tempers. "Don't take up arms and fight!" they said. "Submit the case to experts in tribal law and let them find a way and solve the problem for us! We're not in a position to decide who is in the right. We don't know if priority should be given to guest or protected neighbor." As it turned out, neither did the experts in tribal law, who failed to come up with a solution. Then Abū Zwayyid came forward and helped them find a way out of the dilemma. The poem he composed restored the peace and ever since has served as a beacon to follow. This outcome was achieved through his poem; in fact, by just one of its verses—one verse that set the standard for dealing with the issue. The poem's merit is not restricted to that particular verse, however: it touches on a variety of themes.

5.5   He said:

1   God, You are privy to deepest secrets,
           matters gainsayers hide in their hearts.[30]
       You are the Creator of Paradise and Hell;
           Creator of the world; holder of the end-time.
       You sustain tiny birds with invisible food, God;
           You breathe the breath of life into the locusts' brood,
       Deep in the land, the mother in another land:
           a distant place, in earth's far-flung regions.
5   Your gaze resurrects woeful, prostrate mounts;
           first they're skin and bones, then saddled and run.

Pity a heart forever perplexed and floundering:
    soothing words only make things worse.
My heart is overgrown with prickly bushes:
    a garden covered in Christ's-thorn and acacia.
My eyes smart as if treated with poisonous drops;
    spiny locust legs are thrust into the retina.
Enough of this, rider of a spirited camel:
    loaded with no more than waterskin and saddle,
Reddish-brown, it tackles slopes with panache;   10
    a long-backed red, shoulders steep as bluffs.
Lucky rider lounging as if in a shady cave:
    it does not trudge and does not run amok:
A ball of fire saddled with leather cushions,
    never worn out like a draft animal at the well;
Conical ears like the spathe of a palm
    when wintery cold closes the spathes' sheaths.
Eyes roll, red as a fire's glowing embers,
    like kindling flaring in pitch-black darkness;
Brave men's eyes flashing at neighbors' shouts,   15
    fiendish and resolute fighters in close combat;
On the homeward stretch, its gait is haughty:
    swollen with pride, it veers left and right.[31]
On arrival, share the news with Khālid!
    He has the knack of unraveling secrets.

—Khālid ibn Saṭṭām al-Shaʿlān.

If your guest quarrels with your neighbor,
    by God, seek to escape, your reputation intact!
Be patient—no one gets blamed for patience—
    until time brings counsel and things work out.
Favored by fortune, nicely chugging along,   20
    a soul keeps dreaming and hankers for more.

Virgins none, souls are forever conceiving:

    birth after pregnancies of unknown length.[32]

Semen from evil's breeding grounds sparks

    fierce fighters bent on settling scores, swords in hand;

Plans hatched and spread by word of mouth

    trigger violent outbursts to shatter the peace.

Many boys are bred by a raging cauldron,

    or a gun's hammer cocked to ignite the powder.

25   Calamities are brought about by faulty views:

    wisdom tells us that greed breeds corruption.

Dishonesty spreads far and wide, a way of life,

    running counter to good and generous nature.

Truth lies prostrate on the way, trampled

    beneath falsehood's brazen march.

Fated to live these insipid, rotten times,

    we watch them dissipate, fleeting shadows.

Guests and visitors cannot trust their host:

    no safety from tricksters' false promises!

30   Wolves startle, flee at the sight of a lamb;

    predators are on the run, fair game for all.

Swindlers are hoisted onto saddles of shaykhs;

    stout, steadfast leaders are shunned and spurned.

Cold-hearted good-for-nothings hold sway;

    noblemen's hearths gone, ashes strewn.[33]

You're lost if the Almighty so decrees;

    a relentless tight-fisted grip brings no gain:

I'd pasture ugly Damascus goats in Sinjār[34]

    rather than spend time in miserly company.

He Comforts Turkiyyah, Daughter of Ibn Mhēd, When She Quarreled with Ṣaṭṭām ibn Shaʿlān

Ṣaṭṭām ibn Shaʿlān, the father of Mamdūḥ, migrated in a westerly   6.1
direction and set up camp in al-Hēl, a vast expanse of flat land, I
don't know where exactly. As soon as he arrived, he received vis-
itors from the Sbaʿah, Fidʿān, and both divisions of ʿAnazah: Bishr
and al-Jlās. All of them flocked to see him in al-Hēl. The only visi-
tors from Shammar were ʿAjlān ibn Rmāl and Khalaf Abū Zwayyid.
ʿAjlān came with his famous herd of white camels, called Barrāgāt.
Abū Zwayyid was hard up: the sum total of his possessions was
one male camel. Destitute, he made a living as a conversationalist,
entertaining companies with his stories and verses.

ʿAjlān said, "Abū Zwayyid! Khalaf! By God, I don't feel at ease   6.2
staying here in al-Hēl. Morning and evening I spend in trepidation,
expecting someone to spring a bad surprise on us at any moment.
Our fellow tribesmen of Shammar are a treacherous lot. A Sham-
marī may strike up a friendship with a Rwēlī with the aim of despoil-
ing and blackmailing me.[35] As they say, 'Get hold of the rooster's
leg and you'll haul in the bird whole.' Please God, spare my camels
for as long as we are to stay here this summer!" "Nothing untoward
will happen," said Abū Zwayyid. But ʿAjlān moaned, "Dear brother,
I am so afraid!" As they spoke, a horseman came riding straight at
them from the direction of Ṣaṭṭām's camp. "Abū Zwayyid!" ʿAjlān
cried. "You see, didn't I tell you![36] There you are, the horseman is

heading for us! Oh my God, what will become of us! Oh, what is going to happen to these camels, my sweeties? Oh my God, what if they're stolen, oh no, please no! For sure that rider was told, 'Get going, bring the camels of that kinsman of yours, that Shammarī!'" Abū Zwayyid told him to calm down: "When things get knotty, best to shut up. It's none of your business. Let me deal with it."[37] Ṣattām's man reined in his horse and said, "The shaykh asks you to call on him: you, 'Ajlān, and Abū Zwayyid as well. Go quickly!" "I am the son of Barghash![38] Now it's going to happen!" 'Ajlān said. They found Ṣattām in a sour mood and preoccupied. Already, 'Ajlān saw his worst fears confirmed. The two Shammar visitors sat down.

6.3   Ṣattām had three wives. One was Turkiyyah, daughter of Ibn Mhēd, the shaykh nicknamed "Supper Host" because he was in the habit of inviting all and sundry to partake of his dinner.[39] There was a daughter of Ibn Smēr. The third wife was Jōzā Manhūbah, daughter of a well-known kinsman of the Shaʿlān, Fahd ibn Shaʿlān of the Shiyābah branch.[40] Someone of the Shiyābah had killed a man of the Ṣattām branch and in compensation ceded his daughter Jōzā to Sattām. It so happened that Turkiyyah had left Ṣattām in a fit of anger. She was furious with him and went to stay with one of the slaves of the Shaʿlān clan, a man called Abū Dakhkhānēn, "Man of Two Smokestacks": one fire for baking bread and the other for the coffeepots.[41] Ibn Shaʿlān said, "'Ajlān, my dear, Turkiyyah, the mother of my son Mamdūḥ, became angry with me and flounced out of here yesterday, mad as hell. I want you to go over to her place and persuade her to return to her children, who are stuffing their mouths with grit." "Honest to God, Ṣattām," 'Ajlān said, "my tribe of the Rmāl regards me as a person who brings bad luck, and my own folk don't want me to take part in sensitive missions. If I were to succeed in convincing a woman to rejoin her husband, he'd be sure to leave her; then woe to me. For any other task, I am at your beck and call." Ṣattām said, "Well, then it falls to you, Abū Zwayyid, to bring her back to me." "Me return her to you? Where did you get that silly idea, you 'Anazī? Did things go to your head? You collected this

stable of pedigree fillies, like the mares of the Prophet's compan-
ions, and grew so conceited that you offended the daughter of Ibn
Mhēd and made her flee your home. We came to you thinking you'd
invite us to a roast. We thought no more was expected of us than
washing our hands and eating. As for Turkiyyah, go and fetch her
yourself. Let Hell get her! Why should I be the one to do it? That is
a job for the one who brought her from Ibn Mhēd in the first place,
the man who paid a bride-price of two mares and ten riding camels
for her." Taken aback, Ṣaṭṭām said, "What good are you to me then,
Shammarī? Why didn't you give me this advice earlier, when she
was still with me and I could have put it to good use? Now, even
if I find her amenable to my arguments, I'm afraid she'll give me a
tongue-lashing. That being the case, I fear I'll get mad and divorce
her in a fit of anger, though I truly love her and do not want to be
separated from her." "You'd better keep quiet," Abū Zwayyid said.
"Since you did not regale us with a roast luncheon, your reputation
has been dealt a serious blow."

Ṣaṭṭām told his slave to call another slave: "Go and get ʿAnnād!"   6.4
and ordered him: "Away at once, bring your mistress back to me!
Make for her place quickly, ʿAnnād! Hurry up about it!" ʿAnnād
left and found the daughter of Ibn Mhēd dressed in a body-length
abaya seated and chatting with her lady friends of the Sbaʿah tribe, a
circle even bigger than the men's.[42] "Who comes riding to us?" she
exclaimed. "Ah, I see, it's ʿAnnād. God curse your father, you piece
of dirt!"[43] "Please, mistress!" he said. "What is it you want from
me?" she said. "Well, you see . . ." He hesitated. "Come here, draw
closer, I can't hear you!" she said. As he spoke, she picked up a rock
and smashed it on his head. Blood spurted from him like the thick
tail of a sorrel mare. "Ow, ow, ow!" he cried and slumped to the
ground. When Ṣaṭṭām saw him on his return, he cried, "Good grief!
What happened to you? She bashed you? A curse on you, Turki-
yyah! Good heavens! What will do the trick when it comes to her?"

"Call ʿAjab!" said Ṣaṭṭām. ʿAjab was a blacksmith who had   6.5
worked for the Ibn Rashīd rulers and enjoyed renown as a warrior

on horseback. "Go find Turkiyyah and bring her back!" he ordered
ʿAjab. "No," he said, "I am not going to do that." "Why not?" "First
you must tell me what made her so mad at you. I cannot force her
to come back without knowing what the trouble is." "I'm not going
to tell you what put her into a rage." "In that case, it's up to you. Go
yourself!" "All right then. She became mad at me yesterday because
I gave money to Giṭnah, the daughter of Ibn Smēr: a sum of money
that I had borrowed from her and paid back. She said, 'Why do you
give her money? Do you care more about Giṭnah than me?' She
upset me, then walked out on me." "Right," he said. "If she does
come, will you mollify her by giving her money too?" "No prob-
lem," he said. "There is a problem. Say, 'Yes, by God, I will give her
money.' Only then will I go to fetch her." "I will give it to her." ʿAjab
rode off on his mare. "Here we go again," she muttered. "This time
it is ʿAjab. God's curse on your father and Ṣattām as well." He had his
mare step up to her and poked at her with his lance. "Come on! Ride
with me!" he said. "Why are you so outraged?" "Damn you, ʿAjab,
leave me alone! Get away with you!" "I told you to move or else
I will make you go willy-nilly, by force.⁴⁴ Why are you so cross?"
She said, "Yesterday he gave money to Giṭnah and he didn't give me
anything." "He will make you a present as well," he said. "Just start
moving!" "Twist the promise into your mustache!" she said.⁴⁵ "Just
go!" he said. "The money will come your way."

6.6   When Ṣattām saw them approaching, he was overjoyed. "Ready
the nuptial bed!" he shouted, and the servants laid out the bed neat
and tidy. From where they were seated, Abū Zwayyid and ʿAjlān
watched, and saw Ṣattām's euphoria as she alighted and headed
for the women's quarters. "Bring the money!" ʿAjab said. "Take it
easy, man!" Ṣattām replied. "In God's good time. I will give it to her
tomorrow, when we once again see eye to eye on things." "Don't
play such risky games, Ṣattām!" he warned.⁴⁶ "Give her the money
you promised to assuage her." He was a damned tough fellow, ʿAjab.
He raised his lance and let it hover over Ṣattām's head. "Give her
the indemnities right away, or else I will take her back to the place I

made her come from!" Ṣaṭṭām looked around and noticed that none of his slaves was present. He sauntered toward his chest of valuables to scoop up some money. But before he could do so, up came 'Ajab and with one blow of his lance shattered the strongbox. Ṣaṭṭām called to Turkiyyah: "Come, the money is here: it is yours to take! He was about to stab me with his lance." And cursing 'Ajab, he said, "Damn your father, you lowlife!"[47]

Abū Zwayyid sidled over to Turkiyyah's quarters: "Good day. Peace on you, Turkiyyah!" "Welcome to you, Abū Zwayyid!" "Spring came to this dwelling and burst into flower when you set foot in it," he gushed. "When bliss departs, darkness comes. Welcome, welcome! Hail to this arrival! Cheers for the mother of Mamdūḥ!" "Well, the same goes for you," she replied. "Tell me, what do you have in mind?" "Nothing in particular. All I wished for is to see you, such a highly valued person." He obliquely referred to the money given to her, safely stashed away in the inside pocket of her robe. Then Abū Zwayyid gave her even greater satisfaction by reciting these verses:

6.7

> They asked for counsel but I stopped counseling: 1
>   if my counsel falls flat, they'll stick it to me.
> Shackled mares of the Prophet's companions,
>   pedigree fillies sired by stout and noble steeds.

—*Al-jākhūr* are the irons in which the feet of horses are shackled.

> Foul-tempered and reluctant, they were steered away
>   at a gallop from their carefree homes.[48]
> The first did not come of her own volition:
>   not bagged by a misfit, she's a falcon's prey.

—She did not come of her own accord, but rather because Fahd had killed someone from Ṣaṭṭām's retinue and made up for it by ceding this girl.

5 The second was born to an intrepid shaykh,
    fierce defender of heavily laden camel trains.
The third mends his defects, a fabled mare:
    auspicious, she anchors cavalry in combat;[49]
In times of dearth, her father's call to dinner
    reaches the ears of ʿAnazah far and wide;
In the melee of thrusting and smiting knights,
    his fiery panache blazes a bloody trail.[50]

6.8　"Here, Ṣaṭṭām's money is yours!" she said, and she poured the coins into the fold of the long shirt Abū Zwayyid held up to her. Ṣaṭṭām moaned, "Woe, woe to me! The caravan's treasure has been pilfered! Cursed lady!" He called a slave and told him to load a camel with wheat and bedding for Abū Zwayyid. "When you're done, come to me at once," Turkiyyah instructed the man who attended to the camel. "I want you to add these rolls of textile and small woolen carpets to the load." She did so in appreciation of Abū Zwayyid's poem. ʿAjlān, who had been an onlooker, ventured a request: "My dearest Abū Zwayyid, give me some of that money. I need to go to the markets in Iraq but I'm broke." "Why don't you sell some of your camels, brother?" Abu Zwayyid suggested. "You know you're dearer to me than I am to myself.[51] This windfall has come your way, and I did a lot of work this morning," pleaded ʿAjlān.[52] "All right," said Abū Zwayyid, "take these twenty pounds and off you go!"

How He Obtained Satisfaction for Nūrah, Daughter of Ibn Mhēd, When She Quarreled with Fahd ibn Hadhdhāl

One night, Abū Zwayyid called on Fahd ibn Hadhdhāl for the plea-   7.1
sure of taking part in his circle's conversation, as was the custom.[53]
He at once noticed that the shaykh was preoccupied and wore
a frown. What was the matter? "What's troubling you, shaykh?"
"Well, Nūrah is vexed with me and keeps her distance,"[54] mean-
ing Nūrah, his wife, the daughter of Ibn Mhēd. If the daughter of a
shaykh walks out on her husband, she doesn't return until she feels
like it. She only comes of her own volition. "You know, Abū Dikhīl,
from the moment she stormed out in a huff I've been out of sorts,"
he continued. Abū Zwayyid took his cane and walked toward her
tent. She knew what his visit was about the moment she saw him
approaching. She picked up a camel saddle and put it down for him
to use as an armrest and invited him to enter and take a seat on the
carpet. "Come, come, Uncle dear, make yourself comfortable and
recline on the saddle!" She called him "Uncle dear" because he was
advanced in years and she was still a girl. "Listen, Nūrah," he said,
"I haven't come to sit and chat with you. I've readied a fast camel
that I would like to describe to you. I thought it would be nice to let
you hear what I have to say on the subject before we go our separate
ways."

"Go ahead and show me what you're capable of," she said.[55] "Let   7.2
me hear it."

1   A rider perched on a peerless camel,
          towering on giraffe-like legs,
      Born from a mother raised at al-Sharārāt,
          A father stolen from al-Tīh—free-roaming herds.
      Six years old, fully grown, trained to perfection,
          spared from pregnancy, God's favored racer.
      When others stagger across wastes like invalids,
          her smooth, rounded hooves go at a sprightly step.[56]
5   She zips over the ground, winding like a snake,
          lower lip curled down, and sweeping her tail.
      Wary of violent surges, the rider scarcely brushes his foot,[57]
          like a man eager not to provoke his seething wife.
      Uphill stretches serve to make her run faster still,
          eyes fiery like a hero's, rushing to right a wrong.

—*Al-ʿadīm* is a hero and *al-jnāfah* is a wrong.

      If a shaykh's raiding group celebrates a rich haul,
          rave on about the adulation awaiting them at home,
      Welcome for some is a wife like a hissing snake:
          fangs awash in venom, portent of doom;

—*Al-ḥazf* means snake.

10   Into a mad ruckus of wolves and dogs at first light,
          wolves ruthlessly maneuvering to catch a prey.
      Like a waterwheel her tongue spews evil gossip;
          unashamed, she yells and shouts with abandon;

—*Al-sāyah* is evil gossip and *al-gnāfah* means a shameful act.

      Legs long and spindly, bony shoulders like hangers,
          a hollow back tapering to scrawny haunches.

Sweet smiles of a dazzling beauty await the chief,
    the pearly, chiseled teeth of a shaykh's daughter:
Shaykh of shaykhs, from the mother's side,
    given Nūrah in marriage—a friendly gesture.

—Al-Mhēd is the family of Ibn Hadhdhāl's father-in-law.

A white camel caparisoned with colorful ribbons;   15
    neck and shoulders graced by bell and tasseled rug.[58]
Insouciant, she strides in scented fur dyed yellow;
    breezes stir the longhaired humps of her cortege:
Gazelles of the sands with their supple-necked retinue,[59]
    leading doe, watchful eye trained on distant rims;
She's a fresh stalk, slightly bent, with juicy moisture,
    when swayed by playful puffs of wind.
Never did I see Nūrah's like among kin or friends,
    or ever hear of her equal from anyone.[60]

By way of rounding off his recitation, he planted a kiss on top of   7.3
her head: "May I ask you for a favor, daughter of Ibn Mhēd, now
that I've put my good name on the line with my presence here in
the hope that you'll be persuaded to return to Ibn Hadhdhāl." "I
swear by God, Abū Dikhīl," she said, "that even if you asked me to
jump into a fire I'd do so without a second's hesitation. Just bear
with me a little until I have sent this slave to them. I'll come back
to you straightaway." She instructed the slave: "Go to Shaykh Ibn
Hadhdhāl and tell him that if he wants Nūrah to return to him, he
should give her the mare named such and such, accompanied by a
riding camel carrying textiles, clothing, and provisions, and have
the camel kneel at the tent of Abū Zwayyid. On top of that, give him
a tent and bed covering." After hearing out the slave, Ibn Hadhdhāl
said, "No matter! I'd agree even if she demanded ten horses with
their complement of pack camels. But have her come home. We
don't know which goods she wants to load on the camel." So she

came, with Abū Zwayyid in tow, and they made up. Abū Zwayyid
rejoiced and sang:

> If you're wondering, my camel mount and I are fine,
>> Li'bah and I: smug, sated, quenched.

—Li'bah is a camel of his.

> She built us a big and imposing house,
>> carpeted by one who provides for the penniless.

Abū Zwayyid's Camel, Stolen by Ibn M'abhal, Is Returned to Him by Ibn Mashhūr

Abū Zwayyid's camel was forcibly taken by Ibn M'abhal of the   8.1
Rwalah tribe, who stubbornly refused to return it. In the end, he
recovered his animal through the intercession of a member of the
Ibn Mashhūr branch of the same tribe. In gratitude, Abū Zwayyid
composed these verses:[61]

> Hey, rider of a red-hued thoroughbred camel: 1
>   hardy, swift as an ostrich racing for escape,
> She outstrips pursuers when romping home—
>   Her fur light reddish-brown, tall in the shoulders,
> Loaded with a waterskin and a provisions bag, nothing more,
>   the wood saddle's crosspiece ropes tied taut.
> A tough youngster spurs her on, all night long,
>   inured to brutal rides through simmering plains.
> A regular at hidden waterholes,   5
>   he snatches enemy camels from distant pastures.
> I weep for my mount, poached through trickery
>   by Ibn M'abhal—a grave breach of the honor code.
> Just as graybeards crave for youth, I entreated in vain:
>   "God's censures on him as often as the sands cave in!"

Obstinate in refusal, he drew his sword on me:
   woe to me! And yet, I submit to God's decree.
One cannot pin one's hopes on a callous lout,
   face smeared with soot from his evildoings.
Shame on me for not seeking help from others,[62]
   saviors of poor devils cast about by villainy:
A courageous gentleman such as Rabdā's brother:
   Rabdā's brother shields seekers of his protection.

—The brother of Rabdā is Ibn Mashhūr.

Young, yet a formidable and seasoned fighter,
   most redoubtable when circumstances dictate.

His Poems on a Dispute among Members of His Tribal Group of the Nabhān

Abū Zwayyid always strove to foster harmony among his fellow tribesmen of al-Nabhān. When he was a guest of the Shaʿlān, a traveler arrived and he questioned him: "Did you see my people? How are they doing?" "To be honest, your kinsmen are fine as long as nothing untoward happens and as long as they don't fall out with one another while on the spring pastures." They had become embroiled in bickering and trouble had erupted between Āl Rakhīṣ and Āl Ḍaww.[63] They quarreled over a she-camel and the dispute threatened to spiral out of control. Ibn Rakhīṣ had a neighbor under his protection, a Ḥrērī tribesman from Mesopotamia, Smayyir al-Simdān al-Ḥrērī of the Shammar confederation's tribesmen in Mesopotamia. This neighbor joined a raiding party and had a run-in with a fellow raider of Āl Ḍaww about a she-camel both claimed as booty. At that time, it was not uncommon for Bedouin to fight over spoils. He and the Ḍawwī picked a fight about a she-camel robbed from a tribesman of the Rwalah. Each of them claimed to have been first to tap the camel with his riding stick. "This is my she-camel, and I take possession of her!" said the neighbor. "No way," said the Ḍawwī. "This camel is mine and I will not let anyone else lay hands on her!" They had a heated argument over the animal. On their return, they were told to submit to arbitration. They were advised to seek out an arbiter from among the Shammar tribes and make their case to him. Ibn Shnīnān, a horseman of the Dhirfān clan of Shammar's Zmēl

9.1

branch, trotted behind the she-camel, keeping a watchful eye on her as he drove her swiftly in the desired direction. He made sure to give Ibn Rakhīṣ a wide berth. The claimants submitted the dispute to a competent interpreter of tribal law. The Ḍawwī won and was awarded the camel, and Smayyir al-Ḥrērī lost.

9.2 Ibn Rakhīṣ said, "There is no need for him to litigate his claim. The camel is his whatever the case, without litigation. As our protected neighbor, he doesn't have to prove anything.[64] Our customary law does not apply to my neighbor."

"In God's name, Ibn Rakhīṣ! Litigation is the way people settle disputes!" they exclaimed.

Ibn Rakhīṣ stood his ground: "Our customary law only applies to the settlement of claims among ourselves, in our own group. Claims against a protected neighbor are absolutely unacceptable. Those are matters for God to decide."

"So, what do you suggest?"

"As I see it, he should be allowed to take possession of his she-camel without any need for litigation."

From that point on, matters escalated between the Nabhān, the folk of al-Jrāf, and their branches of al-Ḍaww and al-Rakhīṣ.[65] Al-Ḍaww said, "He won't get the camel." And Ibn Rakhīṣ said, "For sure, you won't get it. Very well then, we'll meet tomorrow when I come to take it."

In the morning, he set out for the camp of al-Ḍaww to seize the camel of his neighbor, come what may. Al-Ḍaww quickly decamped to put themselves under the protection of another tribal group, telling them, "We seek asylum with you from Ibn Rakhīṣ. He is chasing after us, spoiling for a fight, just for the sake of one she-camel."

"What's the problem?" the others asked.

"Just that she-camel," they said.

They begged to differ: "If Ibn Rakhīṣ was roused to act in defense of his neighbor, we also consider that a neighbor enjoys inalienable rights among people like us. We will not condone it if anyone acts in contravention of those rights. We cannot accept responsibility for those who harass a neighbor. We grant asylum only on condition that you return the she-camel.[66] Bring the animal back to Ibn Rakhīṣ!"

They complied and were forced to eat humble pie.

News of their quarrel reached Abū Zwayyid while he was staying with Ibn Shaʿlān. He was not familiar with the details of the case. It seemed that he held Gāsim, the shaykh of the Rakhīṣ, responsible. He might have wondered why the shaykh would assault his own folk. Why on earth would he, on his watch as a chief, let his kinsmen come to blows because of a mere she-camel? He held one of the chief's counselors responsible for misguiding him. He speculated that a scoundrel had insinuated himself into his inner circle. "Would it be some miscreant who sows dissension? It is not in his character to act this way. It must be some villain's evil whisperings." He therefore composed the following poem, in which he questions what happened among his kinsmen and asks God to grant forgiveness to all Muslims, living and deceased.

9.3

> Rider of a mount ravishing beyond description:
>> reddish-brown, she whisks you through mirages;
> Ribs bulging, legs and frame elegantly formed;
>> a skirt of strawberry-red hair flutters below.
> In calm mood, she comforts the lonely rider:
>> on a break, she minds unloaded travel bags.
> Dream of desert crossers far from home,
>> savior of the terror-stricken from the two.

1

—By "the two" he means "fear and thirst." A purebred, well-trained she-camel watches the provision bag. If you unload the bags and let the camel walk free, unfettered, not hobbled, she circles you, browsing on herbage to your left and right, while keeping close to you as if you were her child. She sticks to her rider as he prepares and eats his luncheon until he is done, fetches her, fastens the bundles, loads her, and rides off.

5   Hurtling down daunting, featureless plains,
      her rider fancies leading a cavalry charge;
Bobbing quickly up and down, like a ship
      lifted and tossed by waves far from shore.
Head for my kin, unflinching in the face of danger,
      daredevils renowned for chivalrous feats.
They cool the fury of hotheaded strutters
      And camp in risky borderlands after heavy rains.[67]
Woe, if discord takes hold and insults fly—woe!
      God is my refuge, let's not even think of it!
10 Sound opinion and martial feats bring results:
      pride and might are born from acting in unison;
Tumble into the well of impotence, that's the end:
      a fetid, brackish pool—no one clambers out of it.
If you're lost, ask judges steeped in tribal lore
      for answers: sages keeping God's wisdom in trust.
If peril looms, thoughtful men of experience
      probe customary law for mending solutions.
Seek counsel from humble men who inspire awe;
      avoid fumbling advisers who embroil you in a mess.
15 Keep clear of a wretch who plunges you into disaster:
      if he leads you south, you'll end up north.
Folks, we've duped God with a flood of oaths,
      though the scales to weigh our deeds are His.
Surely, such actions will redound to you:
      your only gain from trespassing is regret.
Hurry! What use are mere lamentations?
      Its moment gone, everything becomes a thing of the past.

He Returns from His Asylum with
ʿAnazah and Heads for Ibn Rashīd

Khalaf Abū Zwayyid made a living from his tongue. He composed   10.1
poems as he followed the trail of shaykhs who gave him presents,
moving from Ṣaṭṭām ibn Shaʿlān to Ibn Hadhdhāl. While he was
with the latter, Ibn Shaʿlān came for a visit. After the greetings, Ibn
Hadhdhāl asked, "Now, Abū Zwayyid, tell me, how was your stay
with Ṣaṭṭām, your impressions? How did he strike you as a person?"
He said, "Ṣaṭṭām ibn Shaʿlān is like foam on camel milk—nice, but
it will not serve you as supper or lunch." "Don't use improper lan-
guage, Abū Zwayyid," Ṣaṭṭām said. "You insult me for no reason. I
didn't say anything bad about you. God is generous." "God is gener-
ous without you. What is this tone of menace? Here I am with the
brothers of Batlā, the Impeccable Hearts.[68] And if I decide to go on
my way to Shammar, between you and me are the Ḍīdān, who split
off from your ancestors' line among the tribal groups; they will pro-
tect me against you."[69] Abū Zwayyid enjoyed himself thoroughly,
pleased as punch with his performance. But he longed to rejoin
his fellow tribesmen. The obstacle was that Ibn Rashīd had been
incensed by his poem in praise of Ṣaṭṭām ibn Shaʿlān. Ibn Rashīd
had sworn that he would kill him as soon as he laid hands on him
and slaughter a fat camel in celebration. The line that kindled his
wrath was: "They never gave birth, nor will they ever, to the equal
of Ṣaṭṭām in the entire world." Abū Zwayyid broached the subject
of his return with Ṣāliḥ ibn Rakhīṣ, a close confidant and adviser of

Ibn Rashīd, and asked him to put in a word on his behalf with Ibn Rashīd.

10.2　Ibn Rashīd set out on a raiding expedition and first headed for Ibn Shaʿlān, who was going to accompany him. At that time, he was on friendly terms with the Rwalah tribe. Jointly, they launched an assault on al-Fawāʿir for their herds on the Shaṭṭ River in Iraq. Once the Shammar tribesmen had rounded up the captured herds, Ibn Rashīd ordered a review of the booty. He made his cameleers stand in two opposite lines and ordered the captured animals to be driven from one end to the other, between the two rows of his men, while he inspected the parade of spoils from where he was seated, reclining on an armrest, surrounded by his security detail.[70] Any animal that caught his attention was reserved for him. He took possession of whatever struck his fancy: "Set that one aside, and that one too, here, to the side!" For instance, a raider who captured two she-camels as his booty would have to give up one of them in the course of the parade, or perhaps one out of every three pilfered she-camels. That's how the spoils pageant operates. Ibn Shaʿlān, whom Abū Zwayyid praised in his ode, was present at the review. "Orders were given for Ibn Shaʿlān's booty to be driven through the lines to be mustered!" In addition, Muḥammad ibn Rashīd reserved for himself the right to send his men to the owners of the plunder if he suspected there were animals of value that had been overlooked during the parade.[71] These he would also claim and seize. Abū Zwayyid feared that Ibn Rashīd would lay his hands on his camel as well, together with those of Ibn Shaʿlān. He confided to someone: "I was never so scared as on that day. I said to myself, 'Your last hour has come; he's going to kill you.'" At that point, Abū Zwayyid turned to Ṣāliḥ ibn Rakhīṣ, one of Ibn Rashīd's intimates and a close advisor. He asked him to intercede for him with Ibn Rashīd.

10.3　One day, Abū Zwayyid made his appearance at the assembly of Ibn Rashīd with a shroud draped over his shoulders.[72] He led a billy goat, the animal slaughtered at one's interment.[73] He did so knowing that Ibn Rashīd had sworn to slaughter an animal on the occasion of his death. He put on his shroud and wended his way through the rows of men in the assembly toward where the prince was seated at the head of two lines. The visitors used to sit on earthen benches that lined the walls of the courtyard. He was moving at a snail's pace. When Ibn Rashīd caught sight of him, he muttered, "Who on earth could that be?" "Abū Zwayyid!" those around him replied. "By God, that cursed creature. 'Splendid women never gave birth, nor will they ever, to Saṭṭām's equal from the world's east to where the sun sets.'" Abū Zwayyid said, "Yes, may you live long! What I actually said was, 'Splendid women never gave birth to Saṭṭām's like, except for the peerless prince of Āl Ḍēgham.'"[74] Ibn Rashīd turned to his cousin. "What do you think, Ḥmūd?" Ḥmūd growled, "Sir, allow me to taste the blood when it drips from this Shammarī."[75] Instead, Ibn Rashīd ordered, "Get out of here, you accursed wretch, you and your locust eyes!"[76] (Abū Zwayyid was walleyed, God show him mercy.) Abū Zwayyid said, "May you live long, Your Highness. It's just that I am not as fortunate as you are, God preserve you! When my father made his escape, in the company of your father, I was neglected by my mother. When she became your wet nurse, she felt too proud to pay attention to me. While she was breastfeeding you, my eyes turned in different directions in hunger. My mother suckled you first, and whatever milk was left she fed to me. She'd say, 'This ugly mutt is just a charcoal burner.[77] If he dies, nothing is lost. I have been chosen to breastfeed the prince of Shammar!' From then on, my eyes popped out like porcelain coffee cups and each eye rolled aside—because as a baby I was kept hungry all the time."[78] Muḥammad ibn Rashīd ordered an animal to be slaughtered. A servant was instructed to cut off a lock of Abū Zwayyid's hair and set him free.[79]

On that occasion, Abū Zwayyid recited these verses: 10.4

> Rider of a camel with thighs full as the letter *jīm*,   *1*
>   with a *kaffah* brand on its leg and a crescent;[80]

—Her thigh looks like the letter *jīm*, with its full belly.

Sired by white Wuḍayḥān, a stallion of Silhēm,
  her grandfather a Shaʿlān stud in Shawwāl's herd.

—Silhēm and Shawwāl belong to the Lḥāwī branch of the Sharārāt.

She's like the leading doe of a herd of sand gazelle:
  a fawn she-camel, of a flaming reddish-brown color.
She outstrips the moon, wind, clouds, all of them,
  faster than sandgrouse driven by hot desert blasts.
5 Point the stick and she goes, the epitome of grace,
  outpacing the pack, running like a cavalry horse.[81]
Her rider a desert pilot known for not losing his way:
  like sandgrouse, he cleaves to the course, unbeatable!
Early morning, she set out from the River al-Khābūr,
  Polestar fixed on the saddle pillow's right.
Leave al-Ghurāb's outcrop not far to your right,
  Wādī al-Miyāh, famed for torrents, to the left.
On reaching Farʿ Ṣwāb, let her trot as she likes;
  in late afternoon, she lengthens her stride for speed.
10 She whisks you at a smooth cadence to al-Khirr,
  there to quaff al-Ḥazl's sweet and limpid water on day five.
From al-Ṣlēb to the spur of Rabdā to Abā Dhēm,
  do not startle at sightings of frightening shapes!
At al-Ḥamāṭiyyah, tribesmen have settled down,
  known for their delicious roasts and rich coffee brews.
My kinsmen, indefatigable captors of enemy herds:
  they brought untold riches to paupers in rags.
Provided with fresh supplies, now hit the road anew:
  alight at al-Bāyiḥ for a midday bite and coffee,
15 And arrive in the afternoon at fat camels' butchers:
  trains of food-laden trays, ceaseless cutting of meat:[82]
Shaykhs come in different shapes and sizes:
  horsemen who outshine camel riders.

Shaykhs and rulers, like steeds chafing at the bit;
  Ḍayāghim, unforgiving if heads are raised in pride.
Camels and small cattle they gift with open hand;
  untold fortunes are distributed among supporters:
Some receive no less than a thousand tents;
  my share is a three-poled, towering house of hair.
I don't say so to stay on his good side,   20
  or out of fear for them, or with trembling knees.[83]

With Muḥammad ibn Rashīd

11.1   The well of Lōgah became the subject of tribal disputes. Muḥammad al-ʿAbdallāh al-Rashīd sent one of his enforcers, Mrēzīg̒, to eject the Sinjārah from Lōgah and allow the ʿAbdah to settle there. It was his intention to have Muḥammad al-Dimānī close to him and to let him set up quarters in Ḥāyil. But al-Dimānī was resolved to keep Lōgah and stay. When the wrangling continued, he sent Mrēzīg̒ and instructed him: "Send him on his way and have him come here!" Al-Dimānī was indignant at being strong-armed into traveling. He saddled his riding camel, pulled out of Lōgah, and sped away in a westerly direction. Aggravated, his fellow tribesmen of Sinjārah joined him where he had set up camp in the west. There the forces of the state detained him.[84] Ibn Rashīd had sent written messages to request his detention. Thus, it happened. After the Sinjārah paid a ransom of eight hundred white she-camels, he was released. All because of Lōgah. On his return to Lōgah, he and Ibn Jibrīn submitted their dispute over the possession of Lōgah to tribal arbitration. They chose ʿGūb ibn Swēṭ to preside as a judge over the litigation of their claims in accordance with customary law. The Sinjārah ended up with the possession of the wells of al-Ḥazl, including Lōgah.

11.2   At the time of this poem, Abū Zwayyid had put himself under the protection of Ibn Rashīd. "Where are your kinsmen staying now, Abū Zwayyid?" Muḥammad asked. Replying in verse, Abū Zwayyid subtly reminded him that clansmen of al-Rakhīṣ had offered refuge to his father as he fled the oppression of Āl ʿAlī.[85]

A brew of poisonous leaves burns my entrails;[86]   1
    mice are gnawing away at my heart's arteries.
My eyes have surrendered to a flood of tears,
    red hot as if a nail were driven into the pupils—
Because God decreed to scatter tribesmen,
    justice enforcers, shields for seekers of protection.
My clan dispersed at the onset of winter;
    They vanished, leaving me without the faintest news,
Like well buckets torn to bits and pieces,   5
    ruined by some well shafts after having thrived;
Bucket broken, wooden crosspieces strewn:
    who'd part with a water bucket, even as a loan?[87]
They ran to men who pamper their neighbors,
    and maul the enemy—let refugees forget about home.

—They sought refuge with the Shaʿlān.

My prince! You spurn kissing an enemy's hand:
    you are like purest homemade gunpowder.
When you are in dire straits, we're at your command!
    Remember when al-Jarādī lit the fires of war?[88]
Ibn ʿAlī planned to poke his fingers in your eyes,   10
    and we undergirded your views and strength.[89]
Thus ʿAbdallah's House rose from its foundations;
    surely, you can't mean to snub such faithful aides.
If, despite all we did, you've lost patience with me,
    God, healer of broken wings, is our last recourse.

In Praise of Saʿūd Abū Khashm

12.1   Hey, rider of a fast, rugged desert crosser[90]
     That's spared from procreation, not suckling young:
Rarest of prizes, she traverses endless wastes,
     smoothly plunging into mirages and reemerging.
If they travel waterless for five days in scorching heat
     to a well crammed with camel mothers drinking,[91]
They turn about, back to a well from which they came,
     for a rest, waiting to slake their thirst with dregs.[92]

5   From my abode she sets out for Saʿūd son of Ḍēgham:
     head straight for Ibn Ḍēgham, give wide berth to misers;[93]
Your destination: Saʿūd ibn ʿAbd al-ʿAzīz ibn Mitʿib;
     God of life-bringing clouds, shower him with glory!
Streaking from the sky, he wreaks havoc on his prey;
     a noble falcon, he usurps all chivalry.
A rampart who shields the purest tribes of Shammar:
     thundering cavalry charges plunge enemies into grief.
My fellows spurn taking milch camels as booty:
     doggedly determined to smite their adversaries.[94]

10   He led Shammar from the front, swollen with fury,[95]
     rekindled Shammar's fire, sputtering sickly and wan.
Called to arms, Ḥāyil's men girded and marched
     into pools of death, a grim reaper at their throats,
Sacrificing life, as the banner's last defense,[96]
     until the enemy ran, thwarted in his quest;

Doom rained down from clouds of death:
    cheers for the single-minded smiting and felling.
Your in-laws are of Shammar's prime lineages,
    noblemen amid moral decay and tribal rot.
In these times of decadence and fading tribes,   15
    father-in-law Zāmil stands as virtue's epitome.⁹⁷
He bolsters virtue with stabs and battle cries,
    restores dimming values to their rightful place.
Esteeming his defense of Arab noble values,
    may God reward him with bounty plentiful.
I have attended assemblies of chiefs galore:
    the deeds of shaykhs make for conversation.
No doubt, he outclasses any shaykhs around,
    makes all traits comprising goodness his own.
His rule scorns shaykhs of dubious repute,   20
    favors the valiant known for proven mettle.
A straight talker who doesn't seek to please,
    not beating about the bush, he tells plain truth.
Honest to a fault, he tells you exactly as it is,
    unlike most shaykhs, whose deeds belie their words.
He is affable and serene or headstrong and truculent,
    standfast when cavalry sows death and destruction.
His white mare kicks off with three legs aloft:⁹⁸
    since foaling once, her womb was kept barren.
Paeans are superfluous: his reception room is teeming   25
    with starving, haggard guests eating until they burst.

Raiding with Gnēṭīr ibn Rakhīṣ

13.1 Abū Zwayyid joined a raiding party led by Gnēṭīr ibn Rakhīṣ.[99] They headed for the Rwalah, but ran out of water and failed to capture any camels. At midday, they took a rest while crossing a barren gravel plain. "When will we finally make it to al-Jawf?" they wondered. "Tomorrow after prayers at daybreak," Jifrān al-Maʿaklī said. "Get a good rest!" Gnēṭīr said. "Let our camel mounts cool their hooves— you rest well, and them too!" They resumed their journey, and at once Gnēṭīr sensed his mount's happy mood. He hit her with his riding stick and she kicked. He poked her in the armpit with the stick and she stamped. Together with Abū Zwayyid, they played with the animals and excited them. They prodded them into a wild stampede and kept up their mad dash for quite a while. When they had calmed enough to once again ride in a close group, Gnēṭīr said, "What do you think about these mounts, Abū Zwayyid? How are they?"

13.2 When they rode as a group again, he said, "Really, I don't know what to say. You went flat out and drove yourselves and them to exhaustion. Dry and shriveled like crumpled, castaway bags. You are bone dry and these damned camels are desperate with thirst."[100]

> 1 Lord, your water-laden clouds bring succor
> to drought-stricken gardens pining for relief.
> I pray, God, that you send us plentiful showers
> to soften the bitter crust choking our hearts.

Lord, You brighten sorrow-clouded minds,
 You are the Savior of those who put their trust in You.
You guide lost souls casting about, bewildered;
 Lord, You loosen knots if people feel strangled.
Humanity lies in Your cupped hand: 5
 You destroy people puffed up with ancient pride.
Some men walk by day as if groping in the dark,
 like travelers at night, bone-weary, distraught;
How come some people, sharp of sight,
 stray from the road as if blind, and yet are guided?
This era has saddled us with woeful leaders:
 measly foxes feast on lions' dinners.[101]
Spare us, God, from trials and adversity:
 beset by anxious thought, my heart boils over.
Mount of my dreams, lean and sinewy,   10
 Barren-wombed, fit to tear into blazing plains.[102]
Hey you, rider of rugged, unflagging she-camels,
 perched on a hump that stretches the saddle cushion:
Legs aflutter like ropes slipped off a pulley;
 panic-stricken ostriches race down empty tracts.
Scolded, they speed up with peeved arrogance:
 you think they're finished? They rally and surge!

—If the camels are scolded—"What kind of running is this?"—and
the riders aim to go at speed, they adopt an arrogant gait. They indulge
in a bout of peevish arrogance: the way they hold neck and tail, strut
like a rutting stud camel, or walk like a conceited, spoiled star.

At night, in empty vastness, they give it their all,
 already worn out by waterless desert crossings,
Leaving behind camel calves scampering about   15
 like orphans in search of food from kindly folk.
The mounts, kneeled by fearless young raiders
 near an enemy camp to snatch away the herds,

Fidget like excited divorcées in the evening,
    hearing of a proposal before bedding down.[103]
Such verse is sweeter than a cool cascade of water
    on arrival at a well, thirsting from the shimmering heat.

On a Raid with Rōḍān ibn Farwān

They left on a raiding expedition led by Rōḍān ibn Farwān. The next   14.1
day, Jifrān came riding hard to catch up with them, an old fellow
who had suffered paralysis of one half of his face but had recovered
from the attack. He had once been energetic and hot-blooded,
but did not look like his former self. Rōḍān was a greenhorn who
started his raiding career by robbing some travelers. Jifrān, on the
other hand, was a heavy hitter, terrifying, the dictatorial terror of
ʿAbd al-Karīm.[104] "Here I am," he said. "I started out this morn-
ing and caught up with you." "Kneel your mount. It is an honor,
Jifrān!" Rōḍān exulted. "Easy, son of Saʿd," the other said. "You are
the up-and-coming one, and my story . . . well, you know." "Dear
brother, your presence comes as a blessing to all of us!"[105] Seeing
that the old fellow was adamant, Rōḍān slid down from the back
of his mount, took the reins in his hand, and made Jifrān's camel
kneel. They set out with the intention of capturing camels from the
al-ʿAlyā herds in the area of the Rwalah tribe or thereabouts, but
returned empty-handed.

It so happened that Shuwardī ibn Jifrān had a brother, named   14.2
Ridn, who lived in the vicinity of the Banū Ṣakhr tribe. Together
with a few others, he rode from there aiming to pilfer camels, head-
ing in the direction of the Shammar tribe, looking for the camels of
another tribe. When they came to Wādī Sirḥān, Shuwardī hit upon
the tracks of the Jirdhān, his fellow tribesmen. He recognized the
traces left by their riding camels. Excited, he told his companions,

"Dear friends, it's your call; as for me, I'm going to follow and catch up with these raiders." As Rōḍān and his raiders were about to leave al-Jawf behind, Shuwardī came hurrying to them and joyously cried, "God's curse on your damned tribe. Hurray! Follow me quickly! Herds of camels right there, idling in those flatlands, for the taking! The camels of the Sirḥān!" He interlaced his words with shouted encouragements, battle cries, exhorting them to join him in his enterprise: "Come on, sons of al-Ghafal, a curse on your father, camels are roaming there freely, unguarded!" My father rode with Shāyish al-Ṣalj, who sat behind the saddle on his camel's back.[106] Abū Zwayyid was a half brother of al-Ṣalj: they were born of the same mother. Shāyish dismounted, took his bag, and fastened it to Abū Zwayyid's camel, preferring to ride with him. The tribesmen of Sinjārah would not be swayed, and continued on their way home. The others protested and appealed to their honor, the old fellows, but in vain, and they hit their camels hard to make them turn in the opposite direction. They were a small group.

14.3   He continued his story: On our way back we came to al-Uḍāriʿ.[107] There the edible *kurrāth* grass grew so thick that if you'd leave a man alone, his hands tied behind his back, he'd find enough to satisfy his appetite: he'd only have to open his mouth and eat.[108] We skirted al-Uḍāriʿ. When we landed amid this plenty, we folded the *kurrāth* grass into bundles, like sandwiches. Whenever one or two camel riders passed by, we made them dismount to feast them on these wraps of edible grass. The last passersby whom we urged to dismount and be treated to these wraps of edible *kurrāth* grass were Ghuṣn al-Sʿadī and his group of five riders. As God would have it, while we were there, in the afternoon the other group was trotting energetically, their mounts swaying from side to side as they came rushing in at a blistering pace. A boy had informed them that the herds were unguarded, except for a few shepherds. Jifrān told them to wait until the camels had been collected at the end of the day. As soon as the animals had flocked together, they hurtled forward and stampeded the herd in the desired direction. Abū Zwayyid had

followed the group that chose to continue on its way back home.
They took a day of rest amid bountiful grasses. The next morning,
all of a sudden, a great mass of animals appeared out of thin air
and came running straight at them. The stolen camels of al-Hwērī.
Nothing like it had been seen since the world was created. Al-Hwērī
was a tribesman of the Sirḥān.

Abū Zwayyid went with the group of losers who had stayed put 14.4
the day before and said:

> Alas, patient camel, I feel my insides boiling,
>> a heart sliced by remorse and frustration.

—He is saying, "Why did I return empty-handed?"

> Losing bets, robbed of my share of camel mothers:
>> well-fed ones, swept up from lush pastures of spring
> By steppe wolves led by a cunning master,[109]
>> a lucky pack always smiled upon by fortune.
> I wronged myself by being such a lazy coward:
>> methinks there is no profit in seeking easy gain.

His female riding camel replied: 14.5

> Khalaf, if only you knew how you hurt me
>> by smearing my name in decent society.
> Sixty nights in a row you slept at my side.
>> [. . .]
> Khalaf, bear with me! Give me nights' rest!
>> Let me grow a towering hump of fat and relax.

Praise God. The capture of al-Hwērī's camels spelled the end of
bad luck and hard times for the Jirdhān clan.[110] The spoils came their
way like water gushing from a plentiful well.

With a Companion of the Rwalah at Ibn Rashīd's Court

15.1 They joined a plundering expedition of Ibn Rashīd. One of the participants was a Rwēlī, al-Ḥisāwī of the Dghimī branch.[111] His fellow raiders camped next to the group of Abū Zwayyid. Their groups were encamped as neighbors who visited one another. The Rwēlī dispatched a qasida with a fleet riding camel. While camped together, the Rwēlī and Abū Zwayyid went to pay their respects to Prince Muḥammad ibn Rashīd. Abū Zwayyid said to him, "Prince, I seek your protection against a stud that insists on mounting a pregnant she-camel"—he meant, like a young male that harasses a pregnant she-camel, a metaphor for a boorish man lacking in discernment. Ibn Rashīd asked Abū Zwayyid, "Who is your opponent?" He said, "This friend of mine, the Rwēlī who appropriated one of my camels. I found one of my riding camels with him, though none of my camels ever fell into the hands of those who falsely claimed their ownership." Ibn Rashīd said, "Let's have it, then!"

15.2   Al-Ḥisāwī al-Dghimī said:

1   Rider of a well-rested, regal she-camel,
        light brown, not for drawing water;[112]
    A delight for the eye is the shine of her fur,
        as she struts like a flirter flaunting a dress.[113]
    Strong and sinewy, her frame slimmed down,
        she cuts through the quivering desert air,

Reddish of hue, fast-paced, neck stretched low,
    across empty flats, as the sun goes down—
Panicky like an ostrich spotting human shapes,
    plumage aquiver and tendons stretched tight —
Toward the hospitable tents of Bedouin
    and white camel herds on rain-fed pastures.

Ibn Rashīd said, "Well, you Rwēlī of the ʿAlyā camels, does this she-camel have any sisters or is she all by herself?"[114] "No, none at all," he said. "This is the only one, all by herself." "Take him with you," Ibn Rashīd instructed the custodian of the spoils, camels captured on his raids. "Take him, and let him choose a she-camel from our booty, whichever he likes best, in compensation for the camel he owes Abū Zwayyid." The Rwēlī's eye fell on a young, half-blind she-camel that was gnawing on a bone, its umbilical cord dangling from the belly, and with an outsized callus on its breastbone. The Rwēlī knew that this inauspicious-looking camel, once grown up, would make an exceptional mount and he confirmed his choice. "What a missed opportunity," the attendants said. "Why don't you take a better one now that this stroke of good fortune has come your way?" "Absolutely not," he said. "I've made up my mind to take this one-eyed camel." He trained the camel and she turned out to be fast and tough, a mount that stood out among all desert-crossing camels.

Then al-Ḥisāwi al-Dghimī composed these verses:

Hey, rider of that well-shaped mount
    with bulging ribs and tall in the back:
Beyond Jwēf, on the plain's home stretch,
    the strong camels speed like mountain goats;
On their last reserves, their pace goes mad,
    as if jinn are tearing at their behinds.
Outlines of vague shapes make them startle:
    bushes on high plains, a stick or branch.
Four days later, the riders of slower mounts
    cook breakfast on a fire of their dry dung.[115]

With Dabbī ibn Fāliḥ

16.1   One year, Abū Zwayyid spent the hot season of midsummer at the well of Tribah while a friend of his from the Shilgān, Dabbī ibn Fāliḥ, encamped at the well of al-Khrēzah. It was a time of severe drought, a terrible period for the Bedouin and other people of that area. The drought killed cattle; all their wherewithal was wiped out. Only the most tenacious camels hung on. Abū Zwayyid lost all he had and became completely destitute. No camels—all his riding camels had perished. Not even one mount was left for riding and travel. When the great heat began to abate in early fall, his children were sitting around listlessly. There was no camel to carry them. While he was at Tribah, it occurred to him to whom he should go. He remembered his friend Dabbī ibn Fāliḥ, who owned quite a number of camels: two sizable herds. Dabbī was a good man. They had been close friends in earlier days. Abū Zwayyid girded up and went looking for him, traveling on foot across the sand dunes toward al-Khrēzah.

16.2   When he got there, he headed for Dabbī, who welcomed him: "How are you? May God look after you. How are you feeling? How are things with you?" "Miserable, as you see; my hands are paralyzed, brother of ʿAlyā. The Bedouin are gone and I have no transportation for my children, who are just sitting around and waiting at Tribah. Jackals are all they have for company. My pack camels died. Not a single camel of mine survived. I came to ask if you could spare any pack camels." "Chin up," he said. "I will help you. Your camels have perished, but you are hanging on. If it is merely a matter of animals, solutions are easy to come by. Here things are not very different. My camels, the ones you saw before, have died. Only the toughest, hardiest ones made it through. Just twenty of them. The twenty mighty, rugged camels with the greatest stamina. If you like, we become as brothers and we divide them: ten for you and ten for me. Or, if you'd rather become my partner, we can share the twenty. We'll be equal partners in one and the same enterprise. Take these pack camels and transport your family on them. Fetch them and bring them here and have them stay with us. Get your family and let's be partners in these twenty camels until God brings us relief." Abū Zwayyid felt it would be improper to take him up on the offer of accepting ownership of half his camels. He did as the other suggested. He took the pack camels and brought his family to stay with Dabbī.

As soon as the weather cooled somewhat in early fall, Dabbī announced his intention of launching a raiding expedition. He said, "Hey, let's go raiding. Join me if you'd like to try your luck in stocking up on God-given booty!" Dabbī was an experienced raid leader. He mounted one of the pack camels, and Abū Zwayyid, who had decided to join, mounted the other. Other tribesmen of Sinjārah who were staying nearby followed his example. When they reached the area of al-Wudyān, they reckoned they had come within striking distance of enemy tribes and their herds. They hid in a dip in the terrain where they would be invisible and sent Abū Zwayyid and someone else ahead to reconnoiter the whereabouts of the camels. Dabbī said, "You, Abū Zwayyid, set off and find out about these camels. These two will come with you. Scout and look around in the distance for the dark blot of a big herd of camels. You search for the camels and we will wait for you here, hidden in this gully, all of today and tonight." The scouts left on their mission to spy out the whereabouts of the herds and enemy forces. Were the camels accompanied by an escort of armed guards or merely by a few shepherd boys? In a successful outcome, when the spoils were divided among the raiders, the raid leader would allot the scouts a bonus

over and above what the other men would receive—an additional
she-camel was added to their share of the spoils. Dabbī picked Abū
Zwayyid for the scouting job as a kindly gesture—doing him a favor
to make sure he would get more than a regular share of the booty.
He gave him a wink, as it were: a signal that he'd get an extra camel
in accordance with the rules. He did him a good turn, because the
one who spies the camels is entitled to more than the others.[116]

16.4   When they had left, Dabbī said, "While our lunch is being pre-
pared, why doesn't one of you climb that lookout?" The man who
volunteered had not even made his way to the top when Dabbī
ran to their mounts in the gully, unfettered them, and drove them
toward his comrades. "Listen, fellows!" he called. "Forget about
your lunch, empty your cups. Mount your camels!" He had noticed
that the man climbing the lookout had seen camel herds. "And?"
they asked the man on his return. "The payoff is this: four big herds
moving in our direction.[117] The shepherds are lazing, stretched out
on the back of their young male camels. Any moment now they may
surface, right there in front of you. Just shepherds. No armed guards
or anything!" They hurried down, and as soon as they emerged from
the gully, they found themselves face to face with the herds. Spur-
ring their mounts, they raced toward their quarry. They yanked the
herds away from the line of their movement, and drove one herd
into another, sowing confusion and panic among the animals, until
by sunset they had rounded up all of the camels. In the gathering
darkness, they made away with their plunder. They had achieved
all they wanted and more—four big herds—and were able to make
their escape with these considerable spoils. They did not spare a
thought for the fate of Abū Zwayyid and his mates.

16.5   Meanwhile, Abū Zwayyid and the other scouts rode a long way
until they reached the edge of al-Wudyān and espied the camels they
were looking for. They swung around and hurried back to inform
their comrades. But they failed to meet up with them; they missed
their assignation. The raiders had ridden strenuously, all night long.
By evening, when Abū Zwayyid reached the place from which they,

the scouts, had set out, there was no one there. The next morning, he started to follow their tracks. By God, he thought, this is the path beaten by the stolen herds as they were being goaded forward. The raiders were driving the camels through the night without rest while the scouts were sleeping. The next day the scouts continued to follow the tracks the raiders had beaten the night before as they fled at high speed. They then crossed the stony plains of al-Ḥjarah, rushed down the bottom of al-ʿAthʿath, and burst into Khabb al-Saḥḥā and Ushaygir, the approximate area where their people were staying in the sands of al-Nafūd, where they finally caught up with them.

They reached them just north of al-Nafūd while they were busy divvying up the looted herds. They had finished dividing the spoils among themselves. Every one of them had a portion of the camels set aside for himself and each knew exactly his share and what had been allotted to others. They had set aside a number of camels for their absent companions, the stragglers. "Hey, Abū Zwayyid," they said, "those are yours. That's your share, the portion you're entitled to. Take them, those are your prize!" All well and good, but one she-camel in particular struck his fancy. And it so happened that it was marked with a ribbon of Dabbī, the raid leader. It was the raid leader's prerogative to select any camel for himself, the camel he liked best. Dabbī, as the commander, had tied his camel rope to this pure-white beauty that was about to give birth to her first young; she was close to delivery. Her graceful neck was as tall as the poles planted at the sides of a well. A self-assured female, she made it her privilege to walk at the front of the camels, the first lady, with a huge black udder hanging below her, the four parts crowned with a teat bursting with milk. Abū Zwayyid looked at her, spellbound, marveling at how she strode at the herd's front. "This she-camel will feed my children," he told himself. He dismounted at her side, took off Dabbī's ribbon, handed it to him, and tied his own rope to its neck. Dabbī understood that Abū Zwayyid had set his sights on her. "Don't you worry. Be of good cheer!" he said. "That's the one you

16.6

deserve, Abū Dikhīl. Sure, you can have her; you are worthy of her,
Abū Dikhīl. Take her and add her to your share of the booty!"

16.7   That is the story at the origin of this poem:

1   Hey, rider of camel trotting through bleak wastes:
         tireless, at an unflagging pace she barrels ahead.
     Red-brown, too tall to be vaulted upon,
         beast fit for recklessly brave youngsters.
     Steer her to ʿAlyā's brother, the grizzled warrior,
         who leads rugged lean camels on risky raids:

—ʿAlyā's brother is Dabbī ibn Fāliḥ al-Shlāgī.

     My friend, your goodness is free of impurities,
         scion of a nest that breeds the noblest strains:
5   Fearless, you plunge into battle's dusty whirl;
         you resolutely put your life at risk without a care
     When hardened fighters' hearts freeze in terror,
         hair whitened from gunpowder hovering in a melee,
     Pools of death swell, sparkling like mighty rivers,
         men humbled and lost, as dimwits stumble about.
     We want you! Not a mean-spirited, grasping miser,
         one who erupts if a moth lands in his clotted cream.[118]
     Wasp-waisted, lily-white beauties dream of you:
         hip-swaying princesses who despise uncouth louts;
10   Combs struggle, stuck in their thick tresses,
         light-brown curls cascading down onto firm behinds;
     Front teeth gleaming, white as sweet camel milk:
         like a young lady suckling a devoted camel mother;

—*Al-bisūṭ* is a suckling camel.

     Rosy cheeks adorned with blue tattoo designs,
         a light touch of dark stains etched by needles.

They ask for men whose strides are long and bold:
    for them they unhook their dress to show a breast.
When saluki hunting dogs rise, stretch, go at a trot;
    when breezes of good fortune stir and begin to blow;
When the she-camel is about to give birth to her calf: 15
    am I not her scout, even if others took hold of her?

—*Mūṭī* is a she-camel ready to deliver her calf.

Never mind that they tied their ribbons to her neck!
    She's mine, an exquisite favor not begrudged.

He means to say: she is my camel, presented to me as a special
distinction by Ibn Fāliḥ. Ribbons, lengths of camel rope, and head-
dresses are tied to camels' necks by raiders who capture them.

With Khaznah al-Fiḍīl

17.1 Abū Zwayyid quarreled with a man of the ʿAbdah division of Shammar about ownership of a she-camel. In the olden days, Bedouin raiders often fought over camels they had captured from other tribes. In this case, they agreed to seek expert advice on how to resolve their dispute. They went to see a tribal judge knowledgeable in matters of customary law. I don't know who it was. Some say they sought out Ibn Shrēm; according to others, they went to see Ibn Jibrīn. I have no idea. But I do know for sure that the judge was from the ʿAbdah division of Shammar. And I know for certain that Abū Zwayyid's opponent was also from the ʿAbdah. The judge knew the other ʿAbdī litigant. They belonged to the same tribal group. But the judge had never met Abū Zwayyid before. The other man said, "We have come to ask your assistance in settling our dispute." "Where is your opponent, ʿAbdī?" the judge asked. "Is it that man?" The judge gestured. "Or this one?" he asked. "No." "Is it him?" "No." "This one then?" The judge kept pointing to important-looking men, those who stood out from the crowd. "Well, tell me who your opponent is." "Here, this fellow here." There he was, Abū Zwayyid, one-eyed, a man with a repulsive, inauspicious mien. The judge had been looking around the assembly to determine to whom the man of ʿAbdah was referring. Naturally, he had passed over the man with loathsome, ghostly features such as he had never encountered before. The other faces in the assembly were familiar to him: they were his fellow tribesmen. "Really, this one?" "Indeed," the other said. "Ah, this kind and generous face, this bright-eyed man! This sparkling mind and vivid presence!"

Angrily, Abū Zwayyid jumped at him. "Listen, deary!" he said. "Must I tell you that I didn't come to have you gaze in admiration at my face! If you're looking for a pretty face, you're better off heading for Khaznah al-Fiḍīl, the daughter of Ibn Rmāl, on whose cheeks the colors red and white vie for preeminence. I am Abū Zwayyid: the wolf-faced bane of his pursuers, a mangy camel in a pen made of thorny bushes where those infected with smallpox are quarantined.[119] I am here with my opponent to seek justice, my rightful share." "Are you Abū Zwayyid?" he exclaimed. "Yes, I am Abū Zwayyid." "You know what, you ʿAbdī," the judge said to his opponent, "I cannot help you with your case. You have lost, and you, Abū Zwayyid, are hereby declared the winner, even without pleading. Honestly, I did not have the faintest notion that you were Abū Zwayyid. I have heard about you, but I had no idea what you looked like. Now that I know that you are Abū Zwayyid, what is it that you are litigating?" "Well, it's about a camel that I claim." "Don't you worry," the judge said. "You'll get your camel, no matter what. It wouldn't make a difference whether you were ruled the winner or loser in the case. If the verdict goes against you, I'll give you the camel. And if the outcome is in your favor, well then, you owe favors to no one."

The story came to the ears of Khaznah al-Fiḍīl, the daughter of Ibn Rmāl. She expressed a wish to have the poet visit her and meet. Khaznah, the daughter of Fiḍīl Abū Hijhūj of the Jārid branch, the sister of Fahd and Jārid—the later Jārid, not the earlier ancestor. She passed the message through a man of her clan who was going to see people who belonged to Abū Zwayyid's group. She said, "If you happen to run into Abū Zwayyid, give him my greetings, as many as there are bushes and stones on your way between me and him." "Very well," he said. "That's an easy errand." He did as he was told: he delivered her message to Abū Zwayyid. While it is true that Abū Zwayyid was a man of good sense and smart, he was also aware of his ghastly and shabby looks. Now this famous beauty, daughter of a shaykh, was making advances at him. He looked bemused, not knowing what to think or say. They had never been in touch: as the daughter of a family of shaykhs, she was in another class, beyond his social rank. Nevertheless, he composed a poem in honor of Khaznah and he set out toward al-Fiḍil with the aim of paying her a visit.

17.4 Khaznah seized the opportunity: This was in the olden days, before Bedouin girls began to cover up and act bashfully, when they still consorted freely with men and spent time in their company, for instance on their way to water the herds or when traveling with the pack camels to stock up at distant markets, just as if they were brothers and sisters. The nice olden ways, free of whispers and base gossip. Those folk would not spread malicious talk. Unlike these days: when a man is seen speaking to a woman, people cast all kinds of unfounded aspersions. See now! Khaznah al-Fiḍil was an acclaimed beauty, widely admired for her grace. She put on her most attractive attire and headed for Abū Zwayyid, flaunting herself like a pure-white, virgin she-camel, in her most coquettish gait. She said, "Welcome, my dearest Khalaf! God brought you here, Abū Zwayyid. You said nice things about me when you were with ʿAbdah. Here, take my necklace!" The kind of necklace that hangs down like a pendant, made of twisted strings of gold. Fahd, his brother, said to him, "You can't do that. As a man, you can't wear Khaznah's necklace! But perhaps she will let you have her camel instead, the huge white stud camel that carries the lady's litter." And he followed this advice. He said, "I am not going to refuse a present given by Khaznah." Shammar tribesmen poked fun at him. They said, "How about it, Abū Zwayyid? You seem to have run out of luck. How could you accept the camel of Khaznah, the camel that carries the lady's litter?" He said, "She has no shortage of pack camels. Her father will easily replace it with a camel he plunders from the enemy. As for myself, the only thing that will do for me is this camel, the one she gave me. Anything else would not suit me."

My heart is beset by worries, driven berserk,
    since being told about a fair, curly-haired maiden.

—Didn't Khaznah say, "Give my greetings to Abū Zwayyid and tell him to pay me a visit?"

She stirred the artist in me to craft verses:
    exquisite lines, not the rhymes of a dabbling hack.
Her breasts are broad and prominent,
    never scratched by the nails of a suckling infant.
Small, finely chiseled teeth with a dewy gleam
    sate a hungry man's craving if tasted and licked.
Her cheeks: daubed in colors of red-hot death,
    dotted with tattoos like traces left by tiny birds;

—The marks of the tattoos are delicate, like the imprints left on soft ground by little birds.

Cheeks tainted red with the slightest touch of white.
    Nose: glint of a sword wielded in close combat.[120]
Eyes agleam, a falcon's gaze on a rocky perch;
    large and wide, shaded by lashes thick and long.
Buttocks bulging like knolls of reddish sand,
    smoothed by breezes, firmed by scattered rain,
Or humps of calves fed by devoted foster camels;
    prickly mothers, not bothered by their owners.[121]
Her tresses tumble down the back in profusion:
    bright chestnut, sprinkled with delicious scents.
Her juicy calves, a palm core's immaculate white;
    haunches broad like benches under palace walls.

—*Al-kbūsh* are the raised benches of clay that run the length of the rulers' palace courtyard.

She's not plump and short or spindly and gangly;
    not fat and sagging or so frail as not to be touched.
With bold strokes her bulging behind was drawn
    by the Lord who separates gold from baser coinage.
Belly lean and taut like a raider's reddish camel,
    a long-backed animal, thirsty from desert crossings.[122]

15   By God, I'd counsel, were it not for some people—
    my fear of scatterbrained folks spilling the beans—

—One comes running for her, then another, all eager to have her.

I'd say, "Be quick! Hasten to the pick of magnificent girls!"
    Ah, wounded by unrequited love, what searing pain!
Wasp-waisted and wide-hipped girls are tantalizing,
    beyond the means of poor devils lacking camel herds.
Seize the day, waste no time weighing pros and cons:
    you can't foretell what future the world has in store.

17.6   Abū Zwayyid joined a caravan of pack camels that traveled eastward in order to stock up at the markets. When the caravan rested during its nightly march, he girded himself, ready for action. "Get up, get up!" he yelled. "What's the matter?" they asked. "By God, Khaznah al-Fiḍīl appeared to me in a dream and told me to carry all of the caravan's loads without further delay." The others understood the message: they rose and loaded their chattel on the pack camels in order to continue on their journey. On this occasion, he composed some lines, addressing them to Khaznah's father, Hijhūj, the shaykh of the Rmāl tribe.

1   Rider of a skittish camel that hates getting hit,
    easily scared, alert and fresh after grueling runs:
Head for the man who shades me in brutal heat,
    my refuge when I feel choked, my breath cut off:

You are a chief who shields camels in a tussle,
    who gains glory by fending off the enemy at the rear.
Yesterday, immersed in the depths of slumber,
    tumbling head over heels down shafts of death,
In my dreams appeared a specter, not a human shape,   5
    to inscribe dictates on my heart, as if on scrolls of paper.
Her folk, it's said, are a deep sea, hard to fathom.
    Don't despair, in peril they rush to your rescue:
Herds robbed from pasture at distant lonely wells,
    beyond huge plains, shimmering mirage, enemies.
You, dear Chief, thrash out matters, cut the knot—
    unfailingly you spot and unmask feckless wiseasses.
A youngster who pours out his heart to an elder,
    his desire to capture riches, to escape penury,
Braced for warnings of danger, thirst, glaring heat,   10
    is told, "Go! Ride a mature mount, tried and tested!"[123]

—A young man tells his guardian how much he'd love to set out on a raiding expedition, in the belief that the elder will urge caution, telling him, "There is plenty of everything you need where we are, my boy. Don't venture out and expose yourself to dangers and risk your life!" Contrary to expectation, his guardian urges him to do so, saying, "Take a she-camel that has given birth five times, a hardy mount, and ride! Don't hang around here, go!"

Not for him long sojourns on rich pasture,
    fattening his sheep and churning butter.

—He speaks about excellent rain-fed grazing covered with lush grasses and plants.[124] Such experts at fattening sheep vie with one another in making profits and keep asking their fellows, "How are your sheep doing?" From six sheep they'd take more than forty pounds of fat, more than six pounds per head of sheep, from each ewe. They'd do so because they pasture sheep on prime pasture grounds soaked by fresh rains.

> Girded up, he boils bubbling milk into dried cheese:
> > the miser's rock-hard chunks dent an axe's blade.[125]

—To make dried cheese, *bigal,* he boils milk until it thickens over the fire. Then he cuts the cheesy mass into pieces like patties, big chunks so hard they would dent the blade of an axe. The only thing he knows and cares about are his goats and the cheese.

> […]
> > Out of sorts, dizzy, he rocks the milk skin forever.[126]

With Mkīdah, Daughter of Jamʿān al-Ghēthī

Abū Zwayyid's poem on Khaznah al-Fiḍīl created a stir. When 18.1
it came to the ears of Mkīdah, the beautiful daughter of Jamʿān
al-Ghēthī, she decided that she too wanted to meet Abū Zwayyid.[127]
She said, "I swear a sincere oath on my life that when I come face
to face with Abū Zwayyid I will greet him warmly on account of the
beautiful words he spoke." She said this without thinking it would
ever happen: just things people say without giving much thought to
it, words carried away by the wind. Sometimes in late spring, these
tribal divisions of Shammar would pick up their goods and chat-
tels and march toward the pools of water left by rains at al-Lmēmā
in the area of Ṣlēb al-ʿAgārib. The flat plain had received a sprin-
kling of rain, a few light showers, the day before. The moisture and
a cool breeze had rippled and firmed the sandy bottom up to where
the sand dunes rose in waving curves. A marvelous sight, the most
delightful scene imaginable.

It so happened that of all people it was Abū Zwayyid who drove 18.2
his small herd of goats to drink from the large pool of water left
by the rains. Someone said to Mkīdah, "Do you see that goatherd
standing there at the rim of the pool, leaning on his cane? Well,
that's Abū Zwayyid. You remember the sincere oath you swore—
that you would greet him if you happened to see him?" "Aren't you
ashamed of yourself, rascal?" she said. "No," he said, "the Lord is my
witness, that's him, none other than Abū Zwayyid." No sooner had

he finished his sentence than Mkīdah waded into the pool, heading straight for Abū Zwayyid at the other side. She was dressed rather flimsily. Her clothes left little to the imagination. The veil covering her mouth had come untied and dangled from her neck. Pulling up her skirt to keep the hem out of the water, she revealed her lower legs and knees, the color of a pure white flower, as she moved toward him. She headed straight for him, prancing like a playful young she-camel.

18.3   "Go, go!" he encouraged her. When she reached him, she said, "My boy, are you Abū Zwayyid?" "True enough, for better or for worse," he said. "Make yourself clear: say, 'By God, I am Abū Zwayyid.'" "Well, if I died right now, you wouldn't get to see Abū Zwayyid." "Ah, honey!" she said. "My darling, my sweet![128] How are you? What are you up to, my savior from misery? Why did you forget us? What made you pay no attention to us? When we'd make short work of any dog that dared bark at you! Do you know, my dear, I made solemn vows that I must come face to face with you at any cost. And now, see! God has fulfilled my wishes!" His looks were ugly: the snout of a hyena and watery eyes that made for poor vision. He stood there squinting and straining to have a good look at that girl as she came hurrying toward him, her skirt lifted from the surface of the water and her shiny legs like lamps illuminated from below. "Little brother dear," she said, "why do you compose verses about speedy camel mounts and daring feats without ever paying attention to us, the girls, in your songs?" As she spoke, she drew closer to him and kept uttering greetings. "Strength, Khalaf![129] Strength, from strength to strength!" She repeated it three times: "Welcome, welcome!" She lowered the veil from her mouth, put her hand behind his neck and pulled him toward her, dipped her nose below his ear and inhaled deeply, then planted three firm kisses on his mouth, cutting off his breath, until his eyes almost sank into his skull, and he let his cane drop. "By God Almighty," she exclaimed, "one by way of a greeting, the second to absolve me from my oath, and the last as a farewell."

They moved away from the pond, chatting all the while as they kept walking over the crest of an elongated elevation of hard stone, its base covered with windblown sands that had been firmed by light sprinkles of rain the day before. They walked side by side, so close that now and then she would bump into him with her shoulder and hips. He could not help noticing her buttocks quivering—like this—with her every movement.[130] "God bless those pack camels that allowed me a chance to see you! I came to collect them and bring them home, but when it was my good fortune to see you, I wanted to have the pleasure of talking with you and getting to know you. But, my dearest, your sheep have started drifting away; they have turned their heads against the wind and are going where they please. Don't let them move off too far: they'll deprive me of our conversation. Fetch your sheep and goats. And I will steer my camels to you, I enjoy chatting with you so much. Do not fret!" He went to fetch his sheep and goats; she likewise turned back and then walked away, disappearing over the top of the low ridge. She had gone, leaving him all by himself. It was late afternoon and the sun was about to set.

On his way back, he hoped to see her again but didn't. He had fallen head over heels in love with her, hopelessly love drunk. He could think only of her. But he had not much to recommend himself. His looks were awful. His eyes were turned to the side, like a locust's. His face was repulsive. But he was a good, decent man. He made a living from his own work and came from a respectable lineage, the Rakhīṣ clan. He was always hard up, poverty-stricken. A thing such as he had tasted just now had never before come his way. It felt like a blast of refreshing cool from an air conditioner at a time of great heat. All he owned were small cattle. Her folks were prestigious camel nomads. The camels moved away with their big strides and left him behind. He rejoined his relatives, carrying his heartsickness with him. He kept running around, looking for people to accost and question, though he felt shy asking about her. He pressed them urgently: "Have you come across a group of Bedouin on their

18.4

18.5

way to water their camels?" "No, we haven't," they said. "Everyone has gathered in one place." Next morning, he set out, riding here and there, making the rounds on his camel, the way someone looks for a runaway camel. He spent all day searching. When the sun began to sink toward the horizon, he was overcome by fatigue and his throat was parched.

18.6   At that moment, he ran into a shepherd who was dozing, belly forward, stretched out on his mount as it circled a herd of camels. "Hey, little brother!" he called to him. "I am in a bit of trouble. Could you spare some water for me to drink?" "Who am I to offer you a draft of water? Weren't you the one whom Mkīdah, the daughter of Khalaf al-Jamʿān, was seen kissing yesterday? What did you say about Mkīdah when she was kissing you? And then you pretend not to know her whereabouts! What did you say? Huh? 'God is great and I am the most fortunate man on earth.' So mightily pleased were you." "Now tell me," Abū Zwayyid said. "Where is the tent of Mkīdah?" "Do you see that tent over there? That's where her folk are staying." "Brother of mine, come here, let me kiss your nose! You have quenched my thirst and taken me on the pilgrimage![131] Such a huge favor you did me."

18.7   The tent owner was Khalaf al-Jamʿān, a friend on whom he used to call and someone who served coffee to visitors outside his tent. He knew that she was his daughter and he headed for Jamʿān's tent. He approached them, leading his mount close to where they were seated, next to the tent, as if he were a casual visitor. But as he dismounted, he was at once recognized as Abū Zwayyid: a charming raconteur, without a malicious streak or vile intent; a good and likable fellow. It is just that he was disadvantaged by his straitened circumstances, as God had decreed. As soon as he appeared, they knew who he was and jumped to their feet. "Over here! Come over here, Abū Zwayyid!" They made him sit down in a prominent place of their circle and pulled over a carpeted camel saddle as an elbow rest for him to recline on and be comfortable. He sat down and they exchanged greetings. Coffeepots were readied and the conversation began. "What has brought you here, Abū Zwayyid?" they asked. "I am on a search," he said, "searching for one that has gone missing." They thought he meant a runaway she-camel or a ewe. "What animal? What shape are its brand marks?" "No, honest to God," he said, "she is without tribal marks, but even so it is clear who she is—she's known to all." "How is that?" they asked.

He answered in verse:	18.8

> Your camel glides, barely touching the ground;	*1*
>   uphill the ruddy beast surges, resolute and fierce:
> A fiery flame to whisk you to faraway lands,
>   its red-hued body wasted after grueling treks.
> Hey, rider, quickly carry my greetings to Mkīdah:
>   Love of her is like a peg hammered into my heart.
> Her smooth belly shines like a cubit of fresh silk,
>   flat and straight, but not for lack of food.

—She's not the kind of girl whose belly button has grown to the size of a camel dropping cluttered with sand on the caravan road.

> Tresses: tail of a mare chafing at its shackles,	*5*
>   restless sorrel horse, impatient to run and chase.
> Lucky are those whose hearts are impervious
>   to fatal spells cast by tattoo-cheeked damsels.
> All celebrate a feast by kissing the one they love;
>   my company are tears streaming down my cheeks.
> Around the wells, joyous crowds mingle and meet:
>   I am haunted by the Bedouin who came and went.

—*Dhīhabān* are the various dispersed migrating groups.

From behind the tent's separation wall, she had overheard the	18.9
words he spoke in her father's circle. She raised her voice: "Listen, Abū Zwayyid, I am not in a position to give you a reward for your

verses. But if my father agrees, I might sleep with you three nights: after that, leave me alone." "By God," her father said, "you've thrown me into the maw of this monster. But honestly, I have no objection. As long as it is your wish to do so, it is fine with me." And he continued: "As long as you accept my condition, with these men here as our witnesses, I will allow you to have her; otherwise not." "Stipulate whatever you like, I'll accept any and all of your conditions." "After I have given her in marriage to you, the two of you will spend three nights in a wedding tent. Then you depart. Really, I do not want to force my daughter on you. If it turns out that she is pregnant, we will send you a message and you stay together. If not, you go your separate ways." "I am only too happy with that, my dearest friend!" They were confined to their marriage tent and after three nights he departed. Two months later they sent a messenger to inform him that his wife was expecting and that he should come to fetch her. She gave birth to his son Dikhīl and other children. She became the mother of his offspring.

His Story with Tarfah, Daughter of Falāḥ ibn Fāliḥ al-Shlāgī

Traveling alone, Abū Zwayyid alighted at Ṭwayyah, a well of the Shilgān, at the approach of the hot season when people, the Bedouin tribes, take up their lodgings around water wells. They had put up seven large tents, each on three tent poles. They were the clan of Falāḥ ibn Fāliḥ of the Shilgān, the uncle of ʿAbaklī. His daughter Tarfah—you wouldn't find such a girl in all of the Arabian Peninsula. She enjoyed legendary fame among all Shammar tribes. At that time, fine girls acquired a name for themselves and were highly valued.

He arrived on his riding camel. His sword—he was armed with a sword—dangled from the mount's haunches. The only other thing he carried was a shriveled water bag. In spite of his unappealing looks, people warmly welcomed him wherever he showed up. That held true for all bards of his ilk: poets like Ibn ʿAngā and al-Hirbīd, who regaled their audience with stories, poems, and wise sayings. At the time of his arrival, the later part of the afternoon, the herds of white camels hurried toward the watering place, Ṭwayyah. At that time of day, masses of camels were on the move and congregated around the pool of the watering place. He brought his riding camel to drink with the other animals. The fodder he had cut for her and his waterskin were on her back when he maneuvered her into the throng of other camels and dismounted. He grabbed his cloak, slid down from her back, and shouted greetings to the men who were seated there, the clansmen of Āl Fāliḥ. While he was busy securing

19.1

19.2

a place for his mount among the other camels, one of the men called to him: "Leave the darned beast! Come over here and have some coffee. I want you to talk to us!" He did as he was told. He dismounted and turned away from his mount, leaving the fodder and the skin on her back. But camels know one another. As he hurried toward the men, he kept throwing anxious glances over his shoulder to his mount.

19.3   The girl, Tarfah, had taken her position in the middle where the camels were drinking, beating back the camels and calling, "Stop! Stop!" At that time her brothers, the sons of Falāḥ, were still little kids; Tarfah was their older sister. As she stood in the pool of water, her legs shone white like the heart of a palm tree. She lifted her skirt to keep it from getting wet and hit the camels with a stick to drive them back. Seeing his mount, she took hold of it, lifted waterskin and fodder from its back, put them in a safe place, and threw her cloak over the fodder. Then she took the reins from the saddle knob and folded them around the camel's neck. She reached for the waterskin, removed it from the mount's back so that it would not be crushed by the camels, and put it down near the water trough. She knew that these were the belongings of a guest. The mount drank and the camels lay down after being watered. She pushed his mount to its resting place for the night. She tied the waterskin to its back and carried the fodder in a fold of her robe. When the other camels were ready to lie down, she made sure to put the guest's luggage at a safe distance from them. Then she brought his mount, couched it, and let the fodder drop from her lap in front of the camel: its dinner.

19.4   Abū Zwayyid had followed her movements attentively. When he sat down with the men, they said, "No, not here. Let's go to ʿAtīg̱, who is preparing coffee. Wonderful to see you, Khalaf. Welcome! How are you, Khalaf? We are glad you joined us, Abū Dikhīl!" And at that, Falāḥ took him by the hand and led him to ʿAtīg̱, the coffee host—ʿAtīg̱ ibn Fāliḥ, Fāliḥ the uncle of Falāḥ's daughter. As he took his seat, he saw his camel mount right in front of him. He watched the girl driving his mount toward the tent, the refilled waterskin attached to the saddle knob. There she kneeled it, and unloaded and covered the gear. "Who is she, Atīg?" he asked. "Is she the lady of the house?" "She is the daughter of this man, Falāḥ, my brother. Tarfah al-Falāḥ."

Abū Zwayyid composed these verses: 19.5

Hey, rider of a proudly prancing camel mount,   1
   fully humped from winter and summer grazing;
Reddish brown, it dashes uphill with raw panache;
   rubbed by saddle ropes, haunches' hair turned gray.
Couched, she tenses up when the saddle's fastened;
   tug at the rope: she fidgets, gurgling and bleating.[132]
She leaves your food bag alone if you take a rest,
   she doesn't vex you with wayward roars and bolts.[133]
Sweet-tempered, she's made for long desert treks,   5
   a sturdy mount, bound to bring you where you wish.
Steer her to ʿAtīg! He'll fulfill your every purpose:
   he lays down his life in the line of chivalrous duty.
A falcon born on high ledges of soaring ambition;
   bands of tight-knit clansmen girded for battle.
You're dearer than all my uncles and ancestors:
   for my lost ones, you are glorious recompense.
I do not hesitate to bare my heart's secrets to you,
   gentle hero of great renown, sung in many odes.
My wound, ʿAtīg, almost healed, was torn open   10
   by a bouncing girl ripping into the tender scar.
Large eyes shine like a glass clockface,[134]
   gaze of a doe sauntering from her place of rest;
Firm breasts almost burst through her robe,
   like eggs of a dove pushing out from the slit.
Ah, smooth stalk in cool meadows, rain-sprinkled
   by nightly clouds, sprouted in a soaked basin.
A glimpse of her stops you in your tracks;
   though you're in a hurry, you turn and linger.

Snatching a look satisfies admirers' appetites:
>   devotees, seasoned watchers of female charms.
A thick tumble of hair cascades onto her behind:
>   fancy seeing her comb the loosened tresses!
Her rump: the hump of a camel calf free to drink,
>   fed by a sheepherder always churning milk.

—*Siktī* is a *shāwī,* the owner of sheep and goats.

Daughter of a chief who leads his men in battle,
>   into crackle of firearms and clouds of powder.

19.6   "On my life, as true as I am the brother of ʿAlyā, go, go, hasten to seal the marriage!" he called. One should know that her uncle, al-Fāliḥ, had no less than seven sons and that each of them had put forward a claim to her. One after the other had taken an oath that she was going to be his prize.[135] But they were good-natured fellows all. When ʿAtīg ibn Fāliḥ, her uncle's son, one of those who claimed her, heard this, he said, "Be of good cheer, Abū Zwayyid, she'll be yours." Not being a fool, Abū Zwayyid said, "Not so fast. Wait a little, son of Fāliḥ—you're as dear to me as my own father. Don't forget that I am married to Zibd al-Mnājī, Cream of Bosom Friends, as the tribesmen of Shammar call her, a sweet woman. Tarfah will not become my bedfellow. But I can tell you in whose position I am now." "To whom do you compare yourself, brother of Mēthā?" he asked.[136] "I am like a shepherd who pampers a she-camel that is not impregnated to save her strength, though he was hired with the promise of receiving her newborn calf as his wages."

A Marriage Proposal Made in His Old Age

In his old age, Abū Zwayyid proposed to a young woman, one of his relatives, but she turned down the offer. Undeterred, he kept pressing her and at long last she agreed, on condition that he give her his riding camel as a dower. She thought that such a disabling condition would put him off. But he tricked her. Having spent just one night in marriage, he sent her on her way, a divorced woman. These are some verses he composed on that occasion:

20.1

> My camel, her gracious legs tried and tested,
>> a blonde I won't barter for a ravishing dame.
> She's mine, kept and kempt to make my living,
>> when stalwarts ride out in search of plunder,
> Sling on their backs travel's bare necessities,
>> in such heat that sandgrouse lose their eggs.
> We fight over the reins in playful tug of war:
>> not one to weary me by running off course.
> Lady proud and highborn, kindly understand:
>> Clear off! You're dismissed without regrets.

1

5

Love Poetry

21.1 Eyes stinging, robbed of sleep, brother of Shammā!
  Worries besiege me in swelling numbers.
As I lie awake, my heart bleeds for a reason:
  what use blaming lovers inflamed by passion?
Spellbound, eyes fixed on her gracious shape,
  mere thought of food makes my insides revolt,
Because of a velvety glow in her doe-like gaze,
  fierce glint of a sea eagle's eye after flight.
5 Hearing her name makes my heartbeat go wild,
  as a prisoner leaps up at news of a ruler's pardon.
By God, who sent us the surahs Kingdom and Tidings:[137]
  as hallowed custom is revered, so I can't forget.

Dirge on Mwēḍī, Who Drowned in the Shaṭṭ River

Woe for our tattoo-lipped beauty queen,   22.1
    carried off by river currents on that evil day.
She was swept along like a ship in full sail,
    a horror to turn gray the hair of a breastfed infant.
In battle, stalwarts vie to rescue her from harm:
    cries of alarm ring out; assailants are put to flight.
Humans are powerless if God wills their perdition;
    I affirm: you're done for if God wills your demise.

His Camel Poems

23.1   Abū Zwayyid has many camel poems to his name. The following are some examples.

> 1   My passion is riding a mighty desert cruiser;
> she's what I like best, pinnacle of my desire.
> Haunches broad, tall, and of massive bulk;
> reddish of hue, soft shoulders cushion the saddle;
> Reddish beast, in her eyes lurks a red-hot stove,
> under black surface, flickering like burning coal.
> Dark waterskins wrapped in cloth for protection,
> nearest desert well fearsome gravel plains away:
> 5   They're led to a remote water hole, known to few,
> by a raiders' captain, fortified by battling foes.
> Lean, hardy mounts kneeled in shade for rest;
> hot noon, whipped by a devil, frenzied, they run.[138]
> Once the fiend lets go, she settles into calmer pace,
> as if the good Lord intervened, granting her respite.
> In midsummer's baked plains where guides are lost,
> beyond the endurance of weaklings from a rotten nest,
> She struts about with a damsel's coquettish gait:
> she loves best riding home from distant journeys.

23.2   And about camels:

Rider of a red-brown camel with a mighty stride,
    not given to sauntering or easily frightened;
Fur aglow with a reddish hue as if silk-coated,
    like a turnout rug woven in Ibn Rayyā's atelier.
If she flags, at once her father's temper shows:
    running like snapping ropes, like plummeting buckets.
No need to kick her flanks with your heels
    or reach backward, hitting with a riding prod.

And this:

Rider of a camel fresh from ages on the pasture:[139]
    years spent piling up layers of fat and strength;
Left bare of womb, they agitate like reluctant brides,
    kicking and crying in a husband's forced embrace,
On crossing vast lonesome plains where hyenas roam,
    blindly confident behind a guide like a string of chickens.

—He means the raid leader: they follow the raid leader like chickens.

And Abū Zwayyid composed these verses on camels:

God help me, my heart has been set on fire:
    beset by manifold torments, it suffers badly.
Anxiety spins the heart around at dizzying speed:
    sternly told, "Stop worrying!" it pays no heed;
Burned by splashes from a pot's furious boil,
    it goes berserk, a frantic, starving desert wolf.
My camel thrived on the herbage of virgin meadows[140]
    all spring, till plants shriveled in scorching heat.
My ardent desire is for a jaunt to faraway lands
    across desert wastes shunned by the faint of heart:
A privilege solely of indomitable braves,
    forever mounted on camels pacing at long stride:[141]

23.3

23.4

1

5

Speedy, inured to thirst, they leave some wells aside,[142]
    scorching across plains, necks held low, like an ostrich.
Short-haired, loaded light with gear and saddle, nothing more;
    in late afternoon they shift from trot to higher speed.

—The mounts are not caparisoned.

Angular bones protrude, as if sculpted by an artisan,
    from gaunt frames tearing along hard, empty tracks:

—Protruding, *nuwāsiʿ*, their necks and shoulders tower up as if chiseled by a carpenter.

10   Haunches broad, calluses on the breastbones
    prominent without hindering their forelegs' elbows,

—*Al-farshāt* are their haunches.

Agitated and twitchy as divorced women
    roused from sleep by a wedding announcement.

Boastful Poems

Abū Zwayyid said: 24.1

> Woe to one for whom we harbor evil: *1*
>   trenchant swords and poisoned blades.
> Bury him under the dust of a dug-out grave
>   or let me drink spiced coffee no more!
> Idiot, snuggled up in his love's embrace
>   as my sleep-deprived eyes burn hot.
> By God, I am driven by love for my clan,
>   desiring to strike at enemies from afar,
> To inflict crushing defeats on tribes: *5*
>   I am sought after to tell of heroic deeds.

And Abū Zwayyid said: 24.2

> My heart feels heavy; there's something wrong;   *1*
>   seething with rage, worn out by churning sorrow.
> Weighed down by worries, I reach for my lyrics:
>   verse creations, not abstruse or silly rhymes,
> Unfit for an audience of floundering dimwits:
>   I am no lout who only cares for food and drink.
> My words are for tribal sons, well-born, well-bred,
>   generous men who spend everything to earn praise;

Whose fires, burning before dawn and at noon,
 bring guests flocking to their hearths in droves;
Coffee dregs heaped high like mounds of ashes;
 they burn through beans in roasting pans and pots,
Brew coffee tender brown, blood of a gazelle
 cut from below, gushing from the heart's arteries.
Tobacco gone up in smoke, yellow leaves will do:
 hubble-bubble in one hand, cup of coffee in the other.[143]
Pour coffee for men proud of their mighty deeds,
 achievers of outstanding feats since ancient times.
If herds of camels are robbed in frenzied turmoil,
 shepherds raise alarm: "Owners, your camels!"
My kinsmen rally, pick the strongest mounts,
 dash off in hot pursuit, sleek fleeting silhouettes:
Purebred she-camels sired by a pedigree stud,
 decked out in colors, an early morning run from Lōgah,
Undeterred by craven naysayers' cautions:
 "How can a band of thirty defeat a thousand?"
Elders of the clan stepped in to voice the solid truth:
 "Tribesmen hold life cheap; they sell it for one riyal.
You sissies, clear off!" Tails between their legs, they went:
 cowards don't recapture stolen high-humped herds.
Red-lipped damsels look to heroes for relief:
 our camels' retrieval was by dint of power and resolve.
At dawn, the shamefaced enemies lick their wounds:
 how did a mere thirty see off an army a thousand strong?
Taken to account by long-haired beauties: what else
 appeases damsels with scented, plaited tresses?
Dim-witted men, beguiled by strength in numbers,
 shocked to see their battle flags teeter, toppled.
A motley mass, bristling with arms, spewing flames;[144]
 the sight alone drives men of sound mind berserk.
We praise the Lord in gratitude for His munificence:
 in war the scales did not tip against us even once.

Enemies crushed, generous hosts all relaxed:
  no reproaches while riding home in scattered parties.
In conclusion, prayers as plentiful as pouring rains
  for the Prophet of Hāshimi descent, the noblest House.[145]

His Poems on the World's Vicissitudes and Contretemps

25.1   Abū Zwayyid said:

1   Do me a favor, coffee maker, hand me a cup:
            make it strong, to lift the haze and clear my mind.
        I was told: "Go for a stroll, make a call!" but "No!
            Fine men thwarted at every turn—where has all the fun gone?"
        I stand in fear of what these times will bring,
            a time when sneaky foxes swagger lionlike;
        Donkey riders aim to fell knights on chargers,
            bandoliered, clad in coats of mail and helmeted;
5   In the market of values, villainy is scooped up in heaps,
            jewelry and precious stones are sold for copper coins.[146]
        Atrocious! Heroes in patterned breeches and scarves
            are being played with, like toys by scrawny kittens.
        Once the world is out of joint it can't be righted:
            no amount of tugging and pulling will straighten it.
        Bear it with patience, all is in the hands of God;
            human affairs depend on the strength of their foundations.

25.2   Abū Zwayyid said:

1   Poor heart assailed by troubles and worries
            nestled deep inside, born of my trials.

Sleepless, eyes burning, dizzy from vertigo;
  slumber eluded me, sped away beyond Hīt.
O God, Creator of heavens and stars,
  You anchored earth with mountain moorings;
O Benefactor who heals broken bones,
  You lift up the oppressed, topple tyrants.
Many amass great wealth only to fall miserably short   5
  in goodness and charity: a rotten breed of devils!
Endure in patience if hard-pressed by the world:
  none but your Provider decides on life and death;
Your fate and subsistence are foreordained,
  written in heavenly script, indelibly yours;
On a tablet, codes of justice have been dictated:
  divine guidance for seekers of moral propriety.
Refuse backbiting, falsehood, wicked practices,
  foolish escapades, feeding minds with vile lies.
The times have lodged enemies inside the house,   10
  pitted folks against one another in vicious strife,[147]
Unhinged modesty's doors, shaming the virtuous;
  trampled upon honesty, deprived truth of life.
Rest in peace, God's mercy on you, martyr of truth:
  dead and buried, you are spared this sound and fury.
The times' depravity has unseated noble virtue,
  left its ropes tattered, threadbare, ready to snap.
Charity's spokesmen, dazed and baffled, wander
  adrift among wild animals in waterless wastes.
Horses sired today fall short of better strains: 15
  studs are led to mares lacking in pedigree.
See, costly Persian carpets are sold dirt cheap,
  puffed-up nobodies and misfits are on their game.
Shockingly, falcons fumble, owls become raptors:
  prey snatched from the claws of perplexed wolves,
Loads of ambergris bartered for sacks of garlic,
  silk sold cheap; cotton bought for princely sums.

My tribesmen are my pride, dashing steeds all,
    hardy fighters, lions crouched for the leap;
20   Forever on the prowl, ramparts for the needy,
    with nothing to their name but chivalrous feats;
Eloquent in Arabic and proficient in Turkish,
    stubborn, immovable during tussles at tangled wells.
If the likes of me, gripped by fear and foreboding,
    sunk in despair, cast about to find a way out,
How does a penniless, downtrodden pauper fare
    whose fellows, insipid idlers, don't care a hoot?
His traces effaced, a ghost among the living,
    still breathing, he is worse off than the dead.
25   Perform the daily prayers, the pilgrimage, the fast,
    repeat the profession of faith morning and evening:
Your records in this world are kept in ledgers
    for final reckoning on the Day of Gathering.

25.3   Abū Zwayyid said:

1   Rider of an outstanding red-brown camel mount,
    a mighty beast, mild-tempered, haunches bulging.
She feels fired up as soon as reins are pulled:
    A mere toe touch and she dashes off at lightning speed.
Head for clansmen, good and generous to a fault:
    my fellows whose mettle is stainless beyond doubt.
We are a coat of mail, closely woven metal rings:
    if anyone's in harm's way, we rush to his rescue.
5   Since olden days, we've shielded refugees from pursuers
    in our redoubt, safe as if ringed by mountain cliffs.
My fellows! Rude reproaches sent flying today
    weaken us when unity is most needed.
Generous men detest falling short in social duty.
    Turn away help-seekers? You'll be shunned!

If names marked in black bask in adulation,[148]
  my friend, thank a world capricious with its favors.
O Lord, your servants bow for You in adoration:
  be kind and spare us from the world's afflictions!
You shower good fortune on a loser—that is Your choice;
  Or bring misery on a lucky head, as You wish.
See how sackcloth has eclipsed silken ware!
  Sheer folly! Threadbare textile leaves you naked!
In markets, lustrous jewelry is spurned by traders;
  iron is king: blunt, but it's enough to cut your throat.
Living a good life means to endure in patience:
  pull hard at the well rope slung over your shoulder!
Cowardice provides no escape from destined Fate:
  your lot is apportioned as the Almighty wills.
If you suffer in silence at being pushed around,
  you deserve a painful blow, smack in the eye.[149]
Oaths and promises with no deeds to match are nothing,
  until you've wearied your hands with maximum toil.

Abū Zwayyid said: 25.4

These verses were molded in the skillful hands
  of a past master of poetry's turns and twists.
Come, my heart, bring out nuggets of wisdom,
  cleverly crafted to satisfy its seekers' demands!
A wolf stretches its neck to release its howls,
  only to be crushed by the hooves of sheep and goats.
Lucky is a person who dies in the true faith,
  fondest desire of those on whom fortune smiles.
Now herdsmen calling "*arr*" to sheep and goats
  are seen strutting with unsheathed swords.
Caught up in evil days without precedent,
  wolves look at sheep with trepidation.

Common folk regard shaykhs with malice:

    tribal chiefs count for less than a tuft of wool.

One understands: past sins come to roost

    if all and sundry act by their own lights.

What's gone is gone, beyond retrieval and repair:

    Goodness! Real men don't waste time on such regrets.

25.5   Abū Zwayyid said:[150]

1   God, You have perfect knowledge of the hidden;

    You steer the world through the Last Day's convulsions;

Creator of the Shiʿah, of Unbelievers and Islam,[151]

    all equally desirous of noble conduct's rewards.

People with good sense cleave to proper ways;

    riffraff can't be trusted to perceive distinctions.

How to dress in cubits of untailored cloth

    without bodice, sleeves, or the correct fit?

5   Big, full-grown sheep and goats are in demand,

    yet the small and skinny are of use as well:

Producing fat, dried cheese, clarified butter;

    from their wool you weave nice houses of hair.

Next to loved ones, hold in highest esteem

    men cushioning your shoulders' heavy burden;

Hawk-eyed, they look after your needs, like a servant:

    they keep you sure-footed, not held in disregard;

By allotting precious shares at spoils' division,

    he adds affectionate esteem to lofty standing.

10   When ropes run over pulleys, I'm ready to hoist,

    unlike impassive slackers, mere corpses on a bier.

I swear, I stay awake with my sleepless friend,

    providing comfort, heartening him as much as I can:[152]

Remember, if you are no good in your life,

    no one needs you in the hereafter.

Abū Zwayyid said: 25.6

Hear my advice if you have aspirations,   1
    guidance when you've lost your bearings:
Rascals made off with what's yours by right;
    you're wronged by a claimant of erring ways.
In grave affairs, seek counselors with solid views:
    fickle advisors compound confusion, lead you
Up the garden path where ruin's shifting sands
    swallow rights lost through one's own doings.
Rights squashed? Claims thrown out of court?   5
    Someone worth his salt takes his matters in hand:
Seek shelter with brave warriors, steeled in battle;
    they comfort a man aggrieved and flustered.
I say so as someone from a clan resolute on revenge—
    we push our foes to the brink as hard as we can:[153]
Our cauldron's steam is as hot as its furious fire;
    other well ropes fall short, ours reach the water.
Our companion is ensconced among the steepest crags;
    we make up for his defects, overlook his missteps;
He's our companion: if he walks on red-hot embers,   10
    duty-bound, we suffer with the protected neighbor.

Abū Zwayyid said: 25.7

Adopt a proper tone toward gentlemen;   1
    avoid the bombastic blather served up by louts;
In addressing them I observe the Prophet's qualities,
    speech valued by the sagacious no less than money.
I do not shy away if called upon for burdensome duty,
    nor do I put store in looking for others' failings.
Our habit is to throw in our lot with friends,
    not to doll ourselves up, swanky, sitting pretty.

5

Peppered with questions by impertinent visitors
    aiming to ferret out secrets of our private affairs,
I face the erring fools brandishing a sharp blade,
    as wielded by a fighter, undaunted by carnage.
Beware of traveling on pitch-dark, moonless nights;
    pincers are used as a tool to extract aching molars.[154]
If I hear foolish babble, meaningless claptrap,
    it feels like a razor-sharp knife slicing my liver.
Three cardinal principles are the pride of the Arabs—
    if these are lost, all truth is lost irredeemably:

10

The rights of neighbors, of guests, and of travel companions
    are held sacred by those of true knowledge.

25.8   Abū Zwayyid said:

1

Humans are prone to err and stray off course
    without guidance from the Beneficent Lord.
God, the road to prosperity begins with You:
    turn Your gaze, let it look with favor on me!
Do so at a gallop, lift up poverty's begrimed torpor;
    quickly, drop my poverty on a good-for-nothing!

—*Al-muṣbiṭ*, "torpor," is slumber, just short of sleep.

Either fortune's camel comes to you willingly
    or wolves erupt in song on seeing you prostrate;

5

One day poverty's ashen gloom is dispelled,
    the next you are forced into bogs of impotence.
Camels: strong mounts for you to go raiding,
    to cross waterless deserts, to irrigate your palms.

—Either you ride her on raids or you use her to draw water to irrigate the fields that provide your food.

Abū Zwayyid said: 25.9

The world is filled with dogs, barking loudly;
    morsels are devoured without touching the teeth:
If things go well, you gladly open Fortune's door;
    a long-suffering person may yet strike gold.
You can't loosen Fate's hold, it is decreed:
    good or bad, ineluctably it comes your way.

Abū Zwayyid said: 25.10

Listen to the charming verses I composed,
    words measured in gold bullion, not in dimes.
Two thousand don't measure up to just one real man;
    of cowards he'd soon dispatch a thousand and one.
A man, perplexed and weak, astray and lost,
    tumbles into a bottomless well of infirmity.

Abū Zwayyid said: 25.11

For hunting choose young peregrines:
    they strike, claws tear prey to pieces.
Let them fly to swoop down on bustards,
    striking them as a fatal bolt from the sky.
Falconry with weaker birds drove me crazy:
    if I call, they evade me, hiding in sagebrush.[155]

Abū Zwayyid said: 25.12

Do not submit grave affairs to oaths and witnesses[156]
    until you've exhausted your own forces all!
If you feel put upon and decide to give in,
    may a hit pierce your underbelly at the bladder.

BATTLE OF AL-JMĒMĀ

26.1 The morning after the battle of al-Jmēmā, Abū Zwayyid visited the shaykhs. On arrival, it was clear that the young prince, Sʿūd Abū Khashm, had been sleeping with his wife: they had married him to Fahdah. She used to say that he liked to play around on her belly and then fall asleep. When he woke up, the slaves gave him a washing. Then he came and sat down with them. Abū Zwayyid was present in the majlis. The young prince called him "my uncle." He would say, "Good morning, my uncle!" The poet said:

1 Hello, hello, hello to you, a hearty welcome,
    a thousand, another thousand, and thousands more!
Sweetheart of a girl with civet-scented breasts:
    how fresh creamy beauties love your raw rutting!
Manly virtue looked down its nose at all suitors,
    then expeditiously sent its camel running to Sʿūd.
How I wish one could summon the dead;
    if only Muḥammad would rise from his tomb;
5 ʿAbd al-ʿAzīz! See the fast horse of hot pursuit!
    Marvel at the tons of booty captured by Sʿūd!
Young camels fringe a long caravan of spoils:[157]
    by God, one struck by him is out of combat.

War of al-Jawf, Poem in
Praise of Abū Khashm

Abū Zwayyid owed money to a slave named Muḥammad ibn Ṣāliḥ,   27.1
who lived in Ḥāyil and was one of the slaves in the service of Ibn
Rashīd. He owed him twenty-six guineas. He kept urging him to
pay back the money and settle the debt, but Abū Zwayyid was hard
up and penniless. He asked his creditor to wait until things eased up
for him, and other similar pleas. People, his own folk, would prod
him gently: "Abū Zwayyid, why don't you pay back what you owe
the slave? The slave who keeps bothering you, give him his money!"
But he replied, "My dear fellows, I don't even have a penny to show
him. And I have never paid off my debts my whole life long. Let me
wait patiently and see. Who knows, tomorrow this fierce falcon may
strike riches in bountiful orchards.[158] Then I will compose some
verses to laud his feats of arms, and as a consequence he will settle
my debts."

As fate would have it, the battle of al-Jawf was fought soon after.   27.2
Abū Zwayyid called on S'ūd and said, "May your life be long, my
congratulations on these blessed spoils!" "God bless you." "By God,
may you live long, I humbly ask your permission to recite some
simple verses that I composed because you are truly deserving of
them." "No problem," he said. "Go ahead." S'ud Abū Khashm was
aware of the debt problem. He knew that the poet hoped he would
settle his debt to the slave. And he did so, a generous deed for which
Abū Zwayyid gave him proper thanks. He opens the poem with

praise for Ibn Rashīd and stresses how deserving he is, and how he routed the people of the north. He stripped Nawwāf ibn Shaʿlān of his possessions and looted all the people of the north. Two good fortunes do not go together: you either win or lose.[159] Abū Zwayyid, awed by the quantity of booty, sang Ibn Rashīd's praises and asked him to pay off his debts.

27.3　When he had finished declaiming, Ibn Rashīd asked him, "What is the amount you owe the slave?" He said, "He wants me to pay him twenty-six guineas." Ibn Rashīd called his servants: "Bring a rifle for Abū Zwayyid!" He meant one of the new rifles, the ones provided by Ibn Laylā that were never used for shooting. "Dearest," asked Abū Zwayyid, "are those for me or for ʿĀmish?"[160] "These are surely for you," he said, and he called for the same to be brought for ʿĀmish. "And bring Abū Zwayyid one of the best riding camels, from the selection!"—that is, the first-class mounts owned by shaykhs. "My dear, is she for me or for ʿĀmish?" "No, for you. And bring a similar camel for ʿĀmish!"

27.4　They brought two riding camels and two rifles. And Ibn Rashīd gave him a piece of paper in his own hand, saying, "Put this in your pocket and give it to the slave when he comes to you. I will take care of the money you owe him. I'll pay your debt; it's not your affair anymore." Thus, he departed with two riding camels and two rifles in recognition of the poem he had composed, and the debt of twenty-six guineas he owed to the slave settled. Ibn Laylā was a man who served the state, the man of the ʿUṣmalī rifles, from the Lubdah quarter in Ḥāyil.[161] The Ottoman Turks sent him to Ibn Rashīd with a thousand rifles, called "Mother of Five (bullets)." Ibn Rashīd stored them in Ḥāyil and distributed them among his henchmen, bodyguards, and Shammar tribesmen. Shammaris who came to visit and pay their respects were given a rifle. The thousand firearms used to be called "rifles of Ibn Laylā," but in reality they came from the Turks, the "Mothers of Five."

27.5　Abū Zwayyid said:

As sand grains are abundant, that often I repeat God's name,   *1*
     grains of the golden dunes, towering hills of sand.
Lord, You are the Creator of humanity;
     You sent down your message in ink on paper.
Glory to father of Mishʿal, who raids far and wide!
     My prayer for him: "Let no head be over his head!"

—Abū Mishʿal is Sʿūd Abū Khashm.

Our ancient debts from time immemorial he settled,
     accounts from the rule of ʿAbbās, said ʿUbayd.

—ʿUbayd (ibn Rashīd) said that in earlier days we abandoned al-Jawbah because of ʿAbbās, ceding it to the Ottoman State, in his verse: "O land, we left you alone because of ʿAbbās; for Ibn Shaʿlān's sake we'd have not left it."

He conquered, gleaming Indian swords in hand;   *5*
     a campaign that settled all unpaid debts as well.
A falcon soaring up from Ajā's crest for the hunt,
     stunning, not one ruffled feather, pure peregrine!
His fare the bleeding flesh of a prey's breast:
     he bagged Abū Tāyih, al-Sharārāt, and ʿAnazah.
War started with Nawwāf marching into town;
     lusting for a brawl, ragtag troops came prowling,
Led by Nawwāf, rutting stud foaming at the mouth:
     you tied his legs, crippled him, ringed his nose.
Nawwāf, what's your gain from reckless charges   *10*
     but malicious gloats, empty claims, and bitter failure?
He charged, goading his troops with rousing chants;
     beguiled, the dazzled fools swung in a *daḥḥah* dance.
Aiming to hunt, he didn't think he'd be hunted:
     how our grizzled huntsmen tore him to pieces!

Abū Mishʿal's feats of arms are certainly true;[162]
    Nawwāf's exploits have tumbled into the gutter.
He ran off by night, pillow and bedcover left behind;
    quiet after earsplitting roars, he gnashed his teeth.

15 They abandoned precious luggage and black tents,
    fled riding bareback on their mounts.
Veering left, they galloped up the wadi bottom;
    veering right, they raced between Nadfā and al-Amḥāṣ.
Heads of black hair turn white at seeing such a rout:
    some plunged into poverty, others wealthy in the blink of an eye.
Shaken, his demoralized troops flagged and wavered;
    they absconded with the prize of failure and frustration.
Pack camels carried passengers, seated among loads,[163]
    installed up there as if with ropes and tent pegs.

20 Muḥammad and ʿAbdallah are your sword's scabbards,
    girded up for you at the well with rope and bucket.

—That is, Muḥammad and ʿAbdallah al-Ṭalāl.

Every inch as eager as you are to collect old debts,
    their ardor for battle cheered each and every fighter.
ʿAbdallah mounted his camel and marched
    with the pick of men, not the chickenhearted,

—Yet ʿAbdallah ibn Ṭalāl was the one who later murdered the prince. On this occasion, he mobilized the men of Shammar, together with Ḍārī ibn Ṭwālah.

Weaklings who cravenly pay for grazing rights,[164]
    submissive appeasers like foxes and scrawny cats.

—As the price for permission to pasture their animals on another tribe's land, they give the owners one of their sheep.

To pay for grazing rights is a shameful deed,
　　blacker than impenetrable dark of night.
On a broad-chested steed came Ṣalfah's brother:　　　　25
　　his nest's feeblest falcon ravages enemy riders.

—The brother of Ṣalfah is Ḍārī ibn Ṭwālah.

At his battle cry, seasoned horses shrink back;
　　diffident, they gallop off, unrestrained by their riders.
Fihrān ibn Hēshān leads the cavalry charge;
　　all-night marches left his horses lean like bows.

—Fihrān ibn Hēshān of al-Ṣdēd of Shammar rushed to the assistance from the Jazīrah area. The pack camels accompanying the horses were so exhausted that they had to be abandoned.

They linked up with Miṭnī, falcon set upon prey,
　　a violent rush of bandoliers and colorful jackets.

—Miṭnī ibn Shrēm.

Horsemen launching the assault came at night
　　with arms for the shaykh of shaykhs:
Maternal uncles did not harm your breed:[165]　　　　30
　　their chivalrous feats paved the way for offspring;
Brothers of Mūḍī, when teeth are clenched;
　　brothers of Mūḍī, when wimps are useless.[166]
Plaudits for Ḥāyil's folks, who live up to the call,
　　who without dismay always gallop into the fray.
Girded with ornate belts, they stop at nothing;
　　shots ringing, they drink from the pool of death.
Your slaves advance like rutting stallions;[167]
　　the least of them lays waste to the enemy's champions.

35   In a crunch, my fellows fulfill the needs of the hour,
     resolute in protecting the princely house.
Each night we sent a herald to your aid:
     we're at your assailant's throat like a cord.
Beauties of ours! Sprinkle your cloth with civet!
     You waited anxiously for sign of Abū Mishʿal:
He sings ditties urging on his horses and men,
     storms forward, striking out at all on his path.
See him dueling on horseback in whirling dust,
     resplendent, while others choke on dried spittle!
40   Among tribes, your equal is nowhere to be found,
     not among the mass of Arabs nor the Banū Yās.
Maidens did not bring forth a boy like you,
     never suckled such an infant at their breast.
You, intrepid warrior, the equal of Abū Zayd,
     victorious over lands of al-Zanātī and Qabbās.[168]
When warhorses are led to every fighter,
     others hold back—you hold dear life cheap.
Once Mūḍī swoons in your sweet embrace,
     pray that she will never burn in Hell's fire.
45   Your friend's back is racked by a wooden saddle;
     I writhe under a heavy load, Abū Mishʿal, my refuge!
O Prince, I am bedeviled by debt owed to a slave;
     an intrepid warrior slave does not easily relent.
Without you, my fire steel cannot strike sparks:
     I beg you, free me from the debt the slave has levied![169]
You are like a valley flooded by torrents of generosity,
     Prince, your stores of fame and glory are almost bursting.
Your noble aspirations will be proclaimed in Heaven,
     when charitable deeds are weighed and measured.

Riposte of Khḍēr al-Ṣʿēlīć to Abū Zwayyid's Poem in Praise of Ibn Shaʿlān

He made a poem in reply to Abū Zwayyid's poem on Saṭṭām ibn   28.1
Shaʿlān:

Rider of a big-humped camel, tough as a wolf,   1
    layered with fat from grazing on pristine enemy land;
Pampered, not grated by a wooden saddle,
    speedy as a male ostrich racing at full tilt;
At staccato pace—no telegraph or steam engine—
    as guns fire deafening salvos.
Make for Abū Zwayyid! Take his verse in reply!
    I made your lies apparent to all the world.
Abū Zwayyid, leave off the spreading of falsehoods!   5
    Do not forfeit honor by swagger and reckless games.
Fear the Lord, privy to secrets and the unknown,
    Never absent—for Him there is no substitute.
No knight as shining as Muḥammad was ever born,
    nor can any creature claim to be his peer.
From south of al-Khurmah to Shaṭṭ al-ʿArab River,
    from Syria to Istanbul, all the way to Kandahar,[170]
Subduers of defiant strongmen flock to him,
    in awe of his vengeful punishment of enemies:
Ruthless and severe with arrogant recalcitrants,[171]   10
    good-natured and gentle with loyal supporters;

For friends sweeter than rainwater in shaded rocks;
  to enemies crueler than flames of blazing fire:
Wholesome drafts made of purest sugar honey;
  or stinging colocynth, bitter apple of biting taste.
Happy are his guests, made masters of the house,
  when seeds are forsaken by the Pleiades rains;[172]
Visitors hasten, spurring camels with their heels
  to run at a frantic pace to the welcoming host.
15 As stars start to twinkle, sparkling like torches,
  misers shut doors, loath to share their coffee,
His axe blades are smeared with camel blood,
  though people make a living from their backs.
Clansmen favored by God, cream of the crop,
  they forced all tribes to concede their lands.[173]
His brother, father of Mājid, rescuers' steed:
  Ever since 'Abdallah's rule his sparks fly.
His routine is wielding polished Indian swords:
  nemesis of enemies, scourge of baleful rogues.
20 Muḥammad is the stud of bell-shaped beauties,
  stylish Bedouin girls and village stunners.[174]
Prayers of the Lord, abundant as the dunes' sand grains,
  for the Prophet, receiver of His revelations.

Riposte of Rāḍī ibn Fārān to Abū Zwayyid's Poem in Praise of Ibn Shaʿlān

Rāḍī ibn Fārān died a long time ago. Before my time—I never saw   29.1
him. He was from Jubbah, but toward the end of his life he moved
to al-Jawf. In these verses, he gives a riposte to Abū Zwayyid's poem
on Saṭṭām ibn Shaʿlān, saying:

Hey, rider flogging a camel with a crop,   1
    not a beast to toil drawing irrigation water,
Nor brought up to suckle her newborn calf
    or harried to carry a needy man's loads.
Like a startled male ostrich, she hurtles down:
    hard-hooved horses can't catch up with her.
Forefeet and legs behind move in rapid sync:
    one desert abode at night, another in the morning.
Find Khalaf among the camp's slanting tents.   5
    Did he forget who nursed him at her breast?
Never did you meet with their disrespect:
    they kept you safe from marauding predators.
Liberal-minded, most hospitable of hosts,
    with spears flying, a rampart from disaster,
He is Mitʿib's mighty brother, fattener of guests:
    no woman suckled his like since Adam's days.[175]
No shaykh, minister, or prince has his stature,
    from the world's beginnings until its very end;

10 A champion stud led to thoroughbred mares
       to sire, without peer among noblest stallions,
   He reigns from Najd to the Iraqi river crossings,
       He quenches grim swords' thirst with enemy blood;
   On horses with heads massive as camels', sounds
       his raucous battle cry, sowing death and doom:
   His orders have no words for "turning back":
       facing the enemy is his tribe's pride and joy.
   God, Creator of layered rain clouds,
       You spread out the earth and raised the sky:
15 Keep Muḥammad from stumbling on the road;
       spread over him Your infallible protective veil.
   As decreed by God, he is His viceroy on earth,
       A walled bulwark to shelter his Shammar tribe.

ʿADWĀN IBN RĀSHID AL-HIRBĪD

His Life

'Adwān al-Hirbīd was a contemporary of Muḥammad ibn Rashīd. He was known for his stories and poems. People eagerly followed his sayings and doings. He was a prolific bard, but during his lifetime he became especially famous for a poem called al-Shēkhah. He hailed from the area of al-Ghūṭah, Mōgag, and al-Amrār, but often traveled deep into the desert. He owned gardens of date palms at Ḥayyah in the Ajā Mountain. Following the late-spring rains, he used to stay in a booth made of palm leaves at al-Khinfah al-Zrēb, where he pastured his animals.[176]

Later in life, he faced much adversity—may God spare us from the world's tribulations—and as his family's sole survivor he had the care of a little boy, Jrēs, the child of one of his brothers. He used to carry the infant around as women do. But his circumstances were much worse. He was one of seven brothers, sons of Rāshid, skilled falconers all. Because he was the elder brother, the others vied to be at his beck and call, eager to impress him favorably by doing odd jobs for him. He was the firstborn. I was told that they lived in a tent with seven main poles.[177] In each of the seven compartments there was a lance. He and his brothers were married men who lived a contented family life. His brothers' quarters were to his right and left. They owned fast riding horses, pack camels, various properties, herds of milk-producing camels that pastured nearby, and large flocks of sheep and goats.

30.1

30.2

One day, he went on a journey to attend to some business. He left the camp where he and his brothers were staying. It was spring, and the desert had bloomed magnificently, but he had to travel to look after his interests. When he had been away for about one year, he ran into someone he had known from before. He asked him how so-and-so was doing, one of his brothers. The other said, "He asks your forgiveness; he is no longer with us."[178] "And so-and-so?" "Ask no more," the other said. "Cruel fate has crushed all your dear ones, may God protect us from its evil. The only ones left are Jrēs, your brother's son, and his mother. The others perished. Except for Jrēs and his mother, not a single one of your close kinfolk have survived." In ʿAdwān's absence, the Shaʿlān of the Rwalah tribe had sprung a surprise attack, killing everyone in the camp and making off with their possessions. "ʿŌjān's gain," he said, meaning that such a criminally wanton and bloody raid merely brought dishonor.

30.4   With the little money he had, he bought a camel and rode back, saying to himself, "Perhaps the boy will grow up and be good. Perhaps God will allow us to perpetuate our family's existence and not cut off our lineage." On arrival, he found their former settlement empty. He gazed at blossoming herbage and thick growth, pools of rainwater that had not yet dried up, slabs of stone from which the cooking pots had been suspended over the fire. No one had dared to set foot in the place since the catastrophe. No one at all. No human being had the courage to come close to it for any purpose. "My God, here is where the animals used to stay, here the cooking pots, here the tent." He sat down, overwhelmed by memories of his loved ones. He thought of their happy days together, their self-assurance and confidence in the future. And now evil fate had carried off his brothers. There he was, all alone by himself.

30.5   He sank to his knees and wept, praying to God for help. These verses welled up in him:

1   A year ago was my last view of our desert abode,
            between hard plains and soft sands of Ashrāf Ḍāḥī.

May rumbling clouds shower you with the rains of Arcturus,
  shaking with anger, and drench you in limpid water.
Abode! Where are your inhabitants' footprints?
  Where the traces herds leave at resting places?
Three stones for cooking pots, like servants' heads;[179]
  a bowl of dust, stirred up by gusty winds—that's all.
Where are the men who sauntered here last year?   5
  Gone from view! Ephemeral as lightning's flicker.
They went, like a dream in a soothsayer's tale,
  thunderlights seen in an early summer evening,
Vanished into a dark maw of night and plague,[180]
  leaving me mortally wounded, felled by a weapon.
Jrēs, my soulmate, over us hover birds of death:
  treacherous are delights of doom-laden nights!
Held by a nose ring, fettered and shackled,
  Jrēs, we're made to swallow horrid brine.
Even if mountains fly, our luck remains prostrate:[181]   10
  Do not fancy that good fortune's gates are still ajar!
My heart is torn to shreds like cheap blue cloth,
  a bucket rent by a well casing's jutting stones.

Some time later he passed their former camp. His brothers had   30.6
died. These were the herds' resting places. An eerie silence reigned,
broken only by breezes whistling around the cooking pots' stone
slabs. He delved into his memories. Yes, here stood their tents only
a year ago. They had space, herbage, and herds in abundance. He
looked at the place. Plentiful rains had drenched the flat desert
bottom, devoid of any sign of human life. The stones that held the
cooking pots were the only mementos of a time when the place bus-
tled with people, cattle, and tents. Only those three slabs of stone,
nothing more.

Then he said: 30.7

    1   Rider of a she-camel with blazing eyes,
           eager to cross wastes at an impetuous pace,
        Vying with sandgrouse swift on the wing,
           thirst-driven to plunge into shimmering heat.
        Jrēs, I roused myself to craft my verse for you;
           like a deft artisan I mold my rhymes;
        Trimmed with an accursed Frank's finesse,
           they're released, and hit the road in single file.

Rider of a she-camel with blazing eyes,
    eager to cross wastes at an impetuous pace,
Vying with sandgrouse swift on the wing,
    thirst-driven to plunge into shimmering heat.
Jrēs, I roused myself to craft my verse for you;
    like a deft artisan I mold my rhymes;
Trimmed with an accursed Frank's finesse,
    they're released, and hit the road in single file.
Gold coins, rounded like pads of camels' feet;[182]
    Never am I told: "Your verses stray off course!"
Jrēs, listen to my complaint, feel for me,
    heed my message, delivered by a hardy mount!
Behold our folk's abode, the mutes don't speak,
    hearthstones, resting places blown about by dust:[183]
Where are the five-poled tents, my cheerful fellows,
    on a grim day, stripped of the dwellings' sweet gaiety?
Swept away like an early-morning deck of clouds,
    dispersed in the afternoon by heady western winds.
I groan, a warrior clasping at his grievous wounds,
    a camel mother gone insane after losing her calf.
Life is bleak, tasteless without human contact:
    from my pillowed bed, God smashed me against the rocks.

—*Jawāḍiʿ* are soft pillows and coverings that give into whatever direction you lean on them.

With Jrēs

Al-Hirbīd always kept a watchful eye on his young relative Jrēs. He made sure that he did not lack for anything. Jrēs was the son of his brother Shēmān, who was among those killed. When Jrēs was a little boy, ʿAdwān used to carry him around. He went to see Jrēs's mother, Bgēshah, and said to her, "Know that I do not feel in the least attracted to you. You are not the wife I'd have chosen for myself. Yet I will marry you for the sake of this orphan boy." And so it happened. He took the mother as his wife and carried her little boy on his back. His fellow tribesmen of al-Swēd joined forces to collect sheep and goats for their use and camels for transportation. At the place where the tribe gathered in early summer, they put up shacks for him and his dependents. In those days, game was still plentiful: in fact, gazelles may have outnumbered the goats and sheep. ʿAdwān, may your life be long, pampered Jrēs as a bird looks after its chicks, year after year. While Jrēs was a child, he always put him in the first and highest place, as if on top of Mount Rāf, as if he built a feathered nest for him in a euphorbia shrub. He felt deeply for the orphan and cuddled him. He'd go to the sands, carrying a rifle, and hunt for game. Year after year, he went hunting and fed the boy on game. If he had shot an ibex ram and people were done eating from it, he would take a chunk of the roast and put it on top of their dwelling. If the boy, his brother's son, woke up at night, he'd reach for it and give it to him, because of his tender feelings toward him: a piece of roast meat set apart for the little one to sustain him in the long nights of winter. He'd give it to him to chew on if he cried. Then he'd be quiet again.

31.2   But Jrēs was not the kind of person you are.[184] Something was missing as he grew up. 'Adwān tried to steer him in the desired direction, urging him to be on good behavior. He did so in verses composed to advise and encourage him by applauding whatever he did well. He did what he could to stimulate him and fan a flicker of ambition. All to no avail. Jrēs's feet were planted on the ground. He wouldn't soar. He was self-absorbed, not the outgoing type. In the olden days, someone might give you a sheep for your personal use. You'd milk it for your household and at a later date you'd return it to the owner. It is given by the owner for a certain period of time, as a charitable deed. 'Adwān's fellow tribesmen joined hands to provide him with four such sheep for his personal consumption, as a loan in his safekeeping. 'Adwān told Jrēs, "Come now, listen to your uncle, take these sheep to find some grazing." One day, when Jrēs was old enough to be sent on such errands, a young adolescent already, and had taken the sheep to pasture a couple of times, he ran into a herd of camels that belonged to men of the Swēd, and he started to mull over his situation. On his return, he said, "Uncle mine, I am not going to take the sheep to graze anymore." "What now? Why is that, my boy?" He said, "If you want me to be a sheepherder, give me some camels as well. It will not do for me to be stuck out there with just a few sheep. They're not even our own. I am through with playing shepherd. You want me to take them to the field? Very well, give me some camels!" And again, he made the point that the sheep were not theirs.

31.3   Taken aback, 'Adwān said, "What do we have here, my boy? Camels are not like pieces of rock, something you pick up from the desert floor. We have reason to be grateful for the comfort we draw from sheep. Thanks to them, we provide for ourselves. True, the owner is someone else; they have been given us on loan. Still, your mother uses their wool to furnish the dwelling that shades us in summer, that keeps us warm in winter, and that protects us from getting soaked by rain. Surplus milk is turned into dried cheese and the fat is stored in skins. This is how we make ends meet." But the boy was adamant. He said, "From now on, things will not go the way you were used to. Say whatever you want, but I am not going to listen. Give me camels or else I won't take the sheep to graze!" ʿAdwān had devoted himself wholeheartedly to the boy's upbringing. "Oh my boy, my boy!" He had nothing to show for his efforts. He was at his wits' end. He said to himself, "Is this what I get in return for the love I bestowed on him? How could I discipline this orphan child after having raised him with tender care? Perhaps someone will talk sense to him, a friend, the boy's mother, or anyone." The old man was left with no choice but to take the sheep to the pasture himself. He did so for days on end. His endeavors had met with complete failure.

He said:

31.4

> I straighten my verses: I am the father of Khzayyim! 1
> Proud moniker, as Ibn Mirdās's cry: "I am Shāyiʿ!"

—Khzayyim was a son who died in infancy.

> Shāyiʿ speaks of his well-intentioned fellows;
> let me tell you about my foul-tempered Jrēs.
> Jrēs, may God forsake you, our sheep are the best:
> lovely animals even though given on loan.
> Much better than begging friends for favors
> and getting sweet words foisted on empty stomachs:
> Your relatives, well versed in smooth talk, 5
> nowhere to be found in your hour of need.
> Shame, nephew! You deserve God's reproach,
> vicious, spiked tongue-lashings left and right,
> All the way to Egypt, chained on camelback,
> to be dumped in the tattoo-tappers' land.

—To Yemen.

> My nephew, for you I bathe in floods of tears;
>> you made my eyes gush in swiftly flowing rivulets.
> My heart, Jrēs, is jolted like a bucket pulled hard
>> by powerful camels, emptied into a basin,
> Plunging down again to the bottom of the well,
>> heavy with water hoisted up by the sturdy beasts,
> Up and down, worn thin and fraying at the ends,
>> its mouth's wrinkled leather torn from the ropes.
> I carried you, innocent child, with my strength:
>> often skinny orphans like you are abandoned.
> Is this my recompense, that you make me cry,
>> searing drops burning open the sluices of my eyes?
> No greater fear is there than being dragged by dependents,
>> hauled, helpless and blind, over beds of thorns.

31.5   ʿAdwān had taken him by the arm to help him. But Jrēs, by God, was a good-for-nothing, useless. He grew up to become a disagreeable, selfish person. They had nothing in common. His uncle was a forceful, enterprising character: a hunter, a gunman.[185] When he became the boy's guardian, ʿAdwān overheard a conversation between Jrēs and other youngsters of his age, who were telling Jrēs how to handle it: "If he wants you to go and graze the sheep, have him give you some camels. If not, let him stumble after those sheep himself!" Some friends put you in a tight spot. Others give you strength: they are of benefit in this world and the hereafter; they do not shy away from difficult tasks. Others speak ill of you and plot your downfall. As the saying goes: "An enemy shows mercy, but a fool is merciless to himself." Jrēs's old uncle had stayed at his side as a devoted father. At this, ʿAdwān compared the boy's friends to the large bag carried by itinerant blacksmiths: the kind of sack you fill with whatever objects you come across that one day may prove useful, like a junkyard where you'd find a metal piece broken off from a hand plane, and that might be turned into a hammer which sparks the powder of a matchlock gun; or scraps from a vessel made of metal sheet for the transport of dates that may come in handy for the manufacture of simple objects like the large needle of a spindle.

He said: 31.6

> Jrēs, hear the cry from my heart—I hear yours: *1*
>> let's leave aside shameful and dishonest talk.
> How often I felt your hands hold my neck—
>> your little fingers gripping me in tight embrace!

—That is, when he was an infant he lifted him up to carry him on his back.

> Jrēs, for you I took your mother as my wife:
>> from love of her progeny.
> Jrēs, you left me in the lurch but how could I leave you?
>> I follow you like a camel in thrall to her calf.
> Often I took aim, eyes glued to my gun's barrel, *5*
>> to not leave you hungry, Jrēs, after a paltry meal.
> Many times I handed you fat chunks of meat
>> so that, spoiled with such dainties, you'd have more.
> Now you loathe me: with your muscled neck
>> came a churlish temper and a peevish obstinacy.
> On your chin you carry the growth of your age,
>> but a beard's dignity depends on the wearer.
> One goat bestowed on you by the Almighty Lord
>> is worth more than a kinsman's small camel herd:

—Even having a goat without milk is better than having nothing at all.

> If he migrates, a friend with camels forsakes you: *10*
>> without camels to carry loads, you remain behind.

God is my refuge, Jrēs! Go! Leave me be!
    No use expecting comfort from brothers' children.
What's my benefit from relatives, close and distant,
    the day a mound of dust is shoveled over me?
Without a friend to lend a helping hand in life,
    a grave's stone slabs seal your utter loneliness.

31.7 His verses received a response from 'Bēd, the chief of Bag'ā, Abū Fahd. May God spare us from this world's evil tricks. Every word they say on this topic, both 'Adwān and the headman of Bag'ā, is very true. The headman's relative Khālid, the son of Fahd and grandson of 'Bēd, killed himself. He had become tired of life. Both of them spoke the truth, each in his own way.

31.8 'Bēd, the headman of Bag'ā, said:

You're better off in life without such a friend,
    spared the evil ways you'd suffer in his company.
Beware if that pack of lies and deceit arrives
    on worn-out riding camels swaying with fatigue:
He buys and sells you, properly, ink on paper,
    without awe of God in his vicious slander.

31.9 As Jrēs reached the age of discernment, 'Adwān took it upon himself to instill in him principles of good conduct, as is one's duty: in speech and by fostering civilized norms in one's heart. He kept reminding him of the many good turns he had done him when he was a little kid. In spite of some unpleasantness experienced from Jrēs, he had not given up on him. He wanted to prod him, to stimulate him to do better. He had pinned his hopes on him. As a youth, Jrēs might be forgiven for committing a folly or indulging some foolish urges. Unfortunately, 'Adwān's efforts did not bear fruit and Jrēs's character defects proved uncorrectable.

31.10 He said:

Rider perched on the back of an Omani camel,   *1*
    six years old, its eyeteeth just broken through,
Capable of scorching speed when given full rein,
    the ideal mount for undaunted emissaries:
Head for a young man bent on my destruction,
    throwing me like a rock into ruin's abyss.
Jrēs, a far cry from his namesake Jrēs al-Yamānī
    or Jrēs, bell of a white camel with fluttering trappings.

—Jrēs al-Yamānī of the ʿIjmān tribe, a generous and brave person.

With God's guidance, I struggled to lift your head,   *5*
    just as a bucket scrapes the walls of a wide-mouthed well.

—He means, while you are a blah-blah-blah.

Thankless tasks! I never severed you from my care,
    a guardianship not brutish, deserving retribution.
Jrēs, remember us frostbitten in ice-cold winter,
    before sun's first peek at dawn or in early darkness?
How we'd seek cover, hide in sprawling bushes
    on high pasture grounds, desperate for shelter?
When starved predators devour weak creatures,
    hosts send guests packing, disreputable as it is.
Me, your uncle! Carrying a powder horn,   *10*
    I stalked game in deserts, on craggy heights,
For a watchful doe, your dinner roast:
    my kill flusters all of her flock of gazelle;[186]
Nourishing you with joints prodigiously fat,
    at nights without supper anywhere in sight.
May God trip up Jrēs for making me cry;
    waylay him for dashing my high hopes.
Surprised your friends don't give camels, Jrēs?
    What delusion to expect help from relatives!

15   Take me, Jrēs! I've relinquished all delights
       but sheep and goats, and likeminded fans,
On meadows clad in green after barren spells,
       lustrous with flowering bushes, plants, grasses;
The faraway hasten back to the land in droves:
       everyone fondly recalls original tribe and abode.
We prance and trot like horses around the herds,
       beating back circling hungry wolves into retreat,

—Around the sheep and goats.

Jrēs, since I don't want to hear: "Al-Hirbīd came,
       a starving scruffy dog begging for sheep on loan,"
20   Nor a supplicant's mutter: "No, he didn't give,"
       or an addressee's denial: "No, he never asked."
If the goat of a niggard lands in your hands,
       walk away a winner, even if it gives no milk.

31.11   'Adwān says:

O Jrēs, do not fear early mornings!
       Graze your sheep, don't be called a slouch![187]
Better to herd sheep than mooch off relatives
       whose tent flaps are shut tight to keep out kin:
Sheep magnates, coddlers of herding dogs,
       risen to a shaykh's status despite their faults.
They prey on me, though I did them no wrong:
       countless bastards schemed to lay me low.

31.12   And he says:

If you're aiming to find the greatest fool,
       among Shammar, Jrēs is first choice by far:

Tried and tested in perverse obstinacy;
    bottomless, unfathomable well of ineptitude!
You're superb at letting down your partner;
    as for myself, I'm a man who boils hoes
In a bubbling pot, to produce meat gravy
    from his axes' thin, albeit blunted, blades.

And he says: 31.13

I ask you, Jrēs, about soldiers on the march:[188]
    you see them walking, Jrēs, as if on crutches.
Clever, they decamped from the land in time;
    yet it took sprightly camels, hardworking men:
Delights for hosts, mustaches dripping with fat,
    and gathered by paupers in their shirts' folds.

A Donkey Driver Cannot Keep
Pace with Camel Nomads

32.1　'Adwān tended to his sheep. When he put up in the southwest of Jubbah that year, the inhabitants gave him palm trees because they held him so dear. They also built him a booth of palm fronds and provided him and his family with plentiful supplies of food. The folks of Jubbah filled his shack with dates and rice. During the day, he would move among assemblies of coffee drinkers and go from one lunch invitation to the next. He entertained people with his stories and accompanied his recitations with tunes from his rebab. You know, in those days people still lived in the time of ignorance. Back then, people were innocent, lacking in awareness. On arrival from his own tribal area, he ran into Hijhūj, Ibn Rmāl. The tribesmen of al-Rmāl came hurrying down from al-Khinfah. They used to spend the hot months of summer in the area of al-Khinfah and the tribal lands of 'Anazah and the Sharārāt, to the west. His arrival coincided with their return, and they all settled down together in Jubbah. Hijhūj stayed put to spend the rest of the summer in Jubbah, may God guide you, with the Rmāl tribesmen, and they enjoyed 'Adwān's company. They knew him from the year before, when he had lived at that place. They said, "You're still here, 'Adwān?" "Yes," he said. "Really, I haven't left with my animals since I last saw you, until you came back right now."

32.2　When they made up their minds to travel once again, he was there with his flock of skinny sheep. They were about to migrate, and this time the Bedouin of al-Rmāl sounded him out to see if he'd be inclined to accompany them. They fondly looked forward to having him with them. They said, "Don't you have a mind to join us, ʿAdwān? If you march along with us, all you'll have are these feeble sheep. Therefore, brother, if you cannot keep up with us and have grown tired, we'll put them in these large camel-borne baskets. We will assign one camel to each ewe. A she-camel for each of your sheep, al-Hirbīd, so you don't have to worry about them and you can have them come with us!" "Really, men," he replied, "I do want to join you on your journey. In any case, I will only allow my sheep to move from here as long as Jrēs is with me to keep an eye on them. And when I weary, by God, you must take the sheep from me or find some way to transport them." One of the Rmāl, ʿAjlān, said, "I will put a riding camel at your disposal so that you can join us, riding at the head of the caravan." Jrūḥ ibn Hazīm, son of Ṣāyil, said, "And I have a strong male camel to carry your gear and the mother of your children." "Fine," he said. "Let's go. I'm with you." They brought pack camels for his luggage and some milk-producing camels for the use of his family. They embarked on the great desert crossing, toward the Nafūd Desert. To his mind, in case of need, there was always the option of returning to Jubbah in order to stock up on dates and rice.

In the olden days, people were always on their guard; there was no security. Therefore, if they came to a sandy prominence and put up the tent of al-Hirbīd, they made sure to place it in the middle of their circle of tents. In the morning, the other tents would milk their animals and send pails full of milk to him, enough to fill all his skins and pots with milk, butter, and other tasty food. Inevitably, the day came when they had to send a camel train to the northeast in order to stock up on the necessary supplies. The Shammar tribesmen marched at a rapid pace to the markets of Iraq and, supplies replenished, hurried back to their camp at the edge of the Nafūd Desert. Next, the Bedouin would disperse; from then on, everyone would only look after his own interests. They followed their

32.3

camels no matter which direction the animals wandered off, at their camels' whim. Back then, the Bedouin used to live in fear; the enemy was constantly on their minds. For that reason, they tended to stick together and move as one group. For instance, if you had a mind to go raiding and capture some camels, and if your folk were sheltered within a larger tribal group, you might be able to embark on your adventure without having to worry about your folk's safety; they would not be helpless when faced with a surprise attack. Those coming at them from one direction would be met by the cameleers bringing supplies, while assailants from the other direction would run into the raiders who had set out from the camp. On the other hand, folk somewhere on their own might be vulnerable to raiders in the absence of their men who went raiding. Families might be robbed while their men were away on a plundering expedition.

32.4   The Bedouin of al-Rmāl had built their camp on the highest spurs of the sand hills. They said, "If we stay here on top of these sand hills, they can pick us off with ease. Some of our Shammar men have set out for the markets while we are in this spot like sitting ducks. We'd do much better marching as they do, along these sandy ridges. Let everyone do as he likes. If you wish to go and stock up at the markets, fine. If someone feels an urge to go raiding, let him do so. No one is under any obligation to stay here." The long and short of it was that they decided to break up camp and move. As the story goes, distant flashes of lightning were observed toward al-Labbah, night after night. They calculated that this spectacle repeated itself every night for fifty days. They deliberated: "It has been fifty nights since we spied the first flashes of lightning. Now there must be enough herbage for the camels to eat their fill. Without further ado, let's move there straightaway. Once we've put up camp in al-Labbah, we are free to go raiding from wherever our camels are grazing and we may also trek to the markets from there. Let's move, the dice have been cast, off we go!" The tribespeople of al-Rmāl did not have any small cattle with them, only camels.

'Adwān told his family, "The Rmāl talk about stocking up in Iraq and raiding expeditions, while we are stuck here with our sheep. Let's turn back and stay between where they are going and our folk in Jubbah. When we start running low on some articles, we can fetch whatever supplies we need from our house in Jubbah." His wife said, "No, by God, never! You want to deprive us of our morning drink of milk, the joy of getting our pots filled with milk and butter?" "Listen, dear cousin," he said, "I have nothing against that. But there is no way we can keep up with them on their journey. Theirs are herds of camels: if they feel like setting course in a certain direction, off they go, without thinking twice, leaving us far behind." She remained adamant: "By God, I won't be of your company if you go your separate way." "As you wish," he conceded. "So be it." That morning, they broke camp and like a rushing torrent filed in a long stream over the sand hills.

Numerous as they were, none of the Rmāl had any small cattle, with the exception of Ḥamdān ibn Ḥāmid. He brought a few sheep, about eight of them, and a small donkey (no offence!).[189] He and Jrēs, as drivers of sheep, were the stragglers at the camel train's tail end. Jrēs, as an orphan in his care for whom 'Adwān felt responsible, was always in his thoughts. He worried lest he should come to harm. On completion of their trek's first stage, they offloaded the camels and waited for Jrēs to arrive with the sheep. Whenever a herdsman passed by, comfortably stretched out on the saddle of his camel, or walking, they asked, "Hey boy, did you see Jrēs by any chance?" "Well, we last saw him yelling to his sheep, somewhere far behind." To any herdsman who came by: "Hey, did you see Jrēs and his sheep?" "O yeah, somewhere behind." The upshot was that Jrēs did not arrive till late at night. On reaching camp, they found all had gone to sleep and the fires were embers. The next day, they did not reach the place where the Bedouin had stopped off the evening before until it was almost morning, and the day after that it was the same story: 'Adwān would retrace his steps to find Jrēs, and would not be back at the camp with him and the sheep in tow until it was morning.

32.7   By then, the Bedouin were ready for early departure on their journey's next stage. The vanguard of the camel train, the tribe's fighting men mounted on fast riding camels, would reach that stage's campsite some time before sunset. There they'd amuse themselves by setting their hunting falcons on prey, one here, one there, while another man might busy himself putting his camel calves through their paces. A little before sunset, the camp was set up. Anxious, 'Adwān retraced his steps to see if Jrēs was approaching. But when he arrived, it was time for morning prayers. Morning had dawned already. The same thing happened that day, the next, and the one after that. And how about Ḥamdān? He turned back on his riding camel to look for the boy. He was greeted by the sorry spectacle of sheep, miserably assembled in disorder at the foot of an oval dune. He called to him, "Hey Fahd!" "Yes? What's up?" "Get out of there! At once, now! Leave them there! Come here, right now, now, now, at once!" "But what about our sheep, Dad?" "Let them go to hell. Food for the wolves or let the devil take them." Eight sheep and a small donkey. They have been drifting about in the wilderness ever since, it is said. Under those circumstances, they did not represent any value, worthless. Good riddance. Ḥamdān was the grandfather of Ṭmāsh, the father of Fahd.

32.8   Deep in thought, 'Adwān returned to the camp. What to do? Even with utmost exertion, they would count themselves lucky if they reached yesterday evening's camp by the next morning. God knows where they would alight the coming evening. He said, "What's our gain from this business? In any case, I am not joining those who want to set out on raiding expeditions. Nor will I be traveling with the company heading for the markets toward the northeast. So what on earth am I doing here? What interest does it serve?" A couple of times that day, he retraced his steps toward Jrēs. At last he said, "Listen, Jrēs!" "What?" he replied. He had understood the magnitude of the problem much earlier and had already given his opinion to his uncle: "Uncle dear, where are you going to take us? To somewhere far away, we don't know where. Let's go no farther. We cannot keep up with the Rmāl and their camel train. They are accustomed to it; it is their routine: one year traveling long distances to the west, the next far toward the east. We can't possibly keep up with them—our sheep are no match for their camels."

'Adwān asked, "Well, what do you suggest?" He said, "My idea is that we should give up trying to accompany them." "Yes," 'Adwān said, "I've just now come to the same conclusion. You're right. God Almighty, it really wasn't my choice that we should keep at it. Now take to the right! To the right, Jrēs! Veer away from their track along the flank of this sand hill! We did so last year. This time, let's likewise go our own way at our own pace. You, woman, listen! When the sheep start moving, unfetter the riding camel and the other male camel! Have them follow the sheep while we load the two pack camels. There we go, on our way back to the plain of Jubbah." And so they did. They branched off from the track to the right, traveling at a leisurely pace to spend the night at a place somewhere between the camel nomads' whereabouts and Jubbah.

Then 'Adwān composed this poem:

> Pity a heart torn loose from its bearings,
>> driven off course by misguided counsel.
> After life in plenitude, walls are closing in;
>> have I strayed, lost the path in bewilderment?
> We take care of scrawny sheep in our keep,
>> anxious, Jrēs, like guests late for dinner.
> Well-fed, the wretches' roast leaves you starved:
>> skinny, some miscarry, some lacking in milk.

—He means, they are like guests who also arrive toward the evening. This kind of sheep, *ḥibṣ*, is the worst of Najdī sheep. Their hair is white and short. The ones that miscarry, lose the embryo, and do not produce milk. The ones that give birth in fall, in autumn, have run out of milk by the time of spring season. It's finished. "Skinny ones" they are called, ewes without milk: those that miscarry and those that give birth in the fall.

5 Breathless, we pant after camels and horsemen
  who raid for sport, cross deserts on mounts,

—Who call to the horses, *ytā'ūn*.

 Camels phantasmic white, a mist when it lifts:
  camels are their pride, Jrēs, curly-haired giants.

—Pure-white camels, the color of white mist, a cloud of white fog.

 Their young shy and jog like hyena cubs;
  men run to catch and check the white imps:

—Camel calves run with a sideways tilt, like hyena cubs.

 Like snakes, they leave winding traces in sands;
  or like the branches torrents drag over desert floors.
 Dashing off at speed, they enrage sheepherders,
  their camp a delight for falconers at day's end.
10 Tribesmen of Ghfēl, they cross vast desert tracts,
  graze camels on strips of green, virgin meadows.
 Raiding, they pick the cream of captured herds;
  their legions flatten growth on low stony ridges.

—They are people of the camel saddle. The saddle they call *shdād*. Herds so big, more than they have use for, like food spilling from their mouths. Don't they bring robbed herds, for instance from the

people of al-Jūbah? Some of the spoils, the captured animals, are
left aside for any takers.

> Come evening, loud dinner invitations fill the air,
> > calls shouted in staccato, fire after fire is lighted.
> Jrēs, we deserve eight resounding belches,
> > short farts and flatuses singing their long song,
> Fired off by a fellow unaware of his flatulence,
> > before straightening up, giving heed, or thinking.
> Aim them at such as me, who did as he was told!   *15*
> > You, Jrēs, are innocent and free of blame.
> Jrēs, tell them to veer off the road and turn:
> > camel nomads do not ride with donkey drivers.

In these verses, ʿAdwān speaks about camels: **32.11**

> My eyes caught sight of a tattooed beauty,   *1*
> > singing her tunes to herds in late afternoon.
> To raise sheep takes dazed idiots such as me:
> > sheepherding is a pastime for boorish egoists.
> Camels, in colors and sorts, are a gift from God,
> > necks graciously curved, their backs elevated.
> Too dear, God knows, to be gifted to friends,
> > though owners live in fear of instant loss:
> Ruthless robbers launching surprise attacks,   *5*
> > thrusting and stabbing, are the camels' scourge;
> They ride hardy mounts at unflagging pace,
> > carrying reins and dry waterskins, nothing more.
> Camels slaughter fighters, adept target hitters,
> > warriors dressed in red silk jackets and long coats.
> They ride from al-Marbūb, skins filled with milk;
> > In the afternoon, looted young camels rest at the well.[190]

He Sings the Praises of Jaz'ah al-Lidhīdh

33.1 One winter, they suffered a long dry spell. 'Adwān spent those days to the north of al-Nafūd near al-Khams or thereabouts. One day, a group of Bedouin put up their tents to his north. He decided to pay them a visit. "Who are they?" he wondered. "What is their tribe?" It did not take long for him to conclude that they belonged to the tribe of Rmāl. Their chief at that time was Hijhūj, Ibn Rmāl. Accordingly, he brought himself to call on them. As he approached their camp, he passed a girl whose task it was to keep an eye on the tribe's pack camels and to water them. Yes, in those days the girls had their role to play.

33.2 He greeted her, and she asked, "Who are you, little brother, visitor? Who are you, man? We haven't seen you before. We don't know you. Surely you are not one of our kinfolk." "By God," he said, "I am one of the ill-starred people cast adrift by fate. I came because I wished to pay a visit to those Bedouin." "Little brother," she said, "whenever you come to pay a visit, you'll find me here on your path, watching over the camels browsing on your way to our place." "Thank God for this blessed occasion!" he said. At that, may God prolong your life, he moved toward those Bedouin and the resting places of their animals. The Bedouin of al-Rmāl at once knew who he was, though. As he approached, they called, "Welcome, al-Hirbīd, a hearty welcome to the poet of Shammar!" As soon as he sat down, he began to regale them with his stories and poems. And whenever he rose and took his leave, he found Jaz'ah al-Lidhīdh and her pack camels on his way. Before continuing, he paused for a chat, surrounded by the white camels. They enjoyed each other's company and conversation. It gladdened his heart and time flew by quickly, as if the world had been born anew.

Then one day, all of a sudden some of their Bedouin who had gone scouting came rushing in. They had gone to reconnoiter an elongated stretch of dunes, al-Hūj, toward the area of al-Khinfah. On arrival at the camp, they exclaimed, breathless with excitement, "God's curse on your fathers all! The herbage there has grown so tall and thick that it has overgrown the bushes! And here we are sitting idle, wasting our time!" The Rmāl jumped up as one man and dashed off with all their belongings. The order was given: "When the morning star appears, we do not want to see even one thread left lying on the campground!" They readied and mounted their camels, and loaded the pack camels with all their gear.

That morning, ʿAdwān came for a visit as usual. On arrival at their place, he rubbed his eyes in disbelief. The campsite was empty but for ravens hopping among the litter. "Good God, as sure as I am my father's son, what happened to them? Had they been raided and stripped bare? Did they run away on receiving a warning?" It was neither. He followed their traces. And then he caught a glimpse of the Bedouins' loaded camel train as it made its way upcountry, the tops of their ladies' litters on the backs of the strongest camels swaying like branches of palm trees laden with heavy bunches of dates. He made no effort to catch up with them. He couldn't have if he wanted to. You're a sheepherder, ʿAdwān! The Bedouin and their camels had gone, leaving him far behind, all alone. Gone were the days when they enjoyed his entertainment and he had been as pleased as punch in their company. The camels had been brought and loaded to carry off his neighbors; he had been abandoned. His gaze fixed on the disappearing camel train, his distressed heart began to tremble. It dawned on him that he had lost his neighbors. They had set off at first light. But he kept the Bedouin in his sights: he had designs on those Bedouin, regardless.

33.5   They had set out on their trek that same morning. Downcast, he returned to his folk and slumped on the ground, huddled deep inside his cloak as if he were ill and bedridden. The next morning, a passing wayfarer told him that he had seen the Rmāl's vanguard marching with mad energy, the train of pack camels straining not to fall behind, with no intention of halting or easing up their pace until they had reached al-Khinfah.

33.6   Ah, yes! Then he said:

1   Separation struck! News of herbage sent them packing:
    may their camels be robbed by champion raiders!

—The lucky raid leader who invariably returns laden with booty is called *miḥrām*. He prays that a redoubtable robber will attack their camel train and herds, which would force them to return and once again be near the poet.

They left the new abode and I'm writhing
    on the camp's remains, my feet unable to move:
Curved, poisonous fangs sank into my flesh,
    venomous slashes from the Angel of Death.

—By the poison of the snake's fangs, he means ʿIzrāʾīl, the Angel of Death, whose bite is always lethal.

A buxom beauty is carried off to al-Hūj
    by white camels taken to distant destinations.
5   They left; so did I, turning to catch a glimpse—
    God! Reunite lovers who throw pining glances!
My darling travels in the suite of a chief, Hijhūj,
    in desert freedom, far from villagers' creaking doors.[191]
Darling, your cheeks are daubed with rose extract,
    thick tresses flowing down your back in waves.

Tall, succulent, she outshines all creamy beauties:
    she's pinned into my vision, whatever people say.
A juicy stalk, dewy with a shower's drops at dawn,
    as balmy breezes dispel banks of morning fog.

He composed these verses on the Bedouin's departure: 33.7

'Āyid, at blush of breaking dawn—the Bedouin: 1
    Oh my! At what pace they pack and leave!
Like birds flying up from a steep peak's ledge,
    they're aflutter when true reports arrive at morning;
Rush off without a thought to bring alms taxes,
    pay obeisance to the shaykh's severe slaves:

—Given orders by Ibn Rashīd, they collect the payments of the zakat.

A male camel was arraigned, mighty and proud,
    tinted a rosy white, an emblem of tribal fame,

—If people want to refer to a certain tribe, they say, "You know, the tribe of that camel, called so-and-so."

Well fed on meadows of Thmēl and Abū l-Gūr,   5
    or brought home from faraway pasture lands,
Halted, penned up at al-Ghūṭah, standing tall:
    outstretched hands can't reach its saddle's lining.

—The camel towers up so high that a man's outstretched hand does not reach the saddle cushion.

POEM ON ṬILGAH AL-BIHIYYĀNIYYAH

34.1 One of ʿAdwān's poems was inspired by a girl from my tribal group, al-ʿMēm. She was a relative of mine.[192] Her name was Ṭilgah al-Bihiyyāniyyah. It was one of his first poems, composed when he was still an apprentice poet and before he had attained excellence.[193] Well, God knows best. He had fallen in love with this girl of my group. No wonder: she was a stunning beauty, without question! The finest doe of the gazelle species.

34.2 He sang her praises in these lines:

1   I commence by saying prayers to God,
           my Lord, as often as new days break,
       Abundant as stars twinkling in dark of night,
           calls to perform daily worship resound.
       Verses I stir up from my heart's recesses:
           selected with finicky care to my taste.
       Inside, they rise thick as clouds of locusts
           coasting to landing grounds late in the day.
5   Weighed in scales for a precise amount,
           they are spun as a string of prayer beads
       Sent expeditiously on its way to my love.
           Her glances bound my heart in fetters.
       Ordered by my eyes to turn and gaze at her,
           I jump as a falcon at a waving piece of cloth.

She looks about, a fierce unhooded peregrine,
    merciless hooked claws to tear bustards apart;
Ravenous from fasting, at her falconer's call
    she strikes bustards like a bolt from the sky.

—The girl is suitable, old enough to be married off. It is only a matter of reciting the marriage formula. He says that the girl has grown up and is ready for marriage consummation. Like someone who is fasting, clutching a date in his hand, who brings the date to his nose to inhale the smell, ready and all set, just waiting for the call to prayers to sound for him to set his teeth in it. By "bustards," or as we say, "the one with spotted feathers," he refers to himself.

Or is it the tender gaze of a gazelle on stony plains,   *10*
    untouched wildness shying from human shapes,
Nibbling at trees on the flanks of a valley bed,
    watercourses moistened by sprinkles of rain?
Cheeks creamy as hearts of palm bursting forth:
    a grating sound, the crack sucks up its sugar.[194]

—*Nuwādī* are stalks of date bunches when the inflorescence, the fruit, appears. The comparison is with a woman who acts absent-mindedly but, as if inadvertently, opens the slit at the side of her robe to show the creamy white of her breast, which is here likened to the white inflorescence of the palm's flowers. The "sugar" is the *jammārah*, heart of palm, which looks as if it is coated in sugar when it rises from the bitter wood of the crack in the tree's stem.

Hidden in green crowns, the land's tastiest dates,
    dense gardens of palms raising thick fronds aloft,

—The *rkhēmī* is one of the best kinds of dates.

Watered day and night by camels and drivers:
    a jet of the well's spout sweeps debris aside.

—He is referring to the camels that draw water for the irrigation of
date palms in such abundance that the fruits are exceptionally tasty.

15   Her plaits: tail of a horse with white-spotted legs,
    swerving in battle, from stabbing to rapid evasion;
Gold sorrel, ready to mount mares young and old,
    tail fanning out and breast wide as if swimming:

—The horse is barrel-chested and runs as if it is swimming.

If the call resounds: "Horsemen, in the saddle!"
    the champion stud pulls away from the pack.

—The horse streaks away from the water holes, gone in the blink of
an eye.

Poem on Mnīrah, the Daughter of Bshayyir

'Adwān traveled to Mōgag on an errand. People from as far as Ḥafr   35.1
al-Nafūd and Bēḍā al-Nithīl went to pay their alms tax in Mōgag. At that
time, Mōgag was of considerable importance, one of the most vibrant
settlements in the region of the mountain. In front of him walked a
group of men who were not aware that he was within earshot. In the
olden days, people used to cover themselves against the sun during
the hottest part of the day and walk with their heads enveloped.

One of them said, "Hey, so-and-so!"

"What is it you want?"

"Make a wish!"

"What should I wish for?"

"Just make a wish! People make wishes just like that."

"But for what?"

"Make your wish now!"

He said, "Oh, how happy I'd be if my wish would be granted!
I want my tent peg fixed in the ground next to these palms with
yellow date bunches so that I have nothing to worry about this
year—so that I can collect these dates and store them in large sacks."

In those days, people had difficulty making ends meet. There was
scarcity of everything.

The other said, "Oh, how fondly I wish for my tent peg to touch
the tree behind yours." The entire garden counted no less than three
hundred trees: the "Garden of Shāyiʿ," it was called.

'Adwān had overheard their exchange of wishes. He said to himself, "May the devil take you! Why not wish for the entire garden?" But he kept the thought to himself.

35.2   After performing the noon prayers, he sat down in a circle of tribesmen of al-Ghfēlāt, a group called al-Marāmshah, inhabitants of Mōgag, and said, "On the way here, I fell in with some strangers, folk not so different from myself, yet I think I'm a little smarter than they are." "What's the story, 'Adwān?" He said, "Well, a group of men walking ahead of me started making wishes. Each of them asked for a date palm in a garden, without saying what they'd give in exchange or how much money they'd pay for it. If I made a wish, I'd ask for the entire garden of three hundred trees, whereas they asked for no more than one tree each. They're not losing any money over it. It is about making a wish. All they wished for was just one tree. It did not occur to them to ask for the entire garden. Not that I'm a much better person than they are; nevertheless, I'd want the entire garden for myself. If it is a matter of expressing a wish, I'm not going to say, 'I can't afford the price.'"

35.3   At that, 'Adwān launched into his description of a farmer's life. He said:

1   I'd wish for a settled life among villagers,
           far from bleating sheep and camel calves.
       I'd wish for the tall pillars at a well's rim:
           four pulley wheels I'd mount over the shaft;
       Wide-mouthed, gushing bottom circle-shaped,
           worked by draft camels, fit and well behaved.
       Elongated leather buckets, no small skins,
           hoisted up, their necks spouting limpid water.

       —The buckets are large and the water is sweet and cool.

5   That'd be my travelers' haven, no mean affair,
           drawing journeyers whose supplies run low;

—*Al-marāmīl* are travelers who have consumed all their supplies on a long-distance journey. They have come from far away.

> At the fire's edge leans a roasting pan for beans,
>> coffeepots—a joyous sight—and porcelain cups.
> My wishful sigh for palms in rows, gardens full,
>> isn't lust for bunches of dates, yellow and lush:
> I'm scheming to steal up closer to Mnīrah;
>> the dream girl sliced my heart into slivers.

—The tree's fruit stalks are yellowish. The girl is Mnīrah, daughter of Zēdān ibn Bshayyir, the headman of Mōgag.

> She's perfect if it weren't for her pristine age—
>> may freshness of budding youth last forever!
> Ah, supple banana stalk planted in fertile soil,
>> tips sprinkled with dew, its roots on a stream.

10

—*Jibīrah* is good, fertile land, not sandy as the dunes or stony, and irrigated from a small channel, *shirć*, water that flows at the roots of the palm trees. *As-sēr* is a synonym of *siriyy*, "small irrigation channel."

> Breasts protrude as truffles in a marshy field,
>> soaked by heavy showers, pop up their heads.

—If it sucks up the moisture from the earth, it pops up: the truffle shows its head. The "throwers of cascading water" are the clouds.

She said, "Well, gunman, you missed the mark. How could you wish for the nice things you crave, and only at the end add me to the list? I cannot accept a poem unless it is entirely devoted to me, from the first line to the last."

35.4

His Poem on the Daughter of Ibn Jwē'id

36.1   'Adwān rented out a draft camel to Ibn Jwē'īd, a sedentary man who lived in Mōgag. He gave him a male camel needed for the irrigation of his grove. On expiration of the loan, as was customary in the season of the date harvest, 'Adwān presented himself at his place to receive payment. On entering the terrain, he saw a girl named Nūrah, the daughter of Ibn Jwē'id. The girl had been recently divorced by 'Bēd ibn Rashīd. She flaunted herself as if she wished to show off her attractions. "Who is this man, Father?" she asked. "He gave us a camel on loan for the irrigation of our palm trees and comes to collect his wages. His name is 'Adwān al-Hirbīd." "Is he 'Adwān the poet?" she asked. "Yes indeed, that's him."

36.2   Now, it is a fact that women go nuts when it comes to poets. Girls would say, "Look there! Al-Hirbīd!" They would show themselves to him: "Who knows, perhaps he will sing some verses about us!" She lost no time in shutting the compound gates. She made sure that no one else came to drop in on them. She chased away all other womenfolk. The garden's gates were barred so that she'd be left alone with him. They cut off bunches of dates, put down the harvest, and started weighing what they owed him for the hired camel. They dropped the dates into a pail and emptied it into big sacks of the sort that are transported on camelback. "No, stop!" she cried. "Don't touch it—I'm the one to do this. Be warned, I am the only one allowed to do this work. Keep off it!"

The pails were carried to her and she filled the sacks. "Ha, there   36.3
we go!" she said in a cheerful voice. She poured the pail's contents
into the sacks, and while doing so she loosened her tresses. Her
beauty was enhanced by the chains and assorted jewelry she was
wearing. "Keep your hands off, you!" she scolded. "I am the one
who is going to sew up the bags and make the right kind of nice
knots in them." This was how she spoke to ʿAdwān, who was sitting
there, watching until they had loaded his belongings and the sacks
onto the camel.

He left, perched on the camel carrying the sacks of dates he had   36.4
received in payment for his loan. Then he said:

> Nūrah, a white camel, flaunts herself for the leader,   *1*
> > anxious to be ahead, to be first to drink at the well.

—The *ʿannāf* is the man who leads a train of camels from the front
by calling to them and chanting.

> Rosy white, in the herd she's sweet and smooth:
> > in morning's push and rush her ankles aren't strapped.
> Tresses curl down in plaits; strips embroidered
> > with copper shine like a robe's costly ornaments.
> Her small teeth, pure white and finely chiseled,
> > are agleam, not too short, nor too broad or long,
> Pure as hail pelted down by rumbling clouds,   *5*
> > sifted fine grains, slightly melted, frozen anew,

—That is, when the clouds are shaken by the wind.

> Between the lips of a delicate lass, not a shepherdess,
> > a charming good-looker from behind and in front.

—He says that she is not a Bedouin girl who must accompany the
camel herds.

Shielded from lovers hunting for prey and gain:
    this curvaceous stunner is beyond reproach.
Fine girl, with bulging buttocks that defy description—
    the blinding flash of Indian swords in a melee;[195]
Voice: clinks of riyals in brisk market trading,
    tinkle of a pile of Maria Theresas gliding through the fingers.[196]

—A pile of Maria Theresa thalers, *al-shūshī*. Back then, they arranged the silver riyals in a pile, like a pillar, for the purpose of counting them.

10   Daughter of a stalwart who sates guests' appetites
    in times of dearth and unaffordable prices.
No need to say more—all and sundry know
    his wont when bulky keys lock misers' doors.

—That is: Without me: there is no need for me, 'Adwān, to tell anyone. He is well known for his generosity, even without my praise for him.

His Poem on Khansā, Daughter of al-Jim'ī

One year, he fell in love with Khansā, daughter of al-Jim'ī, a tribes-man of the Shilgān. Noticing his infatuation with her, people of Shammar and some of his kinfolk told him, "Have you lost your mind, 'Adwān? How could you possibly fancy a girl such as the daughter of al-Jim'ī? He is in the habit of biting his fists, so much so that he has cut up his own hands. He eats his fists, chewing away at them with his teeth. Next thing you know, she'll devour your hands, and your head as well. This is not the sort of girl you'd like to marry and have around in your house. She'll eat you alive, 'Adwān, so keep a safe distance from her! Don't even think of composing verses on her!"

It came to pass that al-Jim'ī decided to travel away from Jubbah and rejoin his own group. 'Adwān thought of asking him to think better of it, but he traveled regardless. 'Adwān could not resist the urge to compose a poem on her:

37.1

37.2

> War is declared on al-Hirbīd, joined by all,
>> a sudden attack grown virulent from whispers,
> Because of a clan hurrying down the sands,
>> at night in westerly winds' freezing bite.

1

—The nights of *al-tsē'ī*, the most severe cold.

I long for Khansā, even if she's biting fists:
    my clenched five with our folk's fists all.
Let her binge on our tribe's fists and fingers,
    fists of the prince's sublime court thrown in.[197]
5   Jrēs, my consoler, stay safe from trouble:
    if I appeal to you, come at once and rescue me!
Tell my darling, if she's beset by lusty beasts,
    to count on me, avenger at her beck and call,
Smart at separating gold guineas from dimes:
    a farmer, what do I care for trifling sums?[198]
Khansā, my damsel, keeps herds for company,
    followers of al-Klāb, camels' loyal devotees.
Her flowing locks cascade down her back;
    infants, Jrēs, have never suckled her nipples:
10   My sweetheart's breasts are silken to the touch,
    imbued with a thumb plant's scarlet glow.[199]

—The red *ṭarthūth* plants are truffles. His cousin, Jrēs, said, "Dear brother of mine, what a thing to say! Your sport is dalliance. You own a capital in animals. You pay zakat from your produce of the land and surplus of dates. All the while, I have to make do with clothes sewn together from pieces of old camel sacks and I'm saddled with these wretched skinny sheep."

37.3   'Adwān impersonated Jrēs when he said:

1   Uncle mine, you're in thrall to female beauty,
    while claiming you're fighting a savage war.
Uncle mine, your hair is flecked with streaks
    of gray, a glistening sparkle on your temples.
Your looks of a rabid dog scare them off:
    vile gray trips up the bravest gentlemen,
Mars gorgeous ladies, sprightly youngsters,
    causes Dhiyāb to retreat in defeat.

—A man who is *shi'shā'* is young, energetic, up-and-coming. Dhiyāb
is Dhiyāb ibn Ghānim.

You want to wheel and deal, to buy and sell: *5*
    with no attractive wares on offer, how can you?
You separate gold guineas from lowly dimes:
    get a cloak to shield me from the freezing cold!
Why gape at budding girls gesturing
    to juveniles hot to trot to their rescue.[200]
Your love plays with us, skimming stones,
    only to abscond, leaving us lost on desert flats.
Interred in a dug-out trench, enclosed, with no escape;
    proud stalwarts checked out before, join them!
If God created you a lost case, lost you'll be: *10*
    God Almighty ruins whomever He leads astray.

His Verses on the Daughter of al-Ṣgērī

38.1   'Adwān was not a poet who hankered to be in attendance at princely courts. Consorting with the high and mighty was not his style. In his compositions, he speaks about what he came across in his life. Once, on a visit to a friend, al-Ṣgērī, he saw his daughter driving camels hoisting heavy buckets from the well for irrigation.

38.2   He said:

> On my way to call on al-Ṣgērī, my mate,
>> I saw your lithe figure, gazelle of the creek,
> Driving draft camels, and stood transfixed:
>> your falcon's gaze at the lure in late afternoon.

38.3   She riposted—that is, he made as if it was her reply, but he composed the lines himself:

> Indeed, you've run into me at the well:
>> I unhooked my shirt and opened the slit,
> Showing you up close my milky breasts:
>> your heart flutters like cloth waved at a falcon.

38.4   He said:

True, girl, by a nose ring you pulled my heart;
   I beseech you, stunner, loosen your cruel fetters!
Eyes of a gazelle, startled from its meadows:
   panicked by human shapes, she dashes away.

She said: 38.5

Your heart cannot suffer in patience, you say,
   though I'm beyond daunting heights and dunes,
Haunted by lying snug between big white breasts,
   to do as you please: morning jaunts, evening rest.
With my cheek's flash of lightning I smite you,
   felled in my loosened tresses' pitch-black night:
A chestnut mare saddled and ready for the ride,
   barrel-chested, she's thrilled by shots and shouts.

His Poem on the Daughter of al-Mārid

39.1 For lack of a camel to draw water, some people at a well asked a girl to do the pulling for them. The girl's large breasts rose up from her ribcage as she heaved at the rope. ʿAdwān was watching her. She knew that ʿAdwān was a poet and she cast hopeful glances at him. However, one of the young men there had claimed her as his bride and was looking forward to the day he'd ask for her hand and she'd be his wife. It seemed that ʿAdwān's presence roused his jealousy.

39.2 She held fast to the end of the rope and he lowered the bucket into the well. She turned her face toward ʿAdwān, while her fiancé lowered the bucket's rope hand over hand into the well. She paid no attention; she was looking the other way. Then he took the rope in a strong grip and pulled so hard that she tumbled to the ground. That pull cut through ʿAdwān. It hurt him as if the rope had been fastened to his ribs—as if he himself had been pulled so violently.

39.3 He said:

1 Bucket man, don't mess up, leave her in peace:
    a brutal pull slammed into the tenderhearted.
  Aghast, seeing the doe-eyed pulled so rudely!
    May the Lord not answer your prayers![201]

—*Ykawwib fazzitak,* as one says, "So-and-so, let him face failure"; that is, the person is no good.

Look, the girls are waiting to take her home.
    Leave the belle alone—wolves eat your guts!
A lean young thing, freshly trained, given rein,
    struggles to keep up with death-defying raiders,
Given no quarter by pitiless, hard-bitten mounts   5
    ridden by boisterous, hookah-smoking toughs:
Racing home, bellies curved as slender crescents,
    bags of skin and bones from saddle to haunches;

—On their return from a raid, the she-camels are wasted.

Fleeting shadows cast by scuds hurtling in the sky,
    lean and mean, they trot to distant lands in a breeze.

Other Love Poetry

40.1   People said to ʿAdwān, "You are an old man by now; how come you're still composing love songs?"

40.2   He intoned:

1   "Repent from passion's way!" "No!" I said.
           "Not until old age stops me in my tracks."
         Chasing love is neither cause for blame nor flaw:
             it's people's inborn trait since Creation.
         My girl is pretty, her sole defect a lack of fault:
             creamy white, adorable of gait and mien;
         Jaunty white camel, with bells, colorful trappings,
             on lush meadows untrodden, refreshed by rain;
5   Beauty's paragon, her worth eclipses herds
             whose diligent shepherds knit hobble ropes.

—While on his mount, the shepherd is twisting rope used for hobbling camels.

         Spurned by Arcturus and late spring's rains,
             my heart is lashed by poisonous hot winds.
         Woe to me if breezes bare her body's curves
             over a belly flat as if born without intestines.
         Her hair fans out like a resolute mare's tail;
             sweet in countenance, her behind is gorgeous.

Black eyes of a gazelle at home in Umm Zingūb;
    gaze of a falcon, its nesting haunts at Umm al-Arsān,

—*Yishbūb* is a gazelle and *shargʿ* is a peregrine falcon.

Her aerie on a ledge beyond seven rocky crags;   *10*
    al-Ḍubbān clapped hands in vain, no falcon came.

ʿAdwān al-Hirbīd said:[202]   *40.3*

I moan as a man forsaken in waterless wilderness,   *1*
    in midsummer, stripped bare by mounted robbers,
Scared by howls of dark predators drawing near,
    flashes of grimace around hooked canine teeth.
Moans of a grieving she-camel, doubly fettered,
    bereaved, not even given her dead calf's skin;
Insane with grief, she runs back and forth,
    from sprightly camels ahead to stragglers behind.
Helpless, my eyes shed tears, for no good reason—   *5*
    because of a pretty face, folks, not a calamity,
In streams, like water gushing from a bucket
    hoisted from the bottom, turning and rocking;
Or a cloudburst pouring down rain in sheets,
    in fall, curtains of steady, rushing drops.
My love's tresses resemble knotted well ropes,
    bunches of early dates fed by water channels;
Svelte beauties braid cluttered hair into plaits,
    ready to swing into dance, swaying their hair;
Thick messy tresses disentangled by fingers—   *10*
    fingers creamy and white like heart of palm.
Glances shot from the languid gaze of dreamy eyes,
    disguised as coy, spells cast through trickery;
Seek my death? Pointless: I'm already dead;
    since seeing her, my insides have refused all food.

She has no peer, her chamomile-white teeth
    arrayed in even rows of finely chiseled ivory.
Eyes with the fierce glint of a lethal peregrine,
    born a fearless chick, taught by falconers.

40.4   On another occasion, a woman, one of his relatives on his mother's side of the Swēd tribe, came for a visit. She dropped her cane at the spot where he was sitting; she did so on purpose, right in front of him. She said, "Hey ʿAdwān, get to your feet and hand me that cane!" "Your servant is at your beck and call!" he said, and immediately reached for the cane and handed it to her. He was secretly amused that she felt at liberty to issue perfunctory orders to him and passed the stick to her. That same evening, he said, "By God, I'd like to go over to those tents where that lady came from and have a chat. The thing is, I feel a bit shy. Anyone want to volunteer to force me, to prevail on me to go there, and to provide me with an excuse?" "Fine with me to do so," one of them said, and he took him over. When they arrived, his companion said, "Listen, men, just now ʿAdwān happened to pass by and wants to go back home. I told him, 'No. No way we'd let you go! We want you here with us! Entertain us for a while!'" He spent the evening telling stories.

40.5   On his return, he said:

1   Date harvest brought al-Mashwī's daughter;
    she roasts my entrails without the need for fire.[203]

—Her father is called al-Mashwī. *Al-ribīd* means the time of the harvest, when the dates are ripening on the trees.

She's not at my feet, nor is she far away:
    search for her among the nomads—you'll know.

—That is, she is close by.

Fellows bold as kestrels brought me—
    may she not be fondled by a despotic brute.
They dragged me to my sweetheart's haunts,
    one leading from behind, the other pulling.
I offered her the staff, my hand touching hers,   5
    a servant most eager to please his minister.

In early fall, her father let her take her seat on camelback, and   40.6
off they went. He stood there, forlorn, watching their departure.
'Adwān said to himself, "Her father is a decent fellow; I hold noth-
ing against him. Her male camel, on the other hand, is a differ-
ent matter. Let me invoke a curse on it—perchance it will die on
the way."

As soon as they had gone, he spoke: 40.7

O Sh'ēb, a lady lashed my heart with two-pronged sticks,   *1*
    Sh'ēb, toward al-Shi'ab it galloped off, O Sh'ēb,[204]

—Al-Shi'ab, a place on the other side of the mountain.

Mounted on a black male; let it be snatched by robbers
    riding fleet, dust-colored steeds of pure Arabian race.

—He wants horsemen to capture her male camel.

Let them spur the camel along vast barren plains,
    horses chafing at the bit, rearing up at cries of war.

—The horses are fired up. On hearing shouts and being called, they
run at full speed, madly as if intoxicated.

Or let it roll and twist in agony from itching mange,
    salt poured in wounds, mixed with watery milk.

—He wants the camel to be infected with mange.

5

Or let it land in the care of butchers to handle:
 knives hacking and slicing chunks from its hump.
Serves him right, abductor of ladies' curvaceous queen,
 so far away, night after night, camp after camp.

40.8 He had his eyes on a girl, knowing that her father was not of the religion: he belonged to a different faith. He said:

How unfortunate, a Jewess's curvaceous behind:
 her faith is another, not our religion of Islam.
Poor daughter of less felicitous ancestry:
 rascals not beholden to our prayers and fasts.
Her name is tucked away in al-Nafūd,
 dunes teeming with flocks of gazelle.

—Her name is Ṭ'īsah, meaning a *ṭi's*, a big dune inside the Nafūd Desert.

I wish her grandfather had our ancestry:
 I'd buy her golden nose rings and bangles.

40.9 He went for a walk late in the afternoon. On the way, he met a girl with her little brother, Ghayyāḍ, and saw her giving the boy a kiss. He knew that her father was a renowned marksman.

40.10 He said:

1

What a shame, Ghayyāḍ! Too bad, too bad!
 What a shame! In front of me! My sweetie's kiss!
Good God! You tasted succulent delight;
 you savored it without asking how I feel!
A juicy twig, suppler than any other sprig:
 scanning her shapely figure calls to mind

Luscious rain-fed stalks, moist in late spring,
    from seamless overcast skies' slanting showers,
On forbidden pastures, kept from intruders
    by fearless hardy fighters on spirited horses;
Daughter of a marksman highly esteemed
    for bagging gazelles in astounding numbers.

'Adwān went on a journey, traveling alone in midsummer. One day, while traversing a swath of empty desert, he ran into another person, a female. He had not expected to meet anyone there. He felt doubtful, wondering whether she was a female jinni, a desert spirit, or a human. That particular stretch of land was empty, uninhabited. He drew closer to the girl and asked her, "Hey girl, are you a jinni or a human?" "Not a jinni," she said. "By God, I am a human." She was about to die of thirst. Seeing her so exhausted, he poured water for her to drink until she was sated. He remained with her for a while until she had recovered somewhat. Then he offered her a ride, a seat behind him on the camel's back, and gave his mount the spurs. "Where shall we go?" She said, "I came from such and such a place and was heading for such and such a place."   40.11

Was she on the run? She must have had a reason to run away. Perhaps a man she did not want to marry, that sort of thing. They journeyed pleasantly enough in good companionship until he had delivered her safely back to her folk. "Our tent is there—that's the place." She pointed. "Kneel your camel for me to dismount, and receive your reward, God willing!" "Look here, my dear girl," he said, "I didn't come to rescue you from perdition in order to gain reward. I did it for the sake of God. Sweetie, allow me to recite a few verses, just a word or two." "What do you want to say?" she asked.   40.12

He said: 40.13

Gazelle, were it not for me,
    fiery heat would have cut short your life.

I let you quaff from my sweet, limpid water.
  By God, let sips from your lips hearten me!
I myself filled the waterskin from a well,
  hoisting rope, pulley wheel, bucket.
My heart scuds like clouds in a northern gale,
  lashed on by deep winter's ice-cold blasts.

—*Aṭ-ṭiwīlēn, ar-rajjāl wa-l-biʿīr*, "The two tall ones, the man and the camel," signify deep winter.

40.14   She replied:

Listen, you poured me a sweet, limpid drink.
  May God quicken your eye for doing good!
Don't ask of me, keep safe from Fate's demands!
  My brave, save your demands for someone else.

A Jerboa's Jumping Dance[205]

This love song is composed on a beat called "dance of the jerboa,"   41.1
the jumping mouse.

> Come back, come back, blissful dell at the happy dunes!   *1*
>> Return, return, forever-lasting days at your camp!
> Where I first saw a girl with budding bust, warm belly;
>> at the tents I saw her moonlit silhouette walking to and fro:
> Buttocks curvy beyond description, plaited locks aflutter
>> like fringed leather cushions of camels on a nightly run.
> Gazelle, you were born from a herd's finest doe,
>> flocks roaming wide plains or among sand knolls,
> In fear of rugged mounts, mustachioed riders, ferocious panthers: *5*
>> God Almighty created you His instrument of my execution.
> Stalk of a banana tree softly astir on circling languid breezes,
>> the beneficent Lord sent you drizzles sieved from sweetest water.
> Last I saw her, she rode a camel marching in a tribal caravan—
>> goodbye, eyes crystal as rock-held water in freshly flooded dales.

Poems on Having a Good Time

42.1 Smokers, leave off! Tobacco isn't any good!
          Want to be classy? Smoking has no class![206]
        Smoke dispels no worry, fills no guest's belly,
          lends no proud luster to ignoble trash.
        Looking for good cheer? I'll teach you,
          though jollity's way needs no guide.
        If you're chasing good cheer, I tell you:
          jolly is riding 'Gēlī camels, trappings astir.
5   If you're chasing good cheer, I tell you:
          horse rugs, silk jackets on noble steeds.
        If you're chasing good cheer, I tell you:
          hitting the enemy with all your might.
        If you're chasing good cheer, I tell you:
          giving attackers a taste of your sword.
        If you're chasing good cheer, I tell you:
          foaming milk from large camel udders.
        If you're chasing good cheer, I tell you:
          creamy brunettes, sporting long plaits.
10   If you're chasing good cheer, I tell you:
          The peal of the pestles pounding coffee beans.
        If you're chasing good cheer, I tell you:
          lounging at high noon in a black goat-hair tent.
        Curved beaks of shining pots awaiting guests:
          coffee's water from the sky, sieved by clouds.

Porcelain cups smudged like the hands of beauties
    daubed with yellow dye matching reddish curls;
Trays carried by men staggering under their weight,
    garlanded with cardamom-sprinkled entrails.
You're looking for good cheer? Listen!   *15*
    Sift for the gist! That's the truth, hard as rock.

—What is sieved is the truth.

A poem composed on the subject of coffee.   **42.2**

Wishing for good cheer, I'd make my choice—   *1*
    though wishful thinking comes to naught—

—*'Alā fōsh* means "for nothing, in vain."

I'd choose pots from Baghdad on the fire,
    immaculately white, with fez-shaped lids,
Beaks curving down, coffee beans from afar,
    handled with skill by fine lads, the cream of youth;
Mortar pounded, proud purchase from town,
    its pestle's peals sounding open invitations.[207]
Tongs to keep hands safe from flames,   *5*
    like the necks of geese with trimmed beaks;

—*Al-mbarriz* is the *milgāṭ*: the fire tongs.

Shallow pan to roast coffee beans over a fire,
    bottom burnt blue by the embers' radiant heat;
Platters to effortlessly serve earless porcelain cups,
    upside down, like a humped white camel herd.

—The herd of white camels are the earless porcelain cups.

Round Yemeni beans, patiently roasted,
    sweating tears, drying to leave gleaming copper coins,

—*Al-gaṭmā* are the coffee beans.

As an unhappy wife yearns for a better man,
    a dashing hero storming resolutely into battle.
10   Spiced with town markets' best, pounded
    peal after peal at the mortar's copper rim.

—*Al-jrūs* is the cardamom and the copper *gōsh* is the mortar.

Joyfully, gentlemen gather at the coffee hearth,
    good-natured company, bright and welcoming;
A slaughtered camel, rib roasts shiny with fat,
    the carved tray's borders sprinkled with grits.
Pour the coffee! For thick-mustachioed stalwarts,
    thrusting cavalrymen who drench their blades.
Pour again for free-spending hosts, heedless of cost;
    in famine they gladly slaughter their finest animals.
15   Such are the delights encountered on leisurely visits,
    a chap's worry-free ramble to happy entertainment.
One is allotted, much or little, by omniscient God;
    His hands hold the strings of all creatures' destiny.

42.3   Having run out of tobacco, ʿAdwān became distracted and restless. On reaching the top of a spur, he espied a tent. As he headed for it, he discovered that it was the camp of Marrān ibn Hazīm, one of the Rmāl, a true shaykh who hospitably entertained guests in a tent always open to visitors. ʿAdwān walked up to him. It was common knowledge at the time that smokers showed unmistakable signs of withdrawal when they'd exhausted their supply of tobacco. Marks of suffering and a bad mood are written all over the face of a person craving a smoke. It did not take Marrān long to notice that something was wrong. He understood right away that his visitor had run out of tobacco. ʿAdwān's face spoke volumes. He knew that he was desperate for the stuff.

He said to himself, "Perhaps he pinned his hopes on something;   42.4
perhaps he smells an opportunity. He does not have himself under
control: his pockets are empty of the stuff and he cannot resist the
urge." He told him, "Listen, 'Adwān, I know that you have run out
of tobacco and that you came to my tent expecting or hoping to find
some here. But I assure you, there is nothing of the sort under the
roof of this tent. I fear that you may hold it against me and start har-
boring wrong ideas. You may suspect me of not being up-front with
you, thinking that in fact I do have some hidden here. But the truth
is, all I have and can offer you are bowls of milk and these sweet
dates. You are most welcome to help yourself!"

Gentle though his tone was, his words did not go down well   42.5
with 'Adwān. Frustrated and deeply disappointed, he turned away
from Marrān. He knew that at times womenfolk carried some of
the stuff for their own use, without men's knowledge. And indeed,
as it turned out, Marrān's wife had tucked away some for her own
consumption! She said, "Look, Marrān, be kind! May God's bounty
come your way! You depend on God for your subsistence." Hearing
that, 'Adwān understood that Marrān had spoken the truth when he
said that he had nothing of the sort. If there was any tobacco in the
house, it was to be found with the mistress.

Their youngest child was called Ṭāmī. 'Adwān lingered and, turn-   42.6
ing to the boy, said:

Almighty God, I was startled from sleep,
    jumping as a prisoner freed from shackles.
I beg Almighty God, beseech Ṭāmī's mother
    to ferret out for me some tobacco in the camp:
Yellow leaves like salad, the stuff of my undoing—[208]
    damn you, yellow poison, how dearly I love you!
I turned to a daughter of hardy desert crossers,
    foes' scourge, lofty astride a high camel back.

In Contemplation of God's Creation

43.1 One day, 'Adwān al-Hirbīd shot a bustard for food. He slit the bird's stomach and in it found a lizard. He cut the lizard and, in its belly, there was a smaller lizard that in its turn had swallowed a spider. Inside the spider was an ant. He discovered that the bustard carried four other species in its belly and that he, 'Adwān, was about to become the sixth species through his consumption of the bustard. Each species had devoured the other and he would be eating the bustard. Amazing, he thought, how one thing leads to the next. These beings were meant to serve as food, the one for the other. Awestruck, he sat down to reflect on God's Creation, praise the Exalted Lord.

43.2 Then he composed these verses:

1 God, Your Creation shows no flaws;
  You keep a ledger of all Your creatures.
 You steer one hundred and ninety species,
  at Your mercy, Builder of soaring peaks.
 Some venture out at first ray of daylight;
  others wait till sunset before eating breakfast.
 Some jaws munch on fruits found in nature;
  some jaws chew what other jaws have eaten.
5 Yet other jaws are too small even to be seen;
  some aren't eaten: what they eat is unknown.

Big animals, tiny insects, all in Your care;
    shy recluses as well as resolute chargers.
You feed all living beings' hungry mouths;
    all of Your creatures' subsistence allotted.
You let bitter Fate remove some beings;
    You bring forth fresh ones of all kinds.
Your world, my Lord, is at Your command:
    one day it's springtime, the next leaves are wilting.
One moment darkness reigns, blinding the eyes;   10
    The next day arrives and bathes Your world in light.
Your world comes and goes, no warning given.
    How futile to seek escape from ordained Fate!
You revive a cripple, make him run again;
    a bird is downed mid-flight, as You decide.
I seek Your refuge from the pit of Hell:
    Do not roast my flesh in those roaring flames!
Be kind to a servant who put his trust in You:
    never has Your loyal slave meant to cheat You.

With Ibn Rashīd

44.1 During the rule of Bandar al-Mit'ib, Muḥammad al-'Abdallah al-Rashīd returned from Ottoman territory. He issued orders for a sizable body of Shammar fighters to join him in Iraq. He needed their assistance for the transport of the goods he had amassed. One of them was 'Adwān al-Hirbīd, but his enlistment turned out to be ill-starred, respected though he was as an energetic and determined person, a man of action. Ibn Rashīd said, "Call 'Adwān!" They were traveling by night. "Call 'Adwān. Let him come—we need his company and entertainment!" They went around shouting his name as they put themselves out to find him. His fellow tribesmen of al-Swēd spurred him on: "'Adwān, you scoundrel! Go over there to Ibn Rashīd! He has given orders to summon you. He wants to enjoy your company!" But the poet stubbornly clung to his refusal: "By God, I'm not going. First of all, he is not the ruler. Second, I am afraid that Bandar will hold a grudge against me if I do and punish me. If he catches wind of it, he'll be angry with me." This episode occurred at the time of Bandar al-Mit'ib's rule as chief of the House of Ibn Rashīd. The poet al-Tbēnānī approached Ibn Rashīd and informed him that, yes, 'Adwān did receive his message, but chose not to answer the call. As a consequence, when Muḥammad became ruler and 'Adwān paid a visit to his court, he was fobbed off with a trifling gift. From the day of his accession to power, Muḥammad never deigned to receive the poet in person. Yes, brother, riding a horse doesn't help if you're scared. If you're smart, you need no prodding.

One day, his al-Swēd kinfolk told ʿAdwān: "Hey ʿAdwān, as a poet you're supposed to be smart. But so far, we have not benefited in any way from having you in our midst." In those days, the al-Rashīd rulers behaved despotically. They'd seize whatever struck their fancy: a nice riding camel, a good horse. His kinfolk said to him, "Until this moment you haven't been any use to us. Therefore, allow us to bring our riding camels and herds, and let them be penned up safely at your place. You'll be paid one riyal for each animal." (At that time, a riyal was worth a thousand riyals of today.) "When Ibn Rashīd's servants come to collect the zakat from us, who knows, they might leave you alone because you are a poet."[209] ʿAdwān was a poor man, devoid of means.

On that occasion, he said:

As a creator of exquisite art, I herewith state:
    Muḥammad and Ḥmūd scatter tribes like chaff.
Unflinching, they rule by dint of mighty swords;
    like it or not, there is no choice but to submit.
On high-humped, long-necked, sturdy mounts,
    they come swooping down on terrified enemies.
Calm when kneeled, strong-paced on the march:
    torrents crashing through a narrow riverbed;
Shammar warriors chanting victory songs
    goad the booty calmly, like herds driven to market.
By your honor, dispense me from paying taxes,
    shiny paper and ink, quill pens wielded by clerks;
From servants barking, "Hey lout, get up, fetch!"
    pulling me up, my mustache in their iron grip.
Diligent and expeditious, pens held at the ready:
    sent on a mission, count on them to perform.

44.2

44.3

1

5

Sibhān, the tax collector, said, "How is this possible, al-Hirbīd? How did you acquire such a large number of riding camels? How did you come by this collection of fine mounts, whereas before you owned no more than one black male camel?" The poet replied, "If they became mine as a result of your kindness, the favor granted me was not yours.[210] And if it was kindness shown to me by the brother of Nūrah: beat it in the name of God, may he not protect you!" And the other left without a further word. His fellows paid ʿAdwān a riyal for each animal and he left riding his camel. He had saved the day for his fellow clansmen.

He Replies to Brikah ibn ʿŌjā

A poet, Brikah ibn ʿŌjā al-Ghyithī, while at the court of Ibn ʿRēʿir,   45.1
composed a few verses, saying:

> We've grown old, our strength was broken,
>> just as a wooden saddle cuts into camels' backs.
> I lowered the serpentine's smoldering fuse,
>> bent over flashpan like a viper coiled to strike.

—That is, I lowered the slow-burning cord used to ignite the powder
in the flashpan. The slow fuse attached to the lock coiled downward
like a snake.

> I'm done; the bucket is slung over my shoulder.
>> Dear fellows with new gear, good luck to you!

ʿAdwān was a hunter before his hair turned gray with age. He   45.2
used to hunt ibexes in the granite mountains, stalking them as they
bounded ahead along steep trails. Then one day, he felt a sudden
stab of sharp pain and his knee buckled. From that time on, he was
no longer able to crawl lying on his stomach so as to go unnoticed
within shooting range of game. Ibn ʿŌjā's lines on the subject of old
age came to his mind.

He said: 45.3

1 Hunting for prey, if that is my verse's game,
  I take my cue from poetry recited by Ibn ʿŌjā.
Climbing steep heights, our strength was broken
  on slippery granite rocks too daunting for most.
Cunning ibexes dodged me and I'd blast them
  with thirsty bullets from my matchlock's barrel.

—He is speaking about matchlock firearms.

Nose in the wind, sniffing, sharp ears pricked up,
  glowing eyes on high alert for sudden threats:
5 A prima donna leads the ibex to bitter mountain wells,
  adults with five annular rings, kids in tow.
I turned back, and left hunting to young devotees—
  bright-eyed, belt-strapped, sporting dagger and powder horn.
If you're not taught how to hunt in your youth,
  forget about becoming a good shot in old age.
On high ridges, my eyes strain for clear vision:
  hazy mirages in distant deserts, wrapped in fog.
A graybeard now, but in halcyon days of old
  I garnered uncounted stout-necked trophies.
10 I'm done; the bucket is slung over my shoulder.
  You, fellows with new gear! Good luck to you!

Reply to His Son When He Had Divorced His Mother and She Married Adhān al-Dhīb

His divorced wife remarried Adhān al-Dhīb of the Ghyithah tribe.   46.1
The man's nickname was Adhān al-Dhīb, "Wolf-eared." 'Adwān's son
'Alī was in tears and kept crying, "I want my mother back!" "Where
is your mother?" he said. "She is with a man of the Dghērāt."

> One wolf in the belly, one on the back:
>> 'Alī, she's with the Dghērāt, unreachable!
> With men forever pouring lead for bullets:
>> ruthless avengers, 'Alī, not to be trifled with.
> Ninety, another ninety grizzled fighters,
>> ninety youngsters sprouting facial hair.[211]

Praise for the People of Jubbah

47.1 He composed a poem in praise of Jubbah and its people. These are the only lines I know:

> Let a steady drum of rain come visit Nāyif,
>   winding torrents race toward Ibn ʿBēkah:[212]
> Let massive clouds tower, layer on layer.
>   [...]

His Date Palms at Mtāliʿ

ʿAdwān al-Hirbīd owned a garden of date palms at Ḥayyah in the   48.1
Ajā Mountain, at a place called Mtāliʿ. He inherited the grove,
al-Mtāliʿiyyāt, planted in hollows surrounded by rocky mountain
slopes, from his father, Rāshid. ʿAdwān named the stately palms
al-Shēkhāt, comparing them to an assembly of high dignitaries.
"Lady shaykhs," you might say, girls dressed in festive attire. Now
the garden lies in ruins. The palms have shriveled. He wished they'd
be irrigated and revived by a torrent following heavy rains:

> I wish for pitch-black rainclouds to visit you,   *1*
>> one angel goading the rear, one leading in front,[213]
> White-blazed crests illuminated at sundown:
>> thickset as mountain shoulders raised aloft.
> White-blazed, choking on its rumbles, exuberant:
>> barrages of rain send foxes scurrying away.
> Let it fall on Hadlā and Hadbā, and Nūrah too,
>> swirling roots of sagebrush in the undergrowth;
> Like my eyes, Nwayyir cries when she's hurt;   *5*
>> I go berserk if someone pokes her in the eye.
> [. . .]
>> creamy camel udders overflowing with milk.

As these lines came to his ears, Rājī ibn Ṭōʿān threw down the   48.2
gauntlet to him:

1 You wish for pitch-black clouds to visit you,
    an angel goading the rear, one leading in front,
  For rain on Ḥayyah's eyes and hinder parts—
    our vale of dense growth and swirling roots;
  Cabins of clansmen who extirpate their foes,
    serve guests grits drenched in melted butter—
  Our inheritance from days immemorial,
    captured by ʿAlī through deeds of cunning:
5 What marvelous loot! The old man's smartest act!
    By shooting, not by pleading in tribal courts;
  By volleys of bullets fired from a trench he dug,
    hit after hit, hardly an enemy escaped unhurt.

—*Ṣanʿ al-bint* means the matchlock.

Your hideout: snakes coiled up inside fissures:
    Qur'an recital does not countervail dented jaws.
  May God unleash against them Hadhrami porcupines
    with a taste for munching on the palms' young shoots,[214]
  Porcupine after porcupine, and yet another porcupine,
    a porcupine digging the base, a porcupine from the side.
10 Flanked by a male with the monstrous grin of Mshārī,
    gruesome hooked incisors inflict grievous wounds.

48.3 Mshārī was an old man with long teeth. Yes, Rājī ridicules ʿAdwān's date palms. What did he mean by "Our inheritance from days immemorial?" Rājī was a member of the Dghērāt, a tribe of the ʿAbdah division of Shammar. Rājī refers to the ancestor of the Dghērāt, the son of Yaḥyā. At first, he lived in Ḥāyil. Resentful of indignities he suffered at the hands of his fellow tribesmen, he, ʿAlī, "forcibly entered," *daghar*. Hence the name of the clan, al-Dghērāt: ʿAlī and his children moved to an area in Ajā Mountain. He started out as a laborer whose job it was to fertilize palm trees for the owner of the garden, Ibn Baggār. From that time on, they were known as the Dghērāt.

They came to al-B'ayyir with Ibn Baggār. One of them was the   48.4
daughter of 'Alī, Salmā, the name that became the battle cry of the
Ghyithah. One of the men in those olden days said, "What a gor-
geous girl! Such a pity she is the daughter of a worker who fertilizes
palm trees." She went to her father, crying. He said, "By God, as
true as I am your father, they are going to rue it; they will not live
to see the next harvest." When the others had left, he took his pack
camel and headed for the highlands of al-Shifā in search of saltpeter,
which he found not far from Khaybar, to the right side, I don't know
exactly where, and he used it to make gunpowder.[215] He rode back,
fetched a quantity of lead from Medina, and melted and cast it to
produce bullets. He kept adding to his stock of ammunition until
the others returned. He was lying in ambush for them, and when
they had drawn close enough, he opened fire from behind a protec-
tive wall, killing them to a man. Thereupon he took possession of
their gardens of date palms. This story explains how they acquired
their tribal name, "Those who enter by force."

'Adwān did not take it lying down and replied: 48.5

I am Abū Ḥzayyim, any aggressor's cure: 1
    mustard oil poison, fatal to the consumer.
Little brother mine, what shall I do with Rājī,
    with his wizened face of a granny mixing snorting powders.
He prays for their ruin by a Hadhrami porcupine,
    ruthless destroyer of palms' every root and branch.
God strike you with a thunderbolt from Hell,
    its flash illuminating sand dunes far and wide.
At his booth, he treats visitors carelessly;   5
    in season, his gifts of dates are laughable.

'Nēg caught fire and burned down the palm trees of Rājī, as every-   48.6
one here knows. One year al-Shēkhāt did not carry a lot of fruit and
the harvest turned out bad. That happened after these poems had
spread. The trees produced a small harvest of unappetizing fruit,

while al-Hirbīd's trees at the settlement of his clan, Ḥayyah, were doing well. He invited buyers to come forward: he wanted to sell off the fruit in advance, so that he could return to the company of his fellow tribesmen of al-Swēd. He sold the coming harvest for one *majīdī*. At that time it was a valuable currency, not a trifling sum of money.

48.7   Rājī went to see Ḥawwās al-Tbēnānī. Ḥawwās had suffered the loss of his eyelashes and Rājī had rheumy eyes, messy with white discharge. It is said that he was capable of wolfing down two trays of food and still have appetite for more. He sought help from al-Tbēnānī, a poet who specialized in this kind of verse, saying, "Ḥawwās, did you hear how al-Hirbīd compared my face to that of a wizened granny who busies herself with mixing snorting powders? This is our chance, now that he has sold for one riyal the harvest of those palm trees that he praised so effusively. We should compose some verses about it, and to do so I need your help, Ḥawwās!"

48.8   "Fine," the other said, and recited these verses:

> Rider of a swift, reddish-brown desert crosser,
>> al-Lḥāwī's stock on father's and mother's side.
> Head for ʿAdwān, pick of prodigious butchers,
>> marksman, nemesis of ibexes bulky as camels.
> You've dishonored your trees and cut their faces,
>> you oaf, selling off their harvest for one riyal![216]

48.9   ʿAdwān understood that al-Tbēnānī had lent Rājī a hand. He said in reply:

> 1   Rider of a red-hued camel cleaving sandy vastness:
>> it burns the miles, dream of messengers in a hurry,
> Swift as bounding hornless gazelles, nose in the wind;
>> or like ostriches startled by distant human shapes.

—The wind: he means the smell of gunpowder.

Go to Rājī, whose laudations tear me to shreds:
    your doings are not a real man's comportment;
Prattle, off the mark, haphazard rock-throwing:
    stay put, do not protest your indisposition!
Take it! My tight-woven verses come flocking   5
    in well-arraigned strings of beads if I lift the pen,
Assiduous, bent over my spring's relentless gush,
    checking that no verse veers off course, goes awry;
Carried by messengers riding fast desert crossers,
    verses sown and waiting for future generations.

—Where is ʿAdwān now? And we are still reciting his poetry!

Take your medicine: rattling venomous bullets,
    pounded saltpeter drains your insides' sap of life.[217]
Down! Smear that mangy face! Roll and writhe!
    Let gray gunpowder make your limbs lame!
Laughingstock, women heap scorn on you: 10
    impotent male, travesty of chivalrous ideals.
You've no inkling how to pasture camel herds,
    how to migrate amid the Bedouin hustle and bustle;
Lure falcons by running and waving cloths,
    take a marksman's aim at fleeing gazelle herds.
Some help you are, real asset to your kinsmen,
    at the tray, gorging on food at plentiful feasts.
I skirted your palms, like a flimsy sagebrush fence,
    drought-stricken, brittle as *ʿarad* acacia shrubs.
We'd rather stay among apple-colored Shēkhāt,   15
    yellow racemes graciously curved, heavy with fruit:
Well-watered gardens of Faḍlī and his spirited kin,[218]
    our treasured property from north to its other end,
Guarded by warriors, unflinching killers in battle,
    amazingly generous in displays of benevolence.

Ḥawwās has the gall to vaunt his tireless mounts:
    fair game to us, we'll maul them with our paws.
Watch your eyes, wormy like locust bellies:
    woe betide your ilk if you spoil for a fight:
20   Senile graybeards, worn out like wooden keys,
    cheeks colorless, vigor spent, wan, debilitated.
We're not bothered by such trifles; we take them lightly.
    Be careful, Abū Gāʿid, you're not in great shape.

48.10   Ḥawwās paid him a visit. He came as a penitent, on his knees, biting his thumbs with regret. He said to ʿAdwān, "I am so sorry for what I did."

His Dispute with Ṣimāʿīn and Sʿēd That Occasioned the al-Shēkhah Poem

Before these events, ʿAdwān had a dustup with Ṣimāʿīn. Initially, the two had engaged in lighthearted banter, but then one verse recited by Ṣimāʿīn rubbed ʿAdwān the wrong way. Ṣimāʿīn was a member of their tribe's ʿUmrān subdivision. Their falling out had to do with the fate that befell ʿAdwān's date palms in al-Mtāliʿiyyāt, his garden in a bottom surrounded by rocky ridges of Mtāliʿ at the western end of the Ajā mountain range. He had given his palms girls' names, such as Nwayyir, Hadbā, and Hadlā, as a token of how much he treasured them: he felt for them as if they were his daughters. He also owned palm trees called al-Shēkhāt in one of the open spaces inside the granite slopes of Ajā Mountain.

In a certain year, ʿAdwān's palm trees burst into fruit all at the same time. Both of his gardens, Ajā and Mtāliʿ, flowered and produced dates. In addition, their fruit promised to be of excellent quality. ʿAdwān had no sons, only daughters. Therefore, he faced the work alone: there was no way he could divide himself in two and be in both gardens at the same time. He argued: "In al-Mtāliʿiyyāt, I am at a far remove from al-Shēkhāt and will miss out on the good cheer and company of my fellows of the Swēd who live in Ajā, near my al-Shēkhāt palm garden. I won't be able to take part in their social gatherings and lively assemblies. On the other hand, if I take up my abode at al-Shēkhāt, the palms of al-Mtāliʿiyyāt will suffer: their fruit will go to waste and bring me no benefit. (There were no other

49.1

49.2

palm gardens in that area; it was an isolated place.) What's my gain? I have no choice but to cut off the fruits, the date bunches, from the trees at al-Mtāliʿiyyāt. There is no other way to make sure that, going forward, both gardens will not bear fruit at the same time, but in alternate years. Thus, the trees of al-Mtāliʿiyyāt will carry fruit in the year that follows the harvest from al-Shēkhāt: the dates we need to regale our guests with." He matched his words with actions. He lopped off the clusters of fruit and left them lying at the bottom of the trees. It was his intention to delay the harvest until the year after, so that the palm trees would produce dates in alternate years.

49.3 Ṣimāʿīn was a dedicated hunter. He spent much time roaming the Ajā Mountain in search of game. He clambered over the rocks looking for ibex. One day, as he came down toward al-Mtāliʿiyyāt, ʿAdwān's garden, and walked past the trees, he was shocked to discover the cut-off bunches of dates, stacked in heaps under the trees. He said to himself, "Such wanton destruction of the trees can only be the work of a man who harbors a deep grudge against ʿAdwān. Let me follow his traces and find out who is guilty of this dastardly deed." He veered off course and went in another direction, following the tracks that remained clearly visible on the soft ground, a mixture of rock and sand. The traces were easy to follow. But as he looked closer, lo and behold, those prints were the steps of ʿAdwān himself, no two ways about it. Men such as Ṣimāʿīn were past masters at the art of reading tracks, having grown up near the Nafūd Desert. He looked again. These were the fruits of his trees, stacked in big heaps at their feet. It dawned on him that it was the work of ʿAdwān himself, and he became convinced that he had done this on purpose.

49.4 Toward the end of that day, he returned to his folk. His kinsmen asked him, "Haven't you brought us any game, Ṣimāʿīn?" He said, "By God, this time I ran into a problem that scuttled my hunting plans." "Why?" they wanted to know. "When I ascended the ridge, during my climb, I heard screams for help. Female voices—females shouting as if in grave danger. At once, I turned sideways toward where the sound came from, thinking that they were being attacked by predators or frightened for whatever reason. When I had come down to the bottom of the narrow valley, the gully of al-Mtāliʿiyyāt, there were no females to be seen anywhere. There was no one in the gully of al-Mtāliʿiyyāt. I wondered where these anguished cries might have come from. Then I heard their tearful voices: 'It us, we are the ones crying, al-Mtāliʿiyyāt.'—Had not ʿAdwān given his palm trees female names: Hadbā, Hadlā, Nwayyir?—So I said, 'Tell me, what's the matter?' They said, 'Look there, brother, do you not see the fruits lying at our feet? God has bestowed on us these riches, but it was our bad fortune that he cut them off, leaving us denuded of any fruit. Not because the harvest was devoured by swarms of locusts. It was his wretched intention to lay us to waste; he did it on purpose.' By God, I saw it with my own eyes, how he had laid into them and brought them to ruin. As soon as I understood the story and what had happened, I decided to come back home." "Very well," the others said. "Any verses?" ʿAdwān was one of the visitors present in the majlis, listening to what so far had been jocular conversation.

Ṣimāʿīn ibn ʿUmrān said: 49.5

    While roaming the mountains on a jolly hunt,   *1*
        I was hit in the stomach by harrowing events:
    I stumbled on tall stems, curved branches
        crying, robbed of their crowns, shaved bald.
    Nwayyir said, "Woe, woe, my shaded fruits!
        With malice, we were ill-treated in the high season,
    Not by locusts, no act of God, not plain rot:
        you hacked them off, you nasty scoundrel."

—They were not laid waste by natural causes. Their fruits were not inferior, nor had they failed to come out. I don't know the poem in its entirety. He calls the trees by their names and makes each of them utter her complaint in a verse. But it is known for certain that this verse is the one that ends the poem.

5

"No honorable man would commit such an offense:
What shame, your lack of real men's noble poise!"

49.6　　No sooner had he finished his declamation than ʿAdwān stood up and left the majlis. Initially, he had put a brave face on it, grinning along with the others and making comments like "God will settle accounts with you" or "My Lord and your Lord is God!" But at the recitation of the last verse, he stood up and walked away, offended and angry. When he had gone, the other men of the Swēd said to him, "What have you done, Ṣimāʿīn? Your words have hurt and angered ʿAdwān! And in his presence at that, as if you couldn't care less about him sitting there. How could you be so insensitive and rude?" "What do you mean? What are you talking about?" he asked. "Your words 'What shame, your lack of real men's noble poise.' Now you run a serious risk of him retaliating with verses of his own. Count on getting a poem in reply or else go and placate the man!"

49.7　　That same afternoon, he mustered up his courage and pushed himself to head for ʿAdwān and call on him. He kissed his head and said, "Truly, honest to God, Abū Khzayyim, I ask your forgiveness. Sometimes I go wrong and then I really act stupidly. It was meant as a joke, honestly. I didn't pay sufficient attention to what I was doing." ʿAdwān said, "It is no problem as far as I am concerned. I did not hold anything against the poem and I'd even say that it hit the mark. I deserved it, considering that I cut off the fruit of the palm trees. It is only when you said, 'No honorable man would commit such an offense: What shame, your lack of real men's noble poise!' Why should you say that?" He said, "I've come to you because you are completely in the right, Abū Khzayyim." (So named after his son Khzayyim, who died in infancy.) "I take full responsibility for what I did. But I dearly wish to avoid a situation where you'd jump me and ride my back." He said, "It's all right. I will let it pass this time, I promise. But be warned, henceforth be careful never to come across my path again and make me cross!" "Absolutely! From now on, I will refrain from touching you in any way. By God, I am not going to rub up against you a second time."

Now we come to the events that gave rise to his composition of the al-Shēkhah poem, may your life be long. At that time, the leadership of the Swēd rested with ʿAssāf al-Hirbīd, Abū Frēḥ, the grandfather of Khalaf, who currently lives in al-Khibbah. They were a small bunch back then: one sheep was sufficient to feed the entire group. People were few in number at that time. They were fond of pampering their camels; those were the days of camels, Bedouin life, tribal warfare, days when people's strides were long. They led extraordinary lives. The tribe stayed in settled country until the rains arrived in fall. The early rains came to al-Khinfah, an area on the way from here to the land of the Sharārāt tribe. At that time, al-Khinfah was known as a dangerous place, infested with enemies. One would only enter it with a show of force. Back then, tribes stood in adversarial relationships to one another. One tribe would plunder the other. Foes clashing on horseback. Each tribe against the other. Ibn Saʿūd poured cold water on those practices, as the poet al-Mshannā said:

> Fortune smiled on buffaloes, maggots, and worms;
>> misers behind locked doors beat Shalwā falcons.[219]
> Ibn Saʿūd has curbed warhorses and chiefs;
>> nobles became servants; bastards went on a spree.

When the fall season started, they were in al-Ghūṭah, north of Mōgag. A camel rider arrived, a wayfarer. He told them, "From al-Khinfah to Jubbah, north to al-ʿWēd, the desert pastures of late spring have remained intact and untouched. There is an abundance of wild cows as they are called, oryxes. Take my word for it, by God, in just about every hollow between the sand hills you'll find five, ten, twenty of them," or so the wayfarer claimed. "Therefore, you'd be well advised, ʿAssāf, to head straightaway for those spring meadows! There's plentiful grazing for your herds, and game meat

for your children and visitors who flock to you while you're there.
So much better than the long journey to Iraq. Consider this! If you
send a camel train to Iraq, it will consume about half of the supplies
on the way back. You're much better off trekking to those mead-
ows: you'll feast on game meat while your camels graze to their
hearts' delight. True, at times it may get a bit risky out there. On the
other hand, think of the plentiful herbage and the many good things
within your grasp."

49.10 Accordingly, the Swēd tribe took the route upcountry, may
your life be long, keeping Jubbah to their right, along the edge of
al-Nafūd. It was in the early days of late fall. They rushed toward
al-Khinfah, marching all day long. They put up camp at al-Ṭiwīl,
an outcrop at the outer rim of al-Jōf, on the way to the tribal lands
of al-Sharārāt and so on. As soon as they came to the middle of
al-Nafūd, they saw that everything was exactly as the wayfarer had
described. Lush herbage of late spring everywhere. It was as if the
flowers had just opened, covering the soil with a carpet of sappy
green plants. No sooner had they arrived than the rains of late fall
drenched the desert floor again. As we were told, they were blessed
with consecutive rains, those of early and late fall. On the heels
of these downpours came the winter rains, followed by the rains
of Arcturus, the rains of spring. More and more growth of herb-
age, renewing itself all the time. A marvelous sight, this profusion
of fresh green: *nuṣiy* grass, *ḥamāṭ*, *khimkhim*.[220] In those days, the
land had retained its lovely original character; it had not yet become
worked and plowed with iron tools. Pure virgin land. They pastured
their animals at al-Ṭiwīl. The soil was in full flower, and they stayed
there for three months. Engrossed in their daily activities, they were
loath to depart and tarried. You know how the Bedouin love to con-
sort with their camels and indulge in endless conversations about
camels. At that time, camels were a relatively rare commodity.

49.11 They spent no less than three months at that location, enjoying
one another's company, in merriment, having endless conversa-
tions and spinning yarns. And great food too: game meat and camel

milk. At the center of the place where the tents were pitched, they had built a pen made of brushwood. Once the camels had safely returned at dusk, they placed their guns against the enclosure. A detachment of guardsmen was always at the ready with the camels in case of an attack by raiders. They entertained themselves deep into the night with song, dance, and festive firing of guns. Come morning, the men girded themselves up for work with the camels. They'd accompany the camels to pasture as protection against the ubiquitous enemies. They did not visit the markets of al-Jūbah, and Ḥāyil was too far away. The reason they gave for staying put was always the same: "Imagine if I'd leave on a journey; I wouldn't have a quiet moment for fear that my folk would come to harm in my absence. Therefore, I must stay close to my camels and their pen." Most of the space in the enclosure was reserved for hunted oryxes. Game was bountiful. There they also kept a store of large vessels filled with camel milk. 'Assāf would entertain them from his sup-plies: coffee and a leather sack stuffed with tobacco. Their caval-rymen filled their pipes and hookahs at his place, lighting up to be ready at a moment's notice to vault onto their horses and charge headlong at the enemy.

Inevitably, time came when the excitement of spring began to wear off and herbage withered. The families of the Swēd did not keep small cattle at their camp; 'Adwān's flock of sheep was the exception. The others were fast-traveling camel nomads who said, "When twigs become dry and brittle, one night's march and next morning is all we need to be back home." The first to notice the change was 'Adwān. He was an alert and clever man whose foresight influenced the opinion of others. One day, looking up at the sky, 'Adwān tracked the stars that were on the descent. As a rule, when the Pleiades are about to set, then that year's season of late spring, and with it the chances of rain, had come to an end. Sometime later, the stars that followed the setting of the Pleiades appeared: an unmistakable sign that the hot season had started. Now they ran the risk of getting mired in the heart of enemy country. What should

49.12

we do if we are attacked and get caught up in the warfare while we are stuck here, so far north? How long will it take us to reach our tribal land near Ḥāyil? For him, a sheepherder, things looked even more ominous than for the others. He measured a lamb's stride between his outstretched thumb and index finger. How long would it take such a small animal to cover the distance from here to Ḥāyil? How could it keep pace with the hardy camels, especially in the hot season heralded by the disappearance of those stars? Spring season had come to an end. One should reckon with the possibility of attack from any direction. They were exposed to red-hot danger from the enemy on the right and on the left: surrounded by Ḍanā Slēmān, al-Rwalah, al-Sharārāt, al-Ḥwēṭāṭ. In those days, tribes had no choice but to rob or be robbed.

49.13   ʿAdwān began to feel anxious. He was a sheepherder, it was getting late in the season, the animals were well fed from grazing on the grasses of spring. He was strongly of the opinion that they should lose no time in moving to their summer quarters before the arrival of the greatest heat, on account of his sheep. He decided to make his pitch: "Hey, ʿAssāf, the weather is getting hot and you have pastured to your heart's content. Your animals have grown so fat they can hardly walk: you'd have to strap their mouths, make it impossible for them to graze. Let it be, now! Let's travel in leisurely stages till we reach our folk back home. Be wary of attacks, of the bite of spotted vipers, of being despoiled of all possessions, stranded and helpless in the midst of this waterless desert! So far, we have remained safe and well. We've been fortunate and have raked in a plethora of good things." With such arguments, he sought to convince ʿAssāf, offering him friendly counsel. Someone overheard what he said, then sidled up to him and said, "Why don't you show them, ʿAdwān? Compose a poem on how stupid they'd be to stay here any longer. Perhaps that way you'd bring it home to them that they'd be well advised to return to their summer quarters." He accordingly composed a poem prompting them to go home. This poem set in motion the train of events that led to the al-Shēkhah poem.

May God keep you safe, their supply of coffee was running out.   49.14
Back then, coffee was a rare commodity. ʿAssāf was the sole person
to carry coffee beans with him and the only guests in his majlis to
be served coffee were perhaps three or four senior men. It was not
served regularly, not as a matter of course. Instead, they'd smoke.
But tobacco was also running out. The story goes that ʿAssāf kept a
tobacco sack with him: a leather bag, a skin stuffed full of tobacco.
In the evening, he'd sometimes allow his visitors to fill their pipes
and light up. He'd say, "Here, this amount will do for you!" Like-
wise in the morning. The smokers would fill their pipes and light
up before setting out to pasture with their camels. ʿAdwān said,
"Worthy fellows, listen! This morning I saw an unmistakable sign
that late spring has come to an end. The stars have set, fellows: it's
time to turn back to our water wells. Everyone knows that if the
stars have disappeared there is no choice but to stay in the vicinity
of water wells. This great heat we experience now heralds the end of
pasture: dry twigs and withered stalks, that's all there is."

'Adwān said: 49.15

We surged from home, trekking to the north,   1
    many stages removed from Ḥāyil's markets.
We thrust ourselves deep into enemy lands,
    set game bounding from inner desert retreats.
We sent our watchmen to the top of dunes
    while others rested in peace and calm;
We pastured to the left of Mkēḥīl at Laghābīb—
    rolling plains where *firs* plants stir in the wind,
Tribal lands of Banū Yaklab and Klāb and Klēb,   5
    fearful of nightly assault and morning raids,
Camels surrounded by stiff-necked strangers:
    ninety nights we did not lay down our arms;
'Assāf led us over robbers' highways to pastures,
    virgin meadows fed by night-traveling clouds.

Let us graze on the lands of awesome fighters
>   where danger lurks in every crag and crevice.
> Our tobacco dwindled, went up in smoke,
>   as we galloped time and again to Abū ʿWēnān:

—Abū ʿWēnān is ʿAssāf al-Hirbīd, the chief of those people, so named after his son Frēḥ, whose nickname was ʿWēnān because he was born at ʿWēnat al-Kalbah, a depression where rainwater gathers, or so it is said. *Aṭ-ṭiyāḥ* are sweet-tempered camels that do not need to be restrained by hobbling them: they won't run off even if they are treated roughly.

10
> Puffs like misty banks or distant coastlines,
>   mingled with wafts of coffee boiled on embers.
> He is a gushing well, the camels' favorite haunt:
>   when desert pools run dry, water is scarce.
> Shigā's brother! See, the Three Females have set:[221]
>   spring gone, no green plants to fatten our herds.

—The brother of Shigā is ʿAssāf. Gemini, the Pleiades, and Sirius are called "the females." When they set, spring has come to an end and the season of great heat begins.

> Chief! Wolves roam along our homebound trek;
>   tell our hip-swaying ladies: "Break up and pack!
> Load the camels, well-trained, wayward ones;
>   file out like camels watered at a rock-dug well!"

49.16   When he had come to the end of his recitation, ʿAssāf said, "ʿAdwān is right, absolutely right. Spring is over. Even early summer has come to an end. The hot days of midsummer are upon us. And look, there we are, lingering in this waterless desert of the Nafūd sands." His arguments were rebutted by Sʿēd, one of the Swēd, a relative of his. Sʿēd al-Wʿēlī was a camel nomad bent on staying there as long as possible with the aim of fattening his camels to the utmost. He said, "Listen, Shaykh, forget about him! The guy is an addict who has run out of tobacco and is angling for a way to leave in search of his stuff. Beat it, 'Adwān, you wretch! Stop scheming to scare the Swēd away from their enjoyment of this last stage of spring! That's how it is—God has ordained that every poet should be a cowardly babbler. Leave us alone to do as we like and to pasture at leisure on these wonderful blessings. Shame on you! Do not scare us away from the *firs* and *ḍimrān* and other herbage!" "Seek refuge with God, S'ēd!" 'Adwān exclaimed. "No, it is not true that every poet is a poltroon. Be specific, and do not include all poets under one heading."

During that session, S'ēd and Ṣimā'īn shared a camel saddle, each leaning against one side of it. Turning aside, S'ēd said, "What do you think, Ṣimā'īn? Isn't it true that every poet is a coward?" Now, Ṣimā'īn was also a poet. He was afraid that if he contradicted S'ēd by denying that every poet is a coward, he'd shoot back that he would say so because he was a poet himself. He had forgotten about his earlier dustup with 'Adwān, the teasing that degenerated into a quarrel between them. He said, "No two ways about it. S'ēd is right; what he says is true. God is my witness: I agree with him when he says that every poet is a coward." They colluded against 'Adwān, each of them affirming that the other spoke the truth.

49.17

"How come then," he argued, "that the Sharifs were poets; the Banū Hilāl were poets; the shaykhs of Shammar were poets; the shaykhs of 'Anazah, 'Tēbah, Mṭēr, the remainder of the tribes. Each of those chivalrous and generous shaykhs was a poet as well." 'Adwān concluded: "I turn toward God and away from these folks with you, S'ēd, and you too, Ṣimā'īn." S'ēd was known as a brave fellow and poet, but also a niggard of the worst kind. And yet, a stalwart man and also a poet. Really, 'Adwān was furious. It cut him to the quick to be told that every poet is a coward. But, may your life be long, he did get back at them with a stinging reply:

49.18

> Ṣimā'īn's conduct lacks a real man's poise;
>> S'ēd's hearth lies fallow, shunned by visitors.

'Adwān walked out on the circle of men. In the evening, he came ambling back, ponderous and looking haggard. By God, everyone understood at once that he was fuming with rage. He made his way to the head of the majlis and kneeled, coming down with a thud, the way a big male camel sinks to its knees, and he groaned, breathing heavily. Someone muttered under his breath, "This bodes ill for us, Ṣimā'īn; these groans are a harbinger of evil things to come."

49.19   'Adwān launched into delivery of the al-Shēkhah poem.

1   A majlis attended by Ṣimā'īn and S'ēd
        is loathsome, though I cherish the company.
    Ṣimā'īn's conduct lacks a real man's poise;
        S'ēd's hearth lies fallow, shunned by visitors.

—He is a miser who receives no visitors.

    Growth of *ḍimrān* and *firs* enticed you, S'ēd—
        may all salty plants of the dunes go to hell!
    Attacking, S'ēd, your words charge and turn,
        though they carry camel loads of cheap crap:
5   Girls hear your words: aren't you ashamed?
        Young men should impress with noble deeds.
    S'ēd, imagine you're hit right in the nipple
        by a spear: a sharp flash, your body lies lame,
    In pristine land roamed by wild cows and game:
        not a soul to ask about your fate, or care.
    I stand in awe of fighters with loaded firearms,
        warriors as truthful in deeds as in words, S'ēd.
    I fear prowling enemies, fresh traces left in sand,
        sudden shadows beyond the dune ridges,

—*Barārīd* are tracks left in the sand.

Grizzled veterans, swift-footed youngsters,   10
    pick of camel riders, sturdy as acacias;
Valiant men, guns slung on the shoulders,
    littering fields with bodies of men dearly missed,
With the irresistible surge of their charge, S'ēd:
    fine noblemen massacred on the day of battle;
A trail of suckling orphans left in their wake:
    debris scattered by massive far-reaching blows.
You're not so bad, S'ēd, just refine your words:
    avoid speech, S'ēd, that's bound to be your undoing.
You've poked your fingers in all poets' eyes,   15
    indiscriminately lumping good with the bad.
You've defamed Nimr, al-Mhādī, and Abū Zayd,
    the Hilālī, the caravan's pride, steadfast in ambush.
Also, 'Rār and 'Mēr, men strong and crafty,
    heavy hitters whose thrusts unsaddle foes;
Al-Ashmal, who cherishes his many opponents;
    Miṭlag plunging into pools freshly filled by rain;
Ṣa'ab of Shammar's Ṣdēd, the enemies' bane;
    'Abdallah, a raging beast, a linchpin in battle.
Shāyi', putting young camels through their paces;   20
    Jārid racing on mighty spirited steeds;
Even the Sharif they rhapsodize, S'ēd;
    Sa'ūd ibn Sa'ūd, accomplisher of major feats.
Don't forget Mish'ān, al-Ṭayyār, and 'Bēd;
    'Antar, who restores balance to sliding loads;
Also, Mghīr ibn Ghāzī and Nōmān, S'ēd,
    rampart of troops gripped by panic and fear;
Or al-'Askarī, Mṣīkh, Hdēb, and Rshēd;
    Ḥsēn, whose onslaught secures the troops' rear.
Remember Jimal, Ibn Ḥithlēn, al-Fighm, Fhēd;   25
    Sājir, patching up his camels' bleeding soles.[222]
Jdē', guardian knight of fat camels in milk,
    when cavalry charges cut deep into sands.

Ḥaṭṭāb, serving layers of dates on his trays;
>> Brēk, who revives worn, emaciated mounts;
Jrēs, his generosity extravagant like a feast;
>> Ḥātim, his irresistible urge to give away all;
Ibn D'ējā, rampart as a sheer cliff of rock;
>> Ibn Smēr in his corner far to our north;
Rmēzān, al-'Arfajī, and famous Abū Zayd;
>> Barjas, fond of camels with speckled udders.
Twenty and another twenty, no less, no more:
>> masterful poets, noble achievers one and all.
In my admiration, S'ēd, for fine gentlemen,
>> tireless hosts of roasts, forever pouring coffee,
O S'ēd, tough men, forever coming and going:
>> men who take and give, both words and deeds.[223]
Even you aren't the worst of your kinsmen;
>> like you, I'm not less than my folk either.
We are as sound as flawless woven cloaks,
>> but without pretensions of higher ranks.

ʿAjlān ibn Rmāl

His Exchange of Poems
with Khalaf al-Idhn

ʿAjlān ibn Barghash ibn Rmāl was a shrewd, opinionated man, a   50.1
conversationalist in the majlis, someone whom shaykhs liked to
have around them, and a poet who also entertained at his own tent.
If people were at a loss how to handle a certain affair, they'd ask for
his opinion and advice. Leadership of spectacular raiding expedi-
tions? No, he was not much of a fighting man, nor someone to com-
mand bands of robbers. He did not aspire to such distinctions, nor
did he covet rich spoils. He had put up camp as a neighbor under
the protection of Khalaf al-Idhn ibn Shaʿlān, who sojourned at
Khashm Ḥadlah. The weather was freezing cold: they had snow and
ice. After a while, ʿAjlān wished to depart from Khalaf's place and
proceed toward the tribal lands of Shammar. "No!" said Khalaf. "No
way I will let you go. You must stay with us. We'll make sure that the
shaykhs take care of your household's necessities and more, includ-
ing money." He meant the shaykhs of the Shaʿlān. ʿAjlān felt trapped.
He said to Khalaf, "Well, how about you go to check out that large
rain pool to our north, to see if it would be any good for us to graze
our animals there. If it is, we can move to that place tomorrow." At
his suggestion, Khalaf rode toward the rain pool to reconnoiter the
terrain.

As soon as he had gone, ʿAjlān called to his womenfolk: "Hurry   50.2
up! Load the pack camels as fast as you can!" At his orders, they
started rushing to and fro, and brought his mare and shackled it

while ʿAjlān waited and rested in Khalaf's tent. He ate a lunch of bread brought by Khalaf's female household, "Ladies of al-ʿAlyā," a female name given to the camel herds of the Shaʿlān. Then he returned to his own camp. The mare stood at the ready, shackled in iron. He jumped into the saddle and raced away. He fled. The folks of his household made off, marching to the east. Their campsite had been in a dip in the terrain—a low hill separated the two camps. The womenfolk of Khalaf's camp did not see them pulling out. On his way home, Khalaf first went to look for the tent of ʿAjlān, but all he found were crows hopping around on the deserted abode. Where was ʿAjlān? The women of his household told him that ʿAjlān had left after lunch at noon. "But I found no one at their camels' resting places," he said. Sometime later, Khalaf rejoined the other tribesmen of al-Shaʿlān. They traveled together as one group and set up camp at al-Hzēm, beyond Grayyāt al-Milḥ.

50.3　During their sojourn there, a group of camel riders called on Khalaf al-Idhn and mentioned to him that his friend ʿAjlān was staying at al-Dhēmī. That news set off an exchange of poems. They visited one another, so to speak, by poem. His fellow tribesmen bickered among themselves: one said Khalaf's riding camel was the better mount; the other claimed it was outpaced by the male riding camel of ʿAjlān. They indulged in that kind of squabbling. Khalaf al-Idhn called to them: "Place your bets, all of you, Rwalah!" "Who will be our arbiter?" they asked. "Don't worry," he said, "they are coming to you and then you'll be able to make your own judgment."

50.4　Khalaf said:

1　　Rider of a red-hued camel, branded al-Slēmī,
　　　　skittish ever since she gave birth to her calf;

—Al-Slēmī is the brand mark of Binī ʿAṭiyyah.

　　　[…]
　　　　massive neck muscles stretch the halter's cord.

It's not far-fetched, a male ostrich might impregnate her,
    but for custodians of her stud's sperm: they know.[224]
Early morning, a fight with her shadow, life or death;
    in the afternoon, a mad rush as if bitten by rabid dogs,
From al-Thāyah reaching al-Dhēmī before dark,   5
    drawn by a shaykh's welcoming fire and supper;

—Al-Dhēmī is a prominent rocky elevation, mixed with sand at its bottom, at the border of the soft, sandy terrain and the stony desert.

Shaykh, son of shaykh, high-born, sharp-witted;
    perhaps to the right of al-Khirr, or else the left.

—Al-Khirr is a dry watercourse that runs from Iraq to al-Nafūd. People refer to its southern end as "glowing embers," meaning *ghaḍāh* bushes, which make excellent firewood, and to its north as "dates"; that is, the date palms of Iraq.

If, after wanderings, he'd settle down with me,
    I'd give my all as reward for such glad tidings.

'Ajlān replied to Khalaf: 50.5

Rider of a red-hued camel branded al-Htēmī,[225]   1
    fasten a small saddle on its back, let it run,
Punishing ground, not the other way around.
    Reddish brown, soft-backed and comfortable,
Grazed from 'Adhfā to Umm al-Ṣirīm in winter,
    browsing al-Labbah's luxuriant green in spring,
Mounted by a consummate young desert pilot:
    come morning, to his left he skirts the bluffs of Kabd.
Departing from al-Markūz in dark before dawn,   5
    she brushes up to al-Thāyah at the end of day,

—Al-Thāyāt are small, flat-topped elevations in the hard plains of al-Ḥamād.

To reach the intrepid hunter of shaykhs
    in melees as camel mothers lose their calves;[226]
Nemesis of the fearless, dispatcher of avengers:
    no vengeance was taken for knights he slayed.
He enthrones neighbors on thrones of respect:
    never does a pack camel of theirs go missing.
In winter evenings bleak with severest cold,
    he butchers his fattest high-humped camels.

10   Beware if his fingers grip his dagger's hilt,
    bloodshot eyes roll in the sockets, terrifying!
His guest basks in the comforts of Paradise,
    savors roasts from young she-camels' humps.
He is my pride, a famed Shalwā falcon of old,
    bold in the frontline attacks on his adversaries.
On broad-chested mares, whinnying at dawn,
    they plunge into darkness thick with eerie shapes;
Sons of shaykhs, who force foes into close combat;
    once the raging ire subsides, they make for gentlest company.

50.6   Lured by the contest, Khalaf Abū Zwayyid joined the fray with a
poem he sent to Ṣaṭṭām ibn Shaʿlān:

1   Rider of a brownish-red camel, well-fed,
    wool covered with chestnut-colored shine,
Short-haired, high in front, gazelle-necked;
    leg muscle: a mouse running up and down.[227]
Set out from Lōgah, at dusk reach al-Hzēm,
    tents soaring up like a flat mountain's tops;
Supper: rice, crushed wheat heaped on trays,
    dripping with drawn butter, poured unstintingly;
5   Bones scattered around like torrents' debris:
    indigent scavengers' favorite abode and haunt.
Shaykh, son of shaykhs of old noble stock:
    Ottoman pashas, hard as nails, are putty in his hands.

Exchange of Verses with Mṭēr ibn Khatlān

The tribe of al-Rmāl wandered through the desert. Every day, silhou-   51.1
ettes of enemy fighters were seen observing them from afar. Still,
they would stay away from each other and avoid a confrontation.
They kept a close watch in these sand dunes. ʿAjlān was not among
them. He had encamped for a long sojourn with sedentary people
near Umm al-Gilbān. While there, he was in poetic correspon-
dence with Mṭēr ibn Khatlān, a tribesman of al-Rmāl, descended
from ʿAmīrah. One day, they received an unexpected visit from a
ṣlubī, a member of the pariah tribe of blacksmiths: "Hey, where are
you coming from?" "By God, from the mountain." "Didn't you see
the camels of ʿAjlān?" "By God," he said, "the pregnant camels of
ʿAjlān are holding up nicely, but the mothers with calves, well . . . ."
"What's wrong with them?" "The guards of Ibn Rashīd do not let
them pasture there. Whenever they draw near, they shout at them
to scare them and chase them off. Camels don't like that: if they are
being yelled at, they refuse to graze." Goodness! What a pity for
ʿAjlān's beautiful camels, the Barrāgāt and Dlāgāt herds. The tribe
counted on having those ready in case of hostilities.

Mṭēr ibn Khatlān sent him these verses: 51.2

> Rider of a camel, smooth-gaited, loose-jointed,   *1*
>> fast as male ostriches startled by human voices;

At full throttle, it outruns bullets of Martini rifles:

    one day al-ʿAbd and al-ʿAbdah, the next at our dunes.[228]

—Al-ʿAbd and al-ʿAbdah are resting places for camel herds at one day's distance from the well of al-Birrīt. The dunes are the sand hills of Gnā and Umm al-Gilbān.

Head for ʿAjlān, hardy wolf waylaying prey,

    regaling companions with entertaining tales.

On spring meadows to Wādī al-Mrā's right,

    we haul in loads of truffles, herbage of all kinds;

5   Grumbling camels wade into gully puddles

    left by white-blazed clouds before darkness fell.

Our fellows, camel owners all, the finest breed:

    dashing horsemen on steeds with bulging ribs;

Marksmen, they feast on delicious roasts of game,

    camp without a care in remote empty hills.

Praise God, we are all in sparkling shape:

    full of vigor, we tackle the trek from al-Birrīt.

Glued to al-Bʿēthah, camels couched at the well,

    you met with peremptory treatment, we heard.[229]

10   Obtuse donkey! Why lay your fine herds to waste

    by settling down between al-Ḥabartī and Dirbās?[230]

Once well-rounded camels were skin and bones,

    al-Gfēʿī banished you to his place's lowest seat.

—*Nigāḍ* means they are very thin, emaciated.

51.3   "I am the brother of Siʿdā!" he exclaimed. "He calls me an obtuse donkey!" And he dispatched his reply:

1   Rider of a camel with a smooth, loose gait,

    hurtling along like a scud in a howling gale;

Not thin and worn out nor grown fat;
    lifting a saddle, a fireball of rare stamina.
Put through her paces down a hill,
    she plunges with dizzying speed like a falcon.
Wave the stick, slacken the racer's reins;
    you'll reach a nomad camp as darkness falls.
Go find Mṭēr, love of creamy-chested girls,   5
    hero of coquettish, sharp-dressed beauties.
I stay at al-Gfē'ī on flat ground ringed by hills:
    Ibn Miṭlag's coffeepots, a pan for roasting beans;
Carefully, pincers pick exquisite dates for me,
    served with assorted grapes, peaches, and figs.
I recline, taking in the view of my couched herd:
    watered in pools, no hassle of pulleys and wells.
Hey, dweller at al-Birrīt, real shithead that you are![231]
    Freeloader, coming and going like Ḥawwās![232]
Don't believe I stand in fear of Martini riflemen!   10
    Bloodsucking bug, your Martini is a mere axe.[233]

His Poems on the Ikhwān and the House of Rashīd

52.1 'Ajlān was in Iraq when the Sauds dethroned the Rashīd and supplanted their rule. A bird called Gēs hoots at night: it is said that the bird calls to his guest's camel. He said:

1 Gēs, clear off to your mother, damn you!
   You're still young, Gēs, but you're smart.
  Gēs, where are the royal fingers' signet rings,
   wide-ranging scouts on reddish thoroughbreds?
  Where the staffs tapping on laden royal trays,
   loud invitations to paupers waiting for food?
  Gone like rising towers of cumulus clouds,
   dissipated by northern breezes, swift and stiff,
5 Their rule doomed by the Lord of Eternal Rule;
   where is the Prophet? Where 'Adnān and Idrīs?[234]

52.2 While sojourning at Lāhah, Kharjā, and al-Tanf, 'Ajlān said:

  Good Lord, such a cold! It chills my bones!
   Frightening, if it's a child of last year's frost!
  God, I yearn for the Nafūd's balsam spurges,
   sleeping, snugly nestled in contented comfort.

—*Al-'ajz* are bushes of large *ghaḍā* trees.

'Ajlān said:

52.3

> O rider enthroned on a wooden camel saddle:
>> look forward to a pleasant rest in late afternoon.
> Beware of dangers lurking in valleys' thickets:
>> choose wide plains for your camel's browsing.

—*Midbil al-shiʿbān* is the lower end of narrow valleys. He is afraid of being caught unawares by the enemy in such places.

> Brisk of pace, she carries you nine nights long
>> to your destination, the courtyard of Nāyif,

—Nāyif ibn Farḥān, the chief of Jubbah.

> Welcomed by scions of our common ancestors;
>> warlike, they oust foes from sweet-water wells.
> Nine lineages sprouted from our ancestor's sons:
>> their white camels' silhouettes etched onto the dunes.[235]
> Breakfast served, the sweetest tastes are on offer,
>> aroma of roasted coffee beans wafting from a fire.
> God, kindly restore to us golden days of old:
>> winter grazing in dunes, curled up in soft sands!
> To hell, Kharjah; may people get lost on your way!
>> Joined by al-Tanf, Ghrāb al-Ḥdālī, and Lāhah!

—Kharjā consists of flat-topped rocky outcrops at the far north of the Ḥamād plains. Beyond it lies the land of al-Shumbul, east of the Syrian city of Homs.

> Cruel lashes of freezing cold whipped my body;
>> snow and ice cover the land like plowed fields.
> At dusk, a cover of white like shredded shirts,
>> in the silence of a windless dusk, the sun sinking away.

52.4   His wife, Frēdah, also called G'ēmīlah, daughter of Ibn Sharayyān ibn Hazīm, said, "Are you sure you want to go east? Wouldn't you prefer to stay in Syria?" She asked because he kept mentioning the flatlands of Jibbah and Gnā. She added, "May the plain of Gnā receive torrents of rain, but without us being there! What does it have to offer us? No more than '*ādhir* and '*algā* plants, whereas these mountains around us produce bananas and apples." He replied:

> May torrent upon torrent flood plains of Gnā:
> > '*algā* are roses and its '*ādhir* costly saffron.[236]
> Dunes crossed by dips, open to the Bedouin,
> > sprout euphorbia bushes like evergreen oaks.[237]
> Like smiling temptresses unraveling thick tresses:
> > a covering of hot weeds, sprinkled with chamomile.[238]

52.5   "Buy us some carpets!" she demanded. In those days, proper clothes were hard to come by. People went scantily clad. "Buy us some carpets to use as blankets to protect us against the cold of these icy, barren plains!" she demanded. "I have sent a message to someone to buy those for us," he assured her. They packed up and traveled, but after crossing the borders of Syria there was still no sign of the messenger he claimed to have sent. "Where are the carpets?" "Ahead of us," he said. They carried on until they set foot in Saudi territory: the villages of al-Nabk, al-Grayyāt, and other settlements of the northern border region. She said, "Now I begin to understand: you were not telling the truth when you said that you had dispatched someone to buy carpets for us." He replied:

> God is One! Plenty of carpets with our folks,
> > readied for us by God—no buying and selling!
> Such nice coverlets aren't brought and spread:
> > they can't be carried by camels well fed in spring.
> Lashed by razor-sharp blasts of northern gales,
> > lofty dunes, our hideout from those fanatics.[239]

—*Al-ʿikṣ* are the big sand dunes.

On arrival in his native land, he soon discovered that his tobacco   52.6
addiction landed him in trouble. In his absence, people of his old
homeland had converted to a religious lifestyle—some of them
members of his own group, others from different clans, but all of
them belonging to the Rmāl tribe. It occurred to him that he might
pay a visit to Hadhdhāl, who had been expulsed by a posse of fellow
tribesmen, one a relative of his, a quite close relative at that. He said:

> My home, sanctuary from telegraph and rail: 1
> I am not cut out to be a maker of bombs.

—*Dānāt* are bombs.

> Island of thirst, not ripped by torrents,
> unassailable to all riders of rugged camels:
> My winter abode, though I come barehanded;
> in fall too, nowhere a single soul in sight.
> Escaping riffraff, shirt hems smeared with shit,[240]
> blockheads wrapped about with pompous turbans,
> I put ten days of riding between me and them,   5
> marching at a grueling pace deep into the night.
> I was told about the brood of the old man Firsīn:
> evil-minded, he trots his white camel in the dark,

—Firsīn is Fāris al-Siṭam, the old man Hijhūj of his group. Perhaps
a relative of shaykh Hijhūj, who did not fall outside the *khamsah*,
fifth-degree relatives bound by the obligation of blood revenge. In
any case, he was one of the religious fanatics with a penchant for
administering bastinadoes on smokers of tobacco.

> Couching the beast halfway between two camps—
> it couldn't be farther apart from Ibn Mirdās.[241]

Ugh, God help you, conflicted by double ancestry,[242]
    while your father stands tall shielding the weak.
Toeing your mean mate's line, you lick up the dirt:
    a stealthy panther-sized cat slinking along a wall.[243]

—His mate was someone unrelated to the local people. He was an outsider, a religious fanatic. If he felt scruples about giving one of his kinsmen, his uncle, a thorough thrashing, he would wink at his mate who was not one of the local people and who had no compunctions about beating him up.

10   From Creation Day there were men and real men:
    the winner won by cowing people with people.

—Akhū al-Anwar, ʿAbd al-ʿAzīz, set people against people to attain his political objectives.

52.7   When ʿAbd al-ʿAzīz had become the new ruler of Ḥāyil, ʿAjlān sent a "camel"—that is, a poem—from his place of residence at Ibn Hadhdhāl's camp. At that time, the Ikhwān sowed dissension and wrought havoc in the area. They would spread all sorts of lies and cast aspersions on people who were in the habit of smoking. ʿAjlān sent these verses, a camel mount, so to speak:

1   Grasp the reins, Sēf, bring the camel al-Ṣiʿīd,
    racer from ancestry of well-preserved sperm!
Hooves shod with pads round as *majīdī* coins,
    trotting, panting like wolves in bursts of speed.

—Shaped like a *majīdī* means that its hoof pads were smooth and round as this coin.

Place the saddle and a small skin with no leaks;
    don't forget two cans of provisions for the road.

A mad-paced ostrich, she streaks across plains,
　　shoulders rocking, wings spread for balance,
Scared to death by bullets whizzing by,
　　stomach cramped though it escaped unscathed.
Head for Ibn Nhayyir and his friend of the Swēd:
　　their religious colony, the door slammed shut;

—Ibn Nhayyir and Frēḥ al-Ḥamzī al-Swēdī founded a religious colony, *hijrah*, at al-Tayyim. If a guest called on them, they would give him a beating. First, they would subject him to an examination of his religious tenets, and if he did not extricate himself from the ordeal to their satisfaction, they'd seize him and administer a severe beating. Even though he came to them as their guest! A guest is a guest from God: entertaining a guest hospitably is one of the mainstays of virtue.

Al-Ajfar, hoped-for farm of fields and palms—
　　earlier, the gazelles of al-Mhādī found it barren—
Excited by the murder of the sons of al-Fdēd—
　　Bedouin of Nāzil, how sorely they are missed—

—Nāzil ibn Thnayyān, the shaykh of the Zmēl, and al-Fdēd of the ʿAbdah were attacked and their sons murdered by Nidā ibn Nhayyir. That is how the Ikhwān were seeking admission to Paradise.

Awed by violent displays of Barjas and al-Fhēdī,
　　they seek Paradise by slaughtering their relatives.

—All of them are at al-Ḥfēr now. Barjas ibn ʿArdān Abū Dirzī belongs to the Salmān branch and al-Fhēdī to the Nimṣān. He is still alive today: he is in the company of al-Sudayrī, the governor of al-Jawf Province, in Uḍāriʿ. Kātib al-Ṣinkh is the name of Fhēdī.

Sweetly was Najd ruled as Ibn Rashīd's dominion!
　　Today, how pitiable! Nakedness dressed up in rags.

I headed for men whose old dresses are like new;
    reclining in comfort, I sing my nostalgic tunes.

—He means Hadhdhāl.

52.8   During his stay with Ibn Hadhdhāl, ʿAjlān composed these verses on the Ikhwān:

1   I'm waiting for a rider on a scrawny, jaded camel
    to tell me about my tribal land, news of events:
Are things, as one says, going smooth and nicely,
    or have the Ikhwān run amok, sowing wrack and ruin?
I marched for ten days and as many nights,
    without halting until the sun went down,
To spite the Ikhwān: worms, sons of worms!
    execrable rogues, may God cancel their youth!
5   Morning and evening busy plucking his mustache,
    upper lip smoothed, he appears with headband on.[244]
Shaykhs of Shammar! Your faces are blackened:
    your faults demolished guests' reception rooms.
Barjas is hunting for plunder in Nāzil's camp,
    slaughtering relatives to gain admission to Paradise.
I swear a sincere oath, as witnesses can confirm:
    this was unheard of among the Prophet's Companions.

52.9   Al-Wḥēr was in Mesopotamia when the verses reached him, and he replied:

1   Spot on, ʿAjlān, not one word off the mark:
    delicious verses made to refresh my mind.
Come to us for a life easier and trouble-free:
    no wanton murder, no snarling dogs at your throat,
Villains of Khatlān's kin or rabble of Silbūd,
    a hotchpotch of foreign twangs and dialects.

—Wasn't the new situation that Shammar tribesmen mixed with men of the Muṭayr and Ḥarb tribes as members of the Ikhwān? These spoke in different dialects. Khatlān and Silbūd were Ikhwān of Shammar.

> Wonderful was Najd in tribal give and take,
>> a refuge where one slept in peace undisturbed.
> Lusterless today, no shelter for the oppressed;
>> let no wayfarer count on hearing "Welcome!"
> I pray, let its soil turn into saltpeter for powder,
>> its rains into inflammable gas for combustion.

Khalaf al-Maẓhūr of the ʿLayyān clan pitched in with a response to both of them. They had made off after being raided by the Zghēbī of the Ḥarb tribe and troops of Ibn Saud, the Ikhwān. The attack occurred at Jildiyyah. Children of Ghaḍbān ibn Rmāl were killed, and his house was set on fire.[245] ʿGāb ibn ʿIjil fled as fast as he could, followed by large numbers of Shammar tribesmen. Under these circumstances, they composed the verses. We were blamed for staying where we were: the tribal sections of Swēd, ʿAmūd, al-Dghērāt. They were continuously harassed by al-Duwīsh and many others, the troops of Ibn Saud. Ibn Saud marched on us, pressing us hard. From al-Githāmiyyah, his onslaught reached al-Nīṣiyyah. We offered our submission. That did not stop al-Duwīsh from stealing twenty-five herds of camels, on that same day, just from the ʿLayyān clan. He came raiding from Yāṭib and drove the camels from Shṭēb Warkān, while fighting was going on at al-Jwēdiʿ and al-Nīṣiyyah. Khalaf al-Maẓhūr ibn Ghāzī said:

> Leave that, rider on a scrawny camel mount,
>> son of a distinguished she-camel, nobly born,
> Say camel experts, from Ṣlēʿ's flawless seed,
>> pedigree offspring of al-Lḥāwī's Sharārī stud;

—Ṣlēʿ is the stud camel of the mentioned pedigree.

> Zigzagging, it races like an ostrich being fired at,
>> frightened on seeing the attackers' vague shapes;
> Fitted out with saddle, bags, and colorful trappings,
>> graced with leather padding for the rider's feet.
> Brought to ʿAjlān by your rugged camel mount,
>> speak to him and talk about our vicissitudes:
> You made a run for it, not bearing the strain;
>> we stayed on, enduring what we had to endure.

5

As a Neighbor of Ibn Hadhdhāl, He Arbitrates between Him and the Jarbā on the Subject of Tribute

'Ajlān migrated with the Rmāl to the Rwalah, and from their tribal   53.1
land he continued to Syria, accompanied by 'Adwān ibn Rmāl, and
once in Syria he made his way to Ibn Hadhdhāl. He took up lodgings
with Fahd ibn Hadhdhāl, the father of Maḥrūt, and sojourned with
him a long time, three or four years, as his protected neighbor, and
married his daughter. Yes, 'Ajlān became a relative of the bey! He
was given the hand of the bey's daughter.

Al-Jarbā and Ibn Hadhdhāl quarreled about the right to levy trib-   53.2
ute from the tribes. The dispute started when 'Agīl al-Jāwar al-Jarbā
and Maḥrūt ibn Hadhdhāl each claimed the right to levy protection
money from both 'Anazah and Shammar. Al-Jarbā imposed trib-
utes on road traffic and salt miners: the transport of salt and other
commodities. That is to say, on those who were not members of his
tribe, Shammar. Hadhdhāl maintained that the tribute flowing into
al-Jarbā's coffers was his by right. Ibn Hadhdhāl lodged a complaint
with an Ottoman official, the governor of Baghdad. He argued his
case at the government's court: "We, the House of Hadhdhāl, rep-
resent the most ancient and deep-rooted noble lineage of the Bed-
ouin Arabs, which entitles us to impose tribute on the Bedouin, on
anyone coming from Najd." The official said, "As long as the Bed-
ouin recognize your right to do so, it is fine with us."

They sent for ʿAgīl al-Jāwar al-Jarbā. He duly came and was told, "We want you to recognize that Ibn Hadhdhāl has the most senior rights and that in earlier days he imposed tribute on you." ʿAgīl said, "Not at all! Ibn Hadhdhāl does not collect any tribute from us! Ever since we made our home in al-Jazīrah, it is I, ʿAgīl al-Jāwar, who take tribute from all comers. We impose it on anyone who for whatever reason crosses the borders of my tribal land: from the moment they set foot within my borders, be they from Shammar or ʿAnazah. Ibn Hadhdhāl's case is very different. If someone from Shammar enters his territory, that person does not owe him anything. He may demand tribute from ʿAnazah only. But Shammar—no! As for myself, within the borders of my land in al-Jazīrah I am entitled to collect tribute from ʿAnazah and Shammar tribesmen. But he has no right to levy anything on Shammar, only on ʿAnazah." Hadhdhāl protested: "What makes you think that you can lay claim to a higher rank in the tribal pecking order?" Al-Jarbā said, "Well, these are old customs rooted in events that happened over a long time." They argued and clashed.

The official said, "The only solution, as we see it, is for you to look for someone to assist you in finding a way out of this controversy. You must choose an arbitrator!" And he continued: "Make your choice, Ibn Hadhdhāl!" Ibn Hadhdhāl said, "As far as I am concerned, I'd look favorably on the choice of ʿAjlān because he is one of the Rmāl, and the Rmāl are renowned for having arbitrators with great expertise in judging matters of tribal law." It so happened that at that time ʿAjlān was staying with him as a neighbor under his protection. Ibn Hadhdhāl therefore reckoned that he would be well disposed toward his case. The official said, "And what about you, ʿAgīl?" ʿAgīl replied, "If Ibn Hadhdhāl has a preference for ʿAjlān, I have no objection. It's all right with me. I can go along. This man lives at your place. Bring him with you to pay us a visit!"

Pleased and gleeful, Ibn Hadhdhāl returned to al-Ṣēhad and told his father of his feat. Fahd ibn Hadhdhāl, the father of Maḥrūt, was blind. Maḥrūt's relatives from his mother's side were from the

Tūmān of Shammar. Triumphantly, Ibn Hadhdhāl painted the tableau of the discussion. However, his father sighed and said, "How I wish you did not try so hard to have this matter referred to ʿAjlān! ʿAjlān knows the history of the case, and what he knows invalidates your arguments. And do not believe that he will jeopardize his honor and credibility for your sake, even though he holds you dearer than half of all Shammar put together. He does not pursue such matters in ways that run counter to his conscience." His son said, "By God, it is too late for that now. I had the case assigned to him." His father said, "Son, go back and tell them that you found that he has left for Ḥāyil. Be quick—ask ʿAjlān to pack up and absent himself for a month or so. During that time, you might arrive at a solution, or if not, perhaps, God willing, another credible witness will take ʿAjlān's place." The son did not follow his father's advice. Instead, he went to see ʿAjlān and said, "Come, ʿAjlān, let's visit ʿAgīl al-Jāwar." Maḥrūt traveled there by car. Back then, automobiles were exceedingly rare. You'd only find them with people like shaykhs. Otherwise, there were no cars in those days. "ʿAjlān," he said, "I feel like going on a jaunt with you. The pasha has invited you. He agreed to see me on condition that I take you along. He wants the entertainment of your conversation, someone well versed in lore. Let's take this jaunt to Baghdad, as he proposed, then come back here." ʿAjlān did not demur: he had not been told what was up, that they had agreed to make him their arbiter.

On being informed that Maḥrūt and ʿAjlān had left, the bey, the old man, said, "Ah, how wonderful, the stories of ʿAjlān! I'll miss them dearly. Didn't all of them leave together?" "Yes," they said. "Mark my words, they will not return together. They will go their separate ways. Before the end of this month—it was the beginning of the month—ʿAjlān's tent will be pitched in the plain of Jubbah or at Umm Gilbān. When he feels aggrieved at Maḥrūt's action, he will be loath to stay here. Not that he will lodge with al-Jarbā or any other shaykh. Rather, he will return to the fold and make his peace with the Ikhwān. He is on the run from the Ikhwān, but after these events he will trace his steps back to them. He feels miserable about the situation, and so do I." These were the old man's words.

53.7   On their arrival in Baghdad, the tribal grandees were waiting, gathered in a large assembly. The Ottoman dignitary called for him to step forward: "'Ajlān!" "Yes," he said. "Look, Ibn Hadhdhāl and al-Jāwar are embroiled in a dispute and they chose you to disentangle them from it. Ibn Hadhdhāl wants recognition of his traditional right to levy tribute from the Bedouin, while al-Jāwar rejects his claims. All they agree on is that you are the right person to find an amicable solution." He said, "By God, I am not particularly knowledgeable about these matters. I'm an ordinary person who carries no special weight. I am not one of the wise elders of Shammar, let alone 'Anazah. I do not have the stature to be chosen for such a role. I'm just a little guy. I never played a part in such momentous issues." The official said, "No, you are the person on whom they have settled. We need your knowledge to extricate them from this imbroglio."

53.8   "By God," he said, "if they bury the hatchet, I will tell them. If one of them might resent what I submit and bear me a grudge, really, I'll just keep my mouth shut." "Honestly," they said, "the issue is buried." The opponents presented their arguments. Having listened to them, 'Ajlān said, "I have the key to a solution, but first they must put in writing and sign that they have given their consent and agreed. Each of them confirms in writing that once I have handed them the key to the solution, he pledges to accept it, without holding it against me in any way. That said, I have evidence I'd like to submit for your consideration. Hopefully it will rid them of their problem." They duly wrote and signed a pledge to abide by 'Ajlān's solution.

53.9   'Ajlān said, "One's good fortune is not like grass, something you cut and it grows again. I am careful not to give others, whether close relatives or outsiders, any say in my good fortune, in issues pertaining to my conscience. The shaykhs of al-Jarbā have levied tribute since the days of Fāris, and after him it was the same under Ṣfūg and 'Abd al-Karīm. As for you, Ibn Hadhdhāl, you have not crossed into al-Jazīrah. When you came to the shore of Shaṭṭ al-ʿArab, you kept to your side of the river. Not once did you make use of the river's crossings to go to the other side. It is correct, Ibn Hadhdhāl, that you collect tribute from ʿAnazah. As for Shammar, no, you do not have an established right to tax Shammar. On the other hand, al-Jarbā takes tribute from both tribes within the borders of his tribal land."

He buttressed his argument by reciting a poem. The outcome was that Ibn Hadhdhāl lost the case. The proof ʿAjlān adduced was a poem composed by al-Grēʿ, a tribesman of ʿAnazah. "Go ahead, recite it!" they invited him. He said, "May your life be long, Fāris al-Jarbā fought a pitched battle against them and imposed a tribute on them at Ghnēm," a place somewhere on the way to Tabūk. "Let us hear the poem of al-Grēʿ!" This is what al-Grēʿ said:[246]   53.10

> Drought! Strike hard at Khaybar's tribes:
>   not a single drop of rain for eight long years!
> Events at Ghnēm gave us no cause for joy:
>   once you've met disaster, food loses taste.
> Shammar threw their weight into battle,
>   seizing full-bodied she-camels and studs.
> Our shape of old dissolved at a stroke:
>   meat gone, knives cut deep and hit the bone.

Those in attendance said, "Isn't it true that al-Grēʿ hails from ʿAnazah, one of your own kin, Ibn Hadhdhāl?" "Yes," he admitted, "I am aware of it and the poem is well-known." The testimony of the verses recited by ʿAjlān resolved the issue for them. Next morning, Maḥrūt reached home, alone. "Hey, where is your companion?" "Well," he said, "he preferred to stay behind and do some shopping to buy household necessities." "How did things turn out?" "By God," he answered, "it went as you predicted, exactly as you said. God Almighty, he did not give short thrift to his luck, he followed the dictates of his conscience. His testimony was that of a righteous man. Only, at the conclusion of his testimony, he said something   53.11

that's been bothering me." "What is it, my son?" He said, "At the end of his exposé, when it transpired that al-Jarbā had won, someone asked me, 'Can you live with this outcome, Ibn Hadhdhāl?' I said, 'Yes, I accept it.' 'We ask especially,' the other said, 'because you were the one to propose him as witness and yet he dashed your expectations.' 'Yes,' I said. 'It reminds me of a verse I once heard:

> Falcon of Ibn Burmān, we brought you here,
>> why did you drop a snake on your master's head?'[247]

"My mind wandered. My recall failed me and I could not recite the entire poem. I fell silent. At that, 'Ajlān sought to comfort me: 'Do not get too worked up about it, Ibn Hadhdhāl. When five have passed, three remain.' My God, Father! From Baghdad until my arrival here I did not see the road I was traveling on for even one moment. I kept asking myself what he meant by the five and the three."

53.12   "Aaargh," said his father. "How could you fail to understand the point? And you are supposed to be a shaykh of shaykhs! Listen, my son, the five and the three are the years of al-Mhādī—al-Mhādī of Ghaṭān, who sought refuge from blood guilt with Shammar and for eight years showed exemplary forbearance in putting up with his neighbor's lapses:

> Eight years we overlooked a neighbor's sins,
>> covering them as women mend torn clothes.

"You were unable to bear with al-Mhādī's equanimity. We are considered a shaykh of shaykhs, but you did not let us treat Ibn Rmāl the way he deserves. Ibn Rmāl is such a wonderful person, and now you have robbed me of his company and conversation. I feel so wretched. I will miss him so much. How can I do without 'Ajlān and his stories!" The old man fell silent, relapsed in his gloom. Around the time of afternoon prayers, they noticed a silhouette moving in the distance. Was it him or someone else? He was told that it was indeed ʿAjlān. Next morning, the tent of ʿAjlān had been taken down and removed.

Fahd exclaimed, "Why did ʿAjlān break up camp? What is the matter with him? You, servant, go, go! Tell him: 'The shaykh wants to know why you are taking down your tent.'" ʿAjlān told the servant, "By God, on the day of my return, the women and children told me that the Bedouin had made up their mind to travel. Accordingly, I pulled down my tent, thinking that we'd travel." "No," the other said, "they are not going to travel!" He said, "Convey my greetings to the shaykh. In any case, I have taken down the tent and put our belongings on the pack camels, in keeping with the opinion expressed by the women and children. But I will move beyond that ridge there, and God willing they will come to me or we will visit. We are not far from one another." And he moved away.

The bey, the old man, said to Sēf, one of his men, "Sēf, my boy, take your camel and ride to ʿAjlān. Make it appear as if you are coming straight from the desert, unaware of what happened, and make sure to be close at hand when he locks his mare in iron at his tent. If, having shackled his horse, he goes on his way to the tent of al-Hadhdhāl, then God willing there is hope. When he lights a fire at his tent, sit down within hearing distance and be sure to prick up your ears. Perhaps, while preparing coffee, he will play a tune on his rebab. Who knows, he might recite some verses. Try to catch the words of his song. Perhaps it will set my mind at rest and allow me to get some sleep tonight." It is told—and we heard it from one of his sons who is an employee at Ṭrēf who came to see us there and treated us to the wonderful entertainment of ʿAjlān's poems and stories—that Sēf said, "When I had come and sat down with him, once he had shackled his mare while I was still at a little distance from him, I heard him tell his wife, 'At the twinkle of the morning star, a little before dawn, I do not want to see even one thread left lying here on our campground.' He was set on traveling. I watched him kindling a fire, then walked over to him and sat down. He prepared coffee, poured himself three cups, filled his pipe, and lit up.

53.15   "When he had finished smoking, he poured another two small cups. Thereupon, he reached for his rebab and sang:

> 1   It was my destiny, Sēf, to come to Baghdad,
>   decreed by His Almighty Majesty's wisdom.
>   Woe is me, tears stream as if from leaky skins:
>   telling my eye, 'Hold!' made it gush ever more.
>   My pounding heart thwarted attempts at sleep;
>   'No! No!' said my eyes as soon as I dozed off.
>   Listen, Sēf! To pack up is wrath's antidote.
>   Travel, rejoice at vast lands, at distant horizons!
> 5   Mere thought of drink and food revolts:
>   staying on as someone unloved is wrong.
>   Sleep, my eye, rest! Noblemen did so before:
>   on foot, one after the other, humbly they went."

53.16   When Sēf had repeated these verses to his master, the old man said, "The case is lost. At first light tomorrow, betake yourself to our Bedouin and have a look around." They were at some distance and the camp of their neighbors was not visible from where they were. They went, came back, and reported, "By God, ʿAjlān is gone." The old man cried out with grief: "Three long days I had to make do without the stories of ʿAjlān. I fear that he'll be robbed on his way before he reaches the tribal lands of Shammar. Once he crosses the border with Saudi Arabia, he'll be safe in the embrace of Shammar and firm government control. It is a different story on the Iraqi side of the border: no authority whatsoever."[248]

53.17   He called his son. Maḥrūt's tent was pitched at a little remove and at times he was still asleep at sunrise. "Maḥrūt! Maḥrūt! Get up quick! Call our men, jump on your horses, and take along camels loaded with large waterskins! I want you to accompany ʿAjlān until you have safely delivered him to Shammar territory. We must make sure he is not robbed on his way back home." They did as they were told, and on reaching the well of Līnah, ʿAjlān said, "Far enough. You can turn back."

Visit to the New Saudi Governor, Ibn Musāʿid

He continued on his journey until he arrived at Umm al-Gilbān, as mentioned, in the low area at the residence of al-Gfēʿī. When he took up his lodgings at Umm al-Gilbān, Ghaḍbān was not present. He was off to Riyadh. ʿAjlān issued an appeal: "Anyone willing to accompany me? I wish to go and pay my respects to Ibn Musāʿid." But they said, "By God, we have no intention of seeing Ibn Musāʿid. There is no one to take you there." He went accompanied by Ḍāfī ibn Ḍabʿān, a cousin. ʿAjlān and Ḍabʿān were sons of Barghash. The son of Ḍabʿān went with his uncle, holding him by the hand, leading him.

54.1

His appearance at the palace gate was announced to Ibn Musāʿid: "ʿAjlān ibn Rmāl wishes to present his respects, may your life be long." "Let him come in," he said. ʿAjlān was ushered in. After the greetings, Ibn Musāʿid said, "So you came after all, ʿAjlān?" Hadn't he made it known in his verses that he had no desire to set foot in Najd again?

54.2

He said:

54.3

Prince, I came to you a chastened man,
longing for soft sands and my grove of palms.

—He means to say, "First, I used to have regard for the Rashīd. Now the Rashīd have abdicated and are like children with their new father."[249] He owned date palms at Umm al-Gilbān.

> Prince, didn't you see lost camel calves,
>> innocent, distraught, clear to every eye?

—The youngsters of the Rashīd family were taken away, all of them. Their fratricidal fathers had assassinated one another. The adolescents were taken to Riyadh.

> What to expect from bullies in baggy coats,
>> beating me with a stick if my daughters sing.

—He refers to the new breed who donned pompous turbans and ostensibly devoted their life to religious practice.

54.4   Ibn Musāʿid said, "Your daughters should be left alone. And put aside your concerns: those calves, the youngsters, are now lodged with their father, treated with respect, and looked after with the greatest care.[250] True, we have no fondness for song and verse, but your exceptional poems always pique our curiosity." But ʿAjlān was in no mood to recite poems to Ibn Musāʿid. Instead, he said, "Father of ʿAbdallah, I came from a paradise on earth. I mean, were I to seek a paradise on earth, I couldn't find a better spot than where I came from. Honestly, I have come as someone who turns his face to the House of God, a remorseful penitent bowing to his Lord. These verses of mine should be understood, however, as a plea to grant me your protection against those who pretend to be devout, whereas in fact they are not true men of religion in any sense. And by now the gates of poetry have slammed shut."

54.5   Ibn Musāʿid said, "Tell me, have you grown old, ʿAjlān?" "Yes," he said, "it is true, I am advanced in years." "What is your age?" "Honestly, I do not know. We kept no records, but if I try to remember the number of years that went by, then, Prince, yes indeed, they are quite a few." "How old were you when we killed ʿAjlān?" he said, referring to ʿAjlān, the representative of al-Rashīd in Riyadh, who was assaulted by ʿAbd al-ʿAzīz and ʿAbdallah ibn Jluwī and killed. "How old were you when we killed your namesake, ʿAjlān?"

"No, no. I am just old!"

Notes

1   "Promised meal" (*idbah*): "food given as payment to laborers." In the
    Arabic edition, the first hemistich of the second verse is missing. It
    was recited to me by an informant in Ḥā'il who was told by old trans-
    mitters that these verses were not addressed to Ibn Saʿūd but to Ibn
    ʿUrayʿir in al-Aḥsā'.

2   If he died in 1942, he must have lived till he was 106. According to
    one editor of his poetry, he lived from 1844 to 1942 (al-Ẓafīrī, *Dīwān
    al-shāʿir Abū Zuwayyid*).

3   The scene repeats itself on the return of ʿAjlān ibn Rmāl from self-
    imposed exile in the Syrian desert, see §54.

4   Lit. "may your tongue be sound!" (*ṣaḥḥ lsānik*).

5   Ibn Rakhīṣ is the family name of the shaykhs of the Nabhān, the clan
    to which Abū Zwayyid belonged. Here and elsewhere, the name Ibn
    Rakhīṣ refers to the shaykh himself.

6   "Always came out the winner": *mā yiflaj hū*, lit. "he is not ruled the
    loser in a court case"; i.e., his arguments are so cogent that tribal arbi-
    ters always rule in his favor. From *falaj*, "to win a dispute submitted
    to a judge."

7   According to Bedouin customary law, a raider who first touched a
    camel with his lance acquired title to claim it as his spoil. However,
    a raid leader (*ʿagīd*) had a mandate to divide the booty among his
    fellows (*ʿazl*).

8   Explained as "your good luck, *ḥazzik*, must be earned, otherwise one may receive blame, *dhamm*."

9   Lit. "if leaving the well after drinking (*taṣdīr*; i.e., acting upon the counsel) were like heading toward the well (*wird*; i.e., taking the advice)." "Save the day": lit. "there would be no need for a medical doctor (*ṭibīb*)."

10   "Young wolves": *niḍāyiḍ dhīb*; *niḍīd*, explained as a synonym of *silīl* (pl. *salāyil*), "offspring"; *niḍā*, "to bring out (the best), produce."

11   "Slouched against the side": *yathwī bi-ṭarg al-bēt*; *ṭarg*, explained as "the place at the side of a tent, under the overhang of the tent cloth."

12   "Take it!": his nickname was Abū Khdhūh, because whenever a visitor came to ask for something, he would say, "*Khdhūh*": "Take it!"; i.e., from his possessions.

13   The reference seems to be to al-Hādī, a son of al-ʿĀṣī, "the rebel," shaykh of the Shammar tribe in Iraq, so called because he refused to cooperate with the Ottoman-Turkish overlords and left it to relatives to deal with them. In 1905, al-Hādi was killed in the course of internecine strife. Al-ʿĀṣī passed away in 1925.

14   It is not clear how this reference relates to the transmitter's assertion that the verses are part of a poem dedicated to al-Hādī al-Jarbā.

15   "Spurred by a falcon": i.e., the poem's subject of praise who charges at these tough warriors.

16   The first hemistich is missing.

17   In this composition, perhaps the poet's best known, the staccato repetition of *ḥamrā*, "reddish-brown (she-camel)," is one of Abū Zwayyid's quirks. The preference for a red steed remains strong: the Bedouin of today favor red GMC trucks. The vocative at the outset of the verse, *yā-rākib* (pronounced with affricated *kāf*, *rāċib*), is the customary address to a rider on camelback ready to carry the poet's verses to its destination. As shown in verse 6, the Shammar consider the Nafūd Desert the northern border of Najd, while Ḥāʾil is part of northern Najd.

18   "Daughter of a legend": Turkiyyah ibn Mhēd.

19   Generally understood as a reference to Muḥammad ibn Rashīd, the most powerful ruler of the Ibn Rashīd dynasty, who was rumored to be sterile.

20   This verse infuriated Ibn Rashīd and made him swear to kill Abū Zwayyid; see §10.1.

21   "Rabid monster": *shīb, shībah*, "mythical wolflike animal" (HA).

22   Also the name given to their herds of camels, especially the white ones (Musil, *Rwala*, 262, 420, 550); e.g., in the battle cry "I am the rider protecting ʿAlyā (camels)" (ibid., 526).

23   As the member of an "enemy tribe," he would need Ibn Rashīd's protection to pasture his camels in the tribal area of Shammar.

24   "Fifth degree": *khamsah*, "five," the group of blood relatives to the fifth degree on whom it is incumbent to exact blood revenge if one of their members is murdered.

25   *Ḍēgham* (CA *ḍaygham*, "lion") is the ancient ancestor and the collective rallying cry (*ʿizwah*) of ʿAbdah, to which the Jʿafar section of Ibn Rashīd belongs. Al-Ḍayāghim are the subject of a cycle of stories and verse in the style of the more famous epos of Banū Hilāl (for an Arabic text of recorded oral traditions of al-Ḍayāghim and Banū Hilāl, see Sowayan, *Ayyām al-ʿarab*, 1025–60).

26   A reference to a goat destined for slaughter that dug up the knife that had fallen and disappeared in the dust. Akin to the phrase "give them enough rope to hang themselves," here it is used by the poet to blame himself for not staying longer with Ibn Shaʿlān (al-Suwaydāʾ, *Shuʿarāʾ al-jabal al-shaʿbiyyūn*, 2:104).

27   This translation is based on communications from Saad Sowayan.

28   ʿGēl (ʿUqayl) is the name for camel traders who mostly hail from the Qaṣīm area. "When the ʿAgejl come to the Shammar they employ many servants and herdsmen. Sometimes they put up their own tents, but not unfrequently they lodge under the tent of some Bedouin" (Musil, *Northern Neǧd*, 135–36).

29   "Futile altercations": *hāt al-līf, ʿadd al-līf*, lit. "give the twig, away with the twig"; similar in meaning to *waddūhā w-hātūhā*, "send it

and bring it back"; i.e., "they talked it up and down, back and forth" (Stewart, *Texts in Sinai Bedouin Law*, 2:8).

30 "Gainsayers": *al-jaḥādah*, frequently used in the Qur'an in reference to people who deny the truth of the revelation. The first hemistich is a frequently used opening formula (see, e.g., Kurpershoek, *Arabian Romantic*, 143).

31 As explained, "they run to the right and the left because of exuberance; they only walk straight if they are fatigued."

32 That is, Fate. Cf. "What the dark nights carry in their bellies is unknown, inseminated at dusk, giving birth at dawn" (Kurpershoek, *Arabian Satire*, 89).

33 Saad Sowayan explains that "Only noble men of good means could light a fire to entertain guests and serve them food and coffee."

34 "Damascus goats": *zgēmiyyāt*, explained as "inferior breed of sheep, with an ugly mouth and appearance, and of little use."

35 In his febrile state of mind, ʿAjlān fears that some ill-intentioned men of the Rwalah will circumvent the rules concerning the sanctity of visitors and guests by employing one of his fellow tribesmen of Shammar for the purpose of robbing him.

36 "Didn't I tell you": *ṣādat*, lit. "it hit, caught the game"; i.e., "it happened, my fears came true."

37 As Sowayan explained, when thirsty camel herds converge on a well at the same time and the herders are in a hurry, the well ropes might get entangled, sparking off violent altercations.

38 A battle cry.

39 The stormy relation between Saṭṭām ibn Shaʿlān and Turkiyyah is told by Alois Musil, who made a prolonged stay in the tribe's camp (*Rwala*, 58, 558–59, 593–603).

40 Manhūbah means "snatched away, robbed."

41 Rulers often employed slaves for important and sensitive tasks. Some home-born slaves were accounted slave brothers of the Ibn Rashīd (Doughty, *Arabia Deserta*, 1:655).

42 The scene is reminiscent of Doughty's description of how he found Hirfa, the runaway young wife of Zeyd, a shaykh of the Fgarā tribe

with whom he was staying, herself the orphan daughter of a shaykh, when he was asked to persuade her to return: "I found Hirfa, a little shame-faced, sitting in the midst of her gossips; old wife-folk that had been friends of her dead mother; they were come together to the aunt's booth to comfort her, and there were the young men her cousins" (*Arabia Deserta*, 277).

43 "You piece of dirt": *ya-thiman al-milḥ*, lit. "the price of salt"; i.e., payment for the purchase of a slave.

44 "I will make you go willy-nilly": *tamshīn w-antī mā tshūfīn al-jāddah*, lit. "you will walk without looking at the path," as in the saying *'alēk b-al-jāddah law ṭālah*, "you have to stick to the prescribed path, no matter how long it takes" (al-Suwaydā', *Amthāl*, 292).

45 "Twist the promise into your mustache": *iftilhin bi-shārbik*; i.e., "give me a solemn promise."

46 "Don't play such risky games": *la tgaṭṭi' al-juwwād*, lit. "do not cut the trails, no shortcuts please"; i.e., "play it straight."

47 *Khaḍīrī*: "someone who does not belong to a known tribe and therefore is not considered eligible to be married to a tribal woman"; in this sense, the term is slightly demeaning (communication from Saad Sowayan). As a blacksmith, a low status occupation, 'Ajab would have fallen within this category.

48 The ladies are compared to thoroughbred horses of the Prophet's companions. Therefore, *ajwāz* ("pairs") probably means that the two forelegs hit the ground at the same time during a spirited gallop.

49 This is Turkiyyah, daughter of Ibn Mhēd.

50 A free translation of a hemistich that many informants were at a loss to explain. The most plausible explanation was, lit., spearheads (*ṣufr*, "yellow, bronze") mounted on shafts (*'ūd*, "branch, twig, shaft") and fire fueled by kerosene (*gāz*); i.e., in battle he is a lethal opponent and a fireball.

51 "Dearer to me than I am to than myself": *yā ba'ad ḥayy*, lit. "may you still be alive (after I and others have passed away)," a Shammar expression of endearment.

52 "I did a lot of work": *ana yābsin rīgī*, lit. "my spittle has dried up."

53   "Pleasure of conversation": *yta'allil*. More than just chatting, it refers to artful storytelling and declamation of poetry that interests and entertains an audience.

54   "Vexed": *ṭāmiḥ*, "a wife thus parted from her husband, but not regularly divorced, is called *ṭāmiḥi*: of this class there are great numbers."

55   "Go ahead": *midd w-ifliḥ*, another way of saying *tifaḍḍal, gil*, "please go ahead, speak!" *Ifliḥ* is also said when inviting someone to start eating (al-Suwaydāʾ, *Amthāl*, 570).

56   "Smooth, rounded": *mithl ash-shuwāshā*, "like Maria Theresa thalers" (sg. *shūshī*); "Maria Theresa dollars, in Arabia are called *riyāl abū shūshe*, in reference to the Empress's being represented on them with her hair brushed up in front" (Musil, *Northern Neǧd*, 3–4); *shūshah* commonly means "bun, tuft" of hair, by analogy with "all that part of a shrub that is above the ground" (Mandaville, *Bedouin Ethnobotany*, 162; similarly, Lane, *Manners and Customs of the Modern Egyptians*, 29).

57   The rider calms the camel by gently touching it with his feet.

58   *Dibdūb*, pl. *dibādīb*: "thick ornamental tufts made of wool of about twenty-five centimeters length tied to the back, behind or in front of the hump as a sign that the she-camel is of exceptional quality and marked for the procreation of similar high-end camels" (HA, 7575). An "ornamented white she-camel" (*waḍḥā umm dibdūb*) refers to an exceptionally beautiful woman (al-Suwaydāʾ, *Amthāl*, 533).

59   "Supple-necked": *khuḍʿ l-argāb*, lit., "necks held low, bowed," a standard expression of praise for camels, but applied to people it denotes submission.

60   The verse echoes a similar compliment paid to Saṭṭām ibn Shaʿlān; see §4.1.

61   This piece is composed with a single end rhyme instead of the more common separate rhymes for each hemistich.

62   "Shame on me": *allāh yilūm lḥiyyitī*, lit. "God blames my beard," similar to the saying "spit two gobs on my beard" (*tiff ʿalā liḥyitī tiffen*), an expression of regret (al-Suwaydāʾ, *Amthāl*, 90).

63 When Ibn Rakhīṣ befriended Ibn Rashīd, chief of the Nabhān, he declared his independence from Ibn Thnayyān, the paramount chief of the Zmēl branch of the Sinjārah division of Shammar. Disaffection between Āl Ḍaww and Ibn Rakhīṣ caused Ibn Rakhīṣ to join the Saudi Ikhwān against Āl Ḍaww (for the full story, see Sowayan, *Ayyām al-ʿarab*, 550–58; there is a shorter version, including Abū Zwayyid's poem, in *al-Ṣaḥrāʾ al-ʿarabiyyah*, 544–47).

64 "He doesn't have to prove anything": lit. "with a blind hand" (CA *makfūf*, "blind"); as explained by Sowayan, "someone higher told him not to do this or that."

65 "Folk of al-Jrāf": *al-jrāf* is the name of the camel markings originally common to all of the Nabhān of the Zmēl of Shammar (Sowayan, *Ayyām al-ʿarab*, 535). As I was informed by Musāʿid ibn Fahd al-Saʿdūnī, the author of *Camel Brandmarks of the Arabian Peninsula, Sedentary and Bedouin* (*Wusūm al-ibl fī al-Jazīrat al-ʿArabiyyah (bādiyah wa-ḥāḍirah)*), *al-jarfah* (pl. *jrifāt, jrāf*) is a tribal marking carved with a knife or sharp object into the skin of a camel—in the thigh, neck, cheek, or any other place—unlike the more usual *wasm*, which is branded into the skin with a red-hot iron. Several other Shammar tribes use the *jarfah* instead of a branded *wasm*.

66 Bedouin will not respect the right to asylum of any individual before he has restored "goods stolen or treacherously obtained," something his tribe should force him to do or expel him from their encampment (Burckhardt, *Notes*, 328).

67 To boast of pasturing in or close to enemy lands is a common trope.

68 "Impeccable Hearts": a moniker of Ibn Hadhdhāl, lit. "Brothers of Batlā, Hearts of Cranes"; *gharānīǧ*, sg. *ghirnūg*, "long-necked aquatic bird; comely youth." Nicknames in the same style are *azwāl aḍ-ḍbāʿ glūb as-sbāʿ*, "appearance of hyenas, hearts of lions," for the Rwalah tribe; *dhabbāḥat al-ḥāyil, naṭṭāḥat al-ʿāyil*, "slaughterers of fat camels, nemesis of aggressors," for all of Shammar.

69 The reference is to al-Ṭimyāt, the paramount shaykh of the Tūmān, one of the four main divisions of Shammar, and the father-in-law of

Ṭārif ibn Shaʿlān. The poet asserts that al-Ṭimyāt will protect Abū Zwayyid from Ibn Shaʿlān.

70   "A mercenary soldier of Eben Rashīd was called *zgurtī*. Prince Muḥammad had kept over four hundred such mercenaries, but the prince at the time of our expedition [1915] kept hardly sixty" (Musil, *Northern Neǧd*, 143); *zgirt*, sg. *zgirtī*, "small trader; irregular troops of ʿGēl [CA ʿUqayl] in Medina" (HA, 4508). Also, *rijājīl*, the men of Ibn Rashīd's bodyguard or private army who are always in attendance at his court, are sent on errands and perform other tasks at a sign of their master (al-Suwaydāʾ, *Manṭiqat Ḥāʾil*, 566).

71   Booty represented a significant share of state income. Muḥammad ibn Rashīd claimed half of the captured horses, one-fifth of the other animals, and all arms, which were partly redistributed among his private army (al-Suwaydāʾ, *Manṭiqat Ḥāʾil*, 543).

72   The scene has been vividly portrayed by European travelers. See, e.g., Palgrave, *Narrative*, 72–73, 97, and, from the poet's time, Blunt, *A Pilgrimage to Nejd*, 217–18.

73   "Slaughtered at one's interment": *hbāṭah*, "sacrificial animal, a sheep or a goat" (HA, 4108).

74   Poetic self-correction is a trope with a long pedigree. Ibn Mayyādah (d. 754 or 766) saved himself on being confronted by women whose private parts he had insulted as "traces left by little lambs" by asserting that in reality he said, not *ka-āthāri l-ṣighār min al-bahmī* but *ka-athāri l-muqaysirati al-duhmī*, "traces left by dark, mature she-camels" (al-Iṣfahānī, *al-Aghānī*, 2:315–16, 3:159).

75   See Introduction, xix.

76   His eyes are turned to the side of the head, like a locust's eyes; *ḥawal*, "walleyed, squinting" (CA *aḥwal*).

77   "Charcoal burner," *faḥḥām*, was considered one of the lowliest jobs, reserved for poor people of humble descent.

78   The poet offers a double plea. He reminds Ibn Rashīd that his father was sheltered from his enemies by the poet's tribal relatives, and he argues that according to the rules of Islam and custom, he is a "milk

brother" of the ruler, since the latter had been breastfed by the poet's mother.

79   Cutting off a prisoner's lock is an age-old custom. Like Ibn Rashīd, Miṭlag ibn Jibrīn, the shaykh of the Mufaḍḍal tribe of the ʿAbdah of Shammar, spared the life of an enemy whom he had sworn to kill and celebrate by slaughtering a camel (*jizūr*), and instead took a knife and cut off a lock of his enemy's hair, saying, "I have forgiven you for the sake of God" (*ʿafēt ʿank li-wajh Allah*).

80   The Arabic letter *jīm* ح has a bulge. The camel brand called *kaffah* ("scale of a balance") is a circle on top of a cross on the animal's right thigh (al-Saʿdūnī, *Wusūm al-ibl*, 155). The crescent, *hlāl*, is one of the most common brands.

81   The second hemistich is a repetition of §9.3, v. 5, a poem with the same end rhyme.

82   The verses echo Ibn Sbayyil's praise for Muḥammad ibn Rashīd: "[trays] heaped with full-grown sheep, legs interlocked, like a shepherd's flock around the well"; "a word from his mouth unlocks the gates of largesse" (Kurpershoek, *Arabian Romantic*, 95).

83   The verse echoes the concluding line of Ḥmēdān al-Shwēʿir's poem of apologies to Ibn Muʿammar, in which he stops short of full surrender to preserve his independence and honor as a poet (Kurpershoek, *Arabian Satire*, 87).

84   The Ottoman State is meant. See the Introduction.

85   As the poet did on other occasions; see §10.3.

86   Sowayan cites this poem together with §9.3, v. 1 in the context of the internal struggles of the Nabhān of the Zmēl (*al-Ṣaḥrāʾ al-ʿarabiyyah*, 546–47). "Poisonous leaves": *rihwind*, explained as "a kind of clarified butter distilled from tree leaves in Iraq; it causes an unpleasant burning sensation in the belly, like that of *umm nār*, 'acid.'"

87   Sowayan comments: "He is talking to Muḥammad ibn Rashīd, blaming him for creating discord with the tribe and reminding him that the tribe would be forced to ally itself with Ḥāyil's enemies. The water bucket is a metaphor for the tribe of the poet."

88 Al-Jarādī: explained as Ibn Jarād, the army chief of Ibn ʿAlī, the ruling dynasty before Ibn Rashīd, who was hunting for ʿAbdallah ibn Rashīd, but took fright when he discovered that Ibn Rakhīṣ had thrown in his lot with Ibn Rashīd.

89 It was explained that the poet reminds (*yiminn*) Ibn Rashīd of past favors received from his kin. In general, *mann* is looked upon with disapproval (e.g., Q Ḥujurāt 49:17, *yamunnūna ʿalayka an aslamū*, "They consider it a favor to you that they have accepted Islam"). Reminding someone of favors received is reprehensible, but in this context it might simply be playful teasing.

90 "Hey": *khlāf dhā*, lit. "after, following that," synonym of CA *daʿ dhā*, "now leave that" (subject), a formula of transition. Perhaps the first section of verse has gone missing. Here the word for "she-camel" is *ʿadmiliyyah*, "peerless, unique"; *bindagin ʿadmiliyyah*, "tried trifle, an old rifle with which the marksman is so well acquainted that he never misses his aim" (Musil, *Rwala*, 225–26; CA *ʿadīm*: "being without"). It resembles the more usual *ʿimliyyah* (CA *ʿamliyyah*), "sturdy she-camel."

91 After four days on waterless pastures, the camels are led to water on the evening of the fourth day.

92 On finding the well crowded, riders and mounts return to the well whence they came and make do with foul-tasting remnants of water scooped up from the bottom.

93 "Ḍēgham": see n. 25.

94 They are driven by desire to pummel their enemies, not by lust of booty. Cf. ʿAntarah, "I enter the fray, then decline the spoils" (Montgomery, *War Songs: Antarah ibn Shaddād*, 11; al-Mufaḍḍal, *Dīwān al-Mufaḍḍaliyyāt*, 1:56).

95 "Swollen with fury": *ṭanā*, "rage, fury," refers to a moniker of Shammar tribesmen, *ṭanāyā*, "those swollen, red-faced with fury."

96 The Rashīdī war banner (*bērag*, CA *bayraq*) was bloodred, with the profession of faith stitched in gold thread. For about seventy years, from the rule of ʿAbdallah until ʿAbd al-ʿAzīz al-Mitʿib, this function was entrusted to a slave family, al-Frēkh (al-Suwaydāʿ, *Manṭiqat Ḥāʾil*, 449–52).

97 The first hemistich repeats the second hemistich of the preceding line. Saʿūd Abū Khashm was married to Nūrah, the daughter of Ḥmūd al-Sibhān. At the time, clansmen of the Sibhān were shoring up the crumbling power of Ibn Rashīd.

98 "Three legs": *tarfā thalāthin bi-khiṭwah*, "(the mare) folds three legs together as she pushes off with one leg for the jump"; cf. the epithet "single-footed" for outstanding horses in *The Iliad*.

99 It is likely that they were riding in a southeasterly direction, across the empty al-Ḥamād plains toward the Nafūd, and possibly toward the wells of al-Ḥuzūl.

100 "Damned (camels)": *mākhūdhātkum* (CA *ma'khūdh*), lit. "may they (f. pl.) be taken, robbed"; *mākhūdh*, a rough, somewhat jocular expression, "that damned animal of yours."

101 "Lions": *ḍarāghīm*, an alternative form of *ḍayāghim*, sg. *ḍēgham*; see n. 25. The poet may have had in mind the decline of the Ibn Rashīd dynasty, which would date this piece to after the death of Muḥammad ibn Rashīd.

102 "Blazing plains": *shihb ar-rahārīh*; the color adjective *shihb*, f. pl. of *ashhab*, "gray, dust-colored," frequently occurs with a connotation of menace.

103 In the text, the next verse is exactly the same as v. 14 and has been omitted.

104 Either ʿAbd al-Karīm al-Jarbā or ʿAbd al-Karīm Qāsim. The two were known as *al-kharābtān*, "the two scourges."

105 "Raid leadership is a matter of good fortune and resoluteness. A lucky leader will always have followers desirous to share in his spoils. At that time, it was the belief that some people were blessed with luck." However, "good fortune also depended on one's devotion to upholding tribal customs and Bedouin values" (Sowayan, *al-Ṣahrāʾ al-ʿarabiyyah*, 660–63).

106 The narrator is remembering having heard so from his father, who personally took part in the raid.

107 "His story": this story, which the narrator heard from his father and tells as if his father is the person telling the narrative.

108   *Kurrāth*: a kind of tall, edible grass; a wild onion from twelve to thirty-three inches high (30–110 cm), with pale green leaves, *Allium sphaerocephalum* (Mandaville, *Bedouin Ethnobotany*, 305).

109   "Cunning master": Jifrān al-Maʿaklī, and see §14.1.

110   "End of bad luck": *ʿilm al-Jirdhān bi-sh-sharr*, explained as "the end of evil and the beginning of good things (*atlā athar*: the tail end of bad things); from that moment, the flow of news (*ʿilm*) about their bad luck had come to an end."

111   A Rwēlī is a member of the Rwalah tribe.

112   "Regal": *jīl bi-s-sūg*, lit. "(did not set foot) at the marketplace for a long time"; i.e., the animal is too grand to be put up for sale. "Drawing water": *darb al-maʿāḍib*, lit. "the path of hardship"; i.e., *al-masnā*: the ramp where camels pull up heavy buckets from the well. This is a metaphor for the "nobility" of mobile Bedouin life as compared to the drudgery of settled life at the oases.

113   "Flirter": *ṭimūḥ*, "woman dissatisfied with her husband and eager to attract the attentions of a better man."

114   "'Alya camels": *rāʿ al-ʿAlyā*, "owner of al-ʿAlyā (camels)," moniker for the camels of the Rwalah tribe and, by extension, members of the tribe itself. "Any sisters"; i.e., lines of poetry other than these verses.

115   On the fourth day, the droppings of this vanguard are dry enough to serve as fuel for the cooking fires of riders on lesser mounts. That is, these high-quality camels cover the same distance in a much shorter time than ordinary riding camels.

116   "As a venture of this kind is very dangerous, every commander must fix the special reward the spy is to get" (Musil, *Rwala*, 644); see Introduction, n. 23.

117   Likely eighty to ninety camels per herd (al-Musallam, *al-ʿUqaylāt*, 87).

118   Making clarified sheep butter (*gishdah*) is associated with the moneymaking activities of owners of sheep and goats (Sowayan, *al-Ṣahrāʾ al-ʿarabiyyah*, 380). A small white butterfly (*ṭēr dhōbah*) may land in the cream to spoil the process (al-Suwaydāʾ, *Min shuʿarāʾ al-jabal al-ʿāmiyyīn*; 3:68; HA, 5722). In Arabic poetry, avarice and

cowardliness, *bukhlun wa-jubnun*, go hand in hand (see, for example, al-Ḥakam ibn ʿAbdal in al-Iṣfahānī, *al-Aghānī*, 2:423); see Introduction, xxxvi.

119   "Mangy camel in a pen made of thorny bushes where those infected with smallpox are quarantined": *ajrab b-ʿinnat majdūr*, a standard expression for situations or persons one seeks to avoid (al-Suwaydāʾ, *Amthāl*, 10–11).

120   The second hemistich fits descriptions of the nose, which remains unmentioned. Other versions read *wa-l-khashm maṣgūl*: "the nose is a shiny sword" (al-Suwaydāʾ, *Min shuʿarāʾ*, 2:90; al-Ẓafīrī, *Dīwān al-shāʿir Abū Zuwayyid*, 180).

121   The calf drinks the milk of two she-camels and in consequence its hump is uncommonly big; cf. al-Dindān's verse: "Her hips bulge like the hump of a camel calf, pampered with the milk of two devoted foster mothers" (Kurpershoek, *Oral Poetry and Narratives from Central Arabia*, 1:149–51).

122   "Long-backed": *simḥūg*, pl. *samāḥīg*, "long, tall," said of people, trees, canes, spears (CA *sumḥūq*, "tall," said of a palm tree; ʿUbūdī, *Muʿjam al-uṣūl al-faṣīḥah li-l-alfāẓ al-dārijah*, 6:378–79).

123   The final verses (§17.6, vv. 11–13) heap ridicule on tightfisted owners of small cattle by way of contrast with "noble" camel Bedouin such as the poem's addressee, the shaykh of the Rmāl tribe. The two vignettes, one about a boy encouraged to go raiding, the other contrasting the noble Bedouin with grasping sheepherders, are in praise of the father of Khaznah al-Fiḍīl.

124   *Msās, mrā*: "good pasture" (CA *maraʾa*, "to be, become tasty"; in a prayer for rain, "bring us wholesome, fertilizing rain," *isqinā ghaythan marīʾan marīʿan*, Ibn Manẓūr, *Lisān al-ʿarab*, 4,166); the opposite of *wkhām* (CA *wukhām*), "bad grazing."

125   The collected product is called *wadyah*, pl. *widāyā*, as in the saying *wadyatuh bi-sgāh*, "butter collected in his skin," meaning that it is too early to tell what sort of person he is (al-Suwaydāʾ, *Amthāl*, 475). In poetry, it has a negative connotation; e.g., the famous Shammar poet Radhān ibn ʿAngā, "those who devote all their time measuring

their sheep's output" (*illī ygawwis wadyatuh kill ḥazzah*) (Sowayan, *al-Ṣahrā' al-ʿarabiyyah*, 380).

126 The first hemistich is missing. As explained, the miser is out of sorts (*miḥtās*, synonym of *balshān*, "stressed, afflicted"), confused and dazed (*ydāyikh*), because he lives in fear of being bothered by visitors.

127 Mkīdah is pronounced with affricated *kāf*, Mćīdah. Jamʿān al-Ghēthī, a member of the Ghyithah, a subtribe of the Yḥayā branch of the ʿAbdah division of Shammar.

128 *Yā baʿad ḥayyī w-mētī*: "you are dearer to me than all other living beings and those that have passed away together," an affectionate form of address to loved ones, relatives, spouses, friends (al-Suwaydā', *Amthāl*, 522).

129 "Strength": *gaww*, a robust Shammar greeting, and in reply, *yā-halā*, "welcome" (Musil, *Rwala*, 455), also used in Sinai (Stewart, *Texts in Sinai Bedouin Law*, Part 2, 17).

130 "Like this": *hā-l-lōn*; here the narrator must have made a movement with his hands to mimic the quiver.

131 *Misgīnan w-ḥājjin bī*: lit. "you have given me something to drink (a synecdoche for all that is pleasant and good) and you have taken me on a pilgrimage (an even bigger favor)."

132 "Couched": *sijūm*, explained as "alert and silent, as if she is fully aware of what is going on and mentally prepared" (CA *asjam*, "camel that does not roar," Ibn Manẓūr, *Lisān*, 1947). "Fidgets": *tihinwiṣ w-tajwīḏ*, explained as "she utters a bèbèbè-like sound and agitates her body"; *jāḏ*, "to be uneasy, squirm"; e.g., a sick person when being cauterized (al-Suwaydā', *Faṣīḥ al-ʿāmmī fī shamāl Najd*, 157).

133 *Tifāḏīḏ*: explained as "she does not *faḏḏ*, is not wayward when getting saddled, does not try to run off, and does not roar, foaming at the mouth and regurgitating half-digested food" (al-Suwaydā' *Min shuʿarā'*, 2:39).

134 Sowayan comments that "when clocks were first introduced to Arabia they were works of wonder, or works of the devil according to some." In 1883, Euting noted the presence of a standing clock in rococo style in the reception room of the Rashīdī prince and later the

successor of Muḥammad ibn Rashīd, ʿAbd al-ʿAzīz ibn Mitʿib (*Tage-buch*, 1:188).

135 According to tribal custom and predilection for first-cousin marriage, they had a rightful claim to the daughter of their uncle; see 19.6. "This reservation is called *jīrah*. If the girl does not accept marriage, the first cousin may abdicate from his right after some time. In rare cases, he will not lift his blockade and will prevent her from marrying another man" (HA, 2547).

136 "Brother of Mēthā" is a rallying cry of the poet's Ibn Rakhīṣ clan.

137 "Surahs": *Tabāraka w-ʿAmmā*, popular names for surahs Kingdom, Q 67, Sūrat al-Mulk and Tidings, Q 78, Sūrat al-Nabaʾ.

138 In this verse the cat-like tearing at the camel's flesh (*yanhash*) is explicitly ascribed to jinn. In classical poetry a cat is given this role: "The idea of a camel's speed being stimulated by having a cat, hirr, at her side, which attacks her with teeth and claws, is one which occurs in a number of passages in the ancient Arabic poetry" (al-Mufaḍḍal, *Dīwān al-Mufaḍḍaliyyāt*, 2:107, 155, 229). Lyall doubts the theory of Geyer that the male cat, hirr, is thought of as demonic, a form of the jinn. Compare §15.4, v. 3.

139 "Ages": *ċihhilin bi-l-jlūs*, "left unimpregnated, childless, for a long time"; i.e., very strong camels (CA *kahl*, pl. *kuhhal*, "middle-aged, man of mature age").

140 "Virgin meadows": *al-khaṭāyiṭ wa-l-agfār* (CA *qafr*, pl. *aqfār*); *khaṭīṭah* is an "isolated area of good grazing surrounded by dry vegetation that is of little use," so called if such a grazing patch is narrow and elongated (Mandaville, *Bedouin Ethnobotany*, 95).

141 Such verse still inspired an unruly late-twentieth-century Bedouin poet, Bandar ibn Surūr, who had replaced his camel with a truck. The vocabulary and phrasing remained unchanged, but the metaphor had overwhelmed the original meaning: "Chivalrous virtue takes undaunted stalwarts, takes what feckless oafs have not: resolve to cross vast deserts and dead emptiness, where cowardly sons of owls fall short."

142 The tough riders and mounts gain time by leaving aside some wells and heading for one farther down the road; see §12.1, vv. 3–4.

143 Similar to Ḥmēdān al-Shwēʿir's "coffee cup in his right hand, hubble-bubble in his left," the ideal state of *kēf* (CA *kayf*), sensual repose (*Arabian Satire*, §17:3).

144 Sowayan comments: "He is talking about an encounter between raiders and owners of the lifted herds, so *ragṭā* here expresses the multitude of raiders wearing different clothes and carrying different weapons."

145 That is, the Prophet Muḥammad.

146 Al-Suwaydāʾ believes these verses were inspired by the internecine struggles in the House of Rashīd that preceded its collapse (*Manṭiqat Ḥāʾil*, 706).

147 Possibly a reference to the internecine strife and murder that brought down the House of Ibn Rashīd.

148 *Taghazzaz lahā sūd*: "for them black (flags) were hoisted."

149 The latter part of the second hemistich is missing and is taken from al-Suwaydāʾ, *Shuʿarāʾ* 1:487.

150 ʿUbūdī, *Muʿjam al-uṣūl*, 11:389, attributes this poem to Khḍēr al-Ṣʿēlič.

151 "Islam": The poet refers to Sunni Islam. The "Unbelievers" are members of other religions, mostly local Christians or visitors from Europe. As the verse makes clear, members of the Shiʿah sect, mostly traders and pilgrims from Iraq and Persia, are seen as a separate group.

152 *Nlizzih lih ʿalā miltizāzih*; *yilizzih*: said of a dismounted warrior who hugs his horse's neck by way of farewell before a battle, in case the horse gets killed. Similarly, cavalrymen would embrace their comrades before charging the enemy, the "farewell greeting," *salām al-widāʿ* (al-Suwaydāʾ, *Manṭiqat Ḥāʾil*, 492).

153 Accepting payment of blood money instead of extracting revenge is regarded as weakness in the tribal view; *gaṭʿ*, "cutting of throats," if the aim is not booty but revenge (Sowayan, "Customary Law").

154 These lines of gnomic wisdom bear no obvious relation to the other verses or to each other. Perhaps they are the remainder of a lost section. This might be an analogue to "aiming to ferret out secrets of our private affairs," something not be done "in pitch-dark, moonless nights"—that is, when one might be caught unawares.

155   The falcons are of the lesser sort, useless for hunting. When called, they do not return to the hunter but instead try to hide in *shīḥ*, a shrublet (*Artemisia*), which happens to fit the end rhyme.

156   The saying goes *al-gḍā midhallah*, "going to court is a sign of weakness."

157   The implication is that S'ūd Abū Khashm was a commander not less capable than his father, 'Abd al-'Azīz, and uncle Muḥammad ibn Rashīd. In fact, S'ūd's court was in parlous state.

158   The reference is to the Ibn Rashīd prince.

159   "Two good fortunes": *as-sa'dēn mā ytarākabin*, a standard expression; i.e., "one side can be fortunate only at the expense of the other."

160   It is not specified here, but earlier 'Āmish was mentioned as one of the sons of Abū Zwayyid (§1.3). Given Abū Zwayyid's advanced age at this point, his son was more likely to make use of the rifles.

161   'Uṣmalī: "Ottoman," from *'uthmānlī* (HA, 6389); here it refers to a version of the Martini rifle produced by the Ottoman Turks, known locally as Umm Khams, "Mother of Five" (bullets), sent to S'ūd Abū Khashm and first used in the battle of al-Jrāb in 1915.

162   Abū Mish'al is S'ūd Abū Khashm.

163   The enemy is ridiculed because usually "the hareem (women) come riding in their train of baggage camels," while "the sheykhs are riding together in advance," called the *salaf* (Doughty, *Arabia Deserta*, 1:261).

164   *Mirti'ah*, here "weaklings," are Bedouin who pay for the right to graze in another tribe's territory; payment of *rtā'ah* is considered a symbol of weakness. "Poets frequently boast of the strength of their tribes, claiming that they graze their herds wherever there is pasture available without paying" (Sowayan, "Customary Law").

165   His maternal relatives were the Sibhān family, who acted as regents while the prince was still a minor.

166   Mūḍī's brothers: S'ūd's regents and the powers behind his throne (al-Suwaydā', *Manṭiqat Ḥā'il*, 436, 513–14).

167   "Slaves": *'abīd*; these are *al-rijājīl*, the personal troops and bodyguards of Ibn Rashīd.

168   Abū Zayd, the legendary hero of the saga of the westward migration of Banū Hilāl.

169   "Strike sparks": i.e., without it he cannot be creative and sing your praises. "Free me from the debt": lit., "Give me a pass [*bāṣ*] (that sets me free) from the debt." *Bāṣ* originally means passport. Here it probably refers to anything that allows him to get by and pay the debt.

170   "Shaṭṭ": *jāri as-sīb*, lit. "vague line seen at the horizon"; i.e., the confluence of Euphrates and Tigris rivers, known as Shaṭṭ al-Arab, as it appears from afar to camel riders coming from the higher desert ground to the river's southwest; see also §49.15, v. 10. Al-Khurmah is a town at the southwestern end of Najd; Kandahar is in Afghanistan.

171   «Arrogant recalcitrants»: *taḥānīb*, lit. "showing a curved back like an angry cat" (CA *taḥnīb*, "crookedness, curving shape").

172   The conceit is that guests are the hosts (*ma'āzīb*, sg. *m'azzib*), since they are told: "you are *rabb al-manzil*, owner of this house." The rains of late fall and early winter (*dalw*, leather bucket; i.e., the constellation of the Pleiades, so called because it catches "water in a large bailing bucket and then pours it over the scorched land," Musil, *Rwala*, 226) did not come to irrigate the grass seeds (*bdhārih*).

173   The tribes were allowed to stay on their lands as the ruler's subjects as long as they paid zakat to Ibn Rashīd.

174   But in his poem in praise of Saṭṭām ibn Sha'lān, the chief of the Rwalah tribe, Abū Zwayyid alluded to the fact that Muḥammad ibn Rashīd remained childless because of sterility.

175   Another instance of this popular hyperbole (see §4.1, v. 13, §27.5, v. 41). It is a rejoinder to Abū Zwayyid's claim that women had never given birth to the like of Saṭṭām ibn Sha'lān, a verse that was particularly irksome to Ibn Rashīd.

176   In late spring and early summer, some nomads used to live in a hut made of palm leaves, *yṣayyir*; also said of a hard-up Bedouin, *ḥaththāl*, forced to make a living in settled country, *yḥathil* (Sowayan, *al-Ṣaḥrā' al-'arabiyyah*, 351).

177   The number of tents with seven poles, such as those owned by paramount shaykhs, is estimated at not more than 2 or 3 percent of all Bedouin tents (al-Suwaydā', *Manṭiqat Ḥā'il*, 583). It might be a

legendary touch given by narrators, as al-Hirbīd did not belong to this class.

178   "Forgiveness": *yaṭlibk al-ḥill*; i.e., *al-bayḥah*, "he asks your forgiveness," an expression used on learning of someone's death, to which the response is *allāh yibīḥ fīh* or *minh*, "may God grant him forgiveness."

179   "Servants' heads": *rūs khiddām*; the Bedouin used to have black slaves, to whom the poet compares the slabs of stone blackened by fire.

180   "Plague": *awhām*, sg. *waham*, "cholera" (al-Suwaydā', *Manṭiqat Ḥā'il*, 657).

181   "Our luck remains prostrate": luck, good or bad, is often portrayed in terms related to the movements of a camel.

182   *Nērāt*: "a gold guinea; originally *līrah*, the *lām* changed into *nūn*" ('Ubūdī, *Mu'jam al-tijārah wa-l-māl wa-l-faqr wa-l-ghinā*, 357).

183   "Hearthstones": *ath-thalāth as-sūd*, lit. "the three black ones"; i.e., the three stones that support the cooking pot, a conventional attribute of the deserted camp scene.

184   A polite interpolation of the narrator, addressed to his audience during recording.

185   *Hāmmah*: "forceful," "a very strong person, camel"; originally "a big, aggressive snake."

186   If the leading she-gazelle is dead, the other gazelles are lost and an easy prey.

187   *Si'būb*, pl. *sa'ābīb*: "saliva that hangs from the mouth in thin threads (also said of cows)," used for a slouch and good-for-nothing (al-Suwaydā', *Faṣīḥ*).

188   The riddle is about locusts. Before being able to fly, they crawl, walking as if on crutches, a reference to their upwardly protruding jumping legs. Young locusts whose wings are just growing, *dibā*, "are so numerous at times that they crawl in a long chain, urging each other on and even riding one on top of the other" (Musil, *Rwala*, 112–13, 627).

189   If in conversation words for repulsive or unclean subjects come up, one offers an apology; e.g., "far be it from you," *bi'īd mn as-sām'īn*,

"at the mention of a dog, donkey, unnamed woman, pair of sandals"
(Stewart, *Texts in Sinai Bedouin Law*, 2:8).

190 This is hyperbole: the raiders leave in the morning and in the after-
noon of the same day are back at their camp where the robbed camels'
young rest after drinking.

191 In poetry, the harsh creaking of wooden doors, big wooden keys,
and screaming wooden rollers of the pulley wheels of wells represent
everything unpleasant and narrow-minded about village life. In Bed-
ouin opinion, doors are shut in order to keep uninvited guests out, a
sign of the worst sin, miserliness (cf. §36.4, v. 11).

192 A note in the source clarifies that the narrator is Ṭlēḥān ibn Mkhallaf
al-ʿMēm.

193 Each of the poem's similes is developed into a minor excursus on
aspects of the *tertium comparationis*. Intricately wrought, this is
hardly an apprentice's work.

194 The sheath that envelops the date stalks breaks through the wood
with a grating sound and sucks up the "sugar" of the heart of palm
(al-Suwaydāʾ, *al-Nakhlah al-ʿarabiyyah*, 96, 228).

195 The traditional simile for the straight nose of a beauty.

196 Maria Theresa thalers, *ibū al-shūshī, al-faransī*; *faransī*, not "French,"
but named after Maria Theresa's husband François III Étienne; see
§7.2, v. 4 and n. 56.

197 In these two verses, the poet indulges in wordplay on the daugh-
ter's family name, al-Jimʿī, the word for fist or clenched hand (*jimʿ*
and the plurals *jmūʿ* and *ajmāʿ*) and other words of the same root,
j-m-ʿ.

198 Another play of words, this time on different coinages and weights:
nērah, Ottoman gold guinea; *arbāʿ*, pl. of *ribʿ*, a quarter of a *ghāzī*
(pl. *ghawāzī*), an Ottoman gold coin minted in Iraq (al-Suwaydāʿ,
Manṭiqat Ḥāʾil, 576); *ribʿ as-sibīʿ*, "a quarter of a *sibīʿ*, a seventh"; i.e.,
"a trifling amount" (ʿUbūdī, *Muʿjam al-tijārah*, 168).

199 *Tarthūth* (*Cynomorium coccineum*), a kind of mushroom also called
zibb adh-dhīkh or *zibb al-ḥmār*, "penis of dog, donkey" (HA, 4663),
referring to the plant's phallic form, "a fleshy, reddish, club-shaped,

and leafless root parasite that grows to about one foot (30 cm) high"
(Mandaville, *Bedouin Ethnobotany*, 329).

200 *Taww ma shadd fazzāʿ*: "(a girl) whose breasts have just begun to
swell and who loudly calls for rescue"; i.e., an innocent enchantress,
she appeals to sprightly young men (*jhayyil al-ʿyāl*).

201 "The expression is literally *ʿatāk al-kōbah*, may you get a skin disease
that makes the hair of your beard fall out" (al-Suwaydāʾ, *Amthāl*, 556).

202 The Arabic edition adds a note that the following poem is also
ascribed to the poet al-Jhēlī.

203 Wordplay: *Mashwī* means "roasted (meat)"; al-Mashwī is the name
of the family of shaykhs of the Shmēlah branch of the ʿAbdah division
of Shammar.

204 Al-Shiʿb means "steep gully"; al-Shiʿab is the name of a mountain
south of Ḥāʾil. Words formed of the root *sh-ʿ-b* occur five times in this
line, conveying a sense of harsh urgency (*shaʿʿab*: "to lash").

205 Sowayan comments in a note to the Arabic text: "This is a strange,
unique poem, in a meter that is not one of the known meters of
Nabaṭī poetry. Perhaps for this reason, there are some irregularities
in its long lines that vary from one transmitter to the other."

206 According to the stories, al-Hirbīd was addicted to his pipe.

207 The coffeepot with its cap-shaped lid is compared to an Ottoman-
Turkish sergeant (*shāyūsh*; i.e., *shawīsh*) who comes strutting in from
town.

208 *Jirjīr*: "arugula" (*Eruca sativa*).

209 Ibn Rashīd's levy on the Bedouin was one riyal, a *majīdī*, for every five
camels. Teams of tax collectors, with a scribe and helpers, went out
to the tribes at the end of spring to assess the herds. Dodging the tax
collection, called *ḥōsh*, carried a penalty of paying double the amount
and other punishment at the discretion of Ibn Rashīd (al-Suwaydāʾ,
Manṭiqat Ḥāʾil, 464–65, 555, 577).

210 The ascendancy of the Sibhān family dates from the appointment of
Zāmil al-Sibhān to the Rashīdī treasury. It is unlikely that he or one
of his relatives would have been dispatched in person to the poet's
cattle enclosure.

211 "Ninety" is used here and throughout these corpora as a formulaic number with the general meaning of "many."

212 *Tanfiḍ ʿaskarih*: "raindrops that hit the ground like an army preceded by a rain of bullets" (CA *nafaḍa* "to shake").

213 Explained as "Mikāʾīl, the angel of rain, who calls at the clouds as a herdsman calls his camels, to make them follow in his steps, with a sound *urrrhooo!*"

214 As explained, if the porcupine eats the core, *jummār*, of a date palm, the tree dies. They eat from the palms if there are not enough grasses and plants to serve them as food, and they only choose plants that have not been directly exposed to sunlight.

215 Al-Shifā means "a flat top of a long ridge"; it is the name of the country that slopes up to the crest of the al-Tihāmah mountain range. In poetry, "salt of al-Shifā" is another word for gunpowder made by the Bedouin (e.g., Zēd al-Khshēm, a sedentary poet of the Gfār in Shammar Mountain, Sowayan, *al-Ṣaḥrāʾ al-ʿarabiyyah*, 424).

216 *Khāmid ar-rīḥ*, here translated as "oaf," is the "listless" wind in summer when the grasses have dried up. It is the opposite of *hābb ar-rīḥ*, the animated wind that brings rainclouds and the good things in life, corresponding to *bushrā*, the wind of "glad tidings," as in Q Aʿrāf 7:57.

217 *Mrattināt*: as explained, the Bedouin connect the plural of the Martini gun with *rattan*, "to speak in an incomprehensible tongue, with a rattling sound." *Dharānīḥ*, sg. *dharnūḥ*: "poison." *Ḥallāb al-ablāl*: lit. "milking (the body's) fluids"; i.e., the blood and contents of the abdomen are "milked" by gunpowder.

218 "Faḍlī": the name of an ancestor.

219 "Shalwā falcon": *ṭēr Shalwā*, an expression for a mighty and noble achiever.

220 *Nuṣiy* is a perennial that "thrive[s], with flowers and green forage, well into June," while "annual grazing plants are generally dead and gone by the end of May." *Ḥamāṭ* is a weed that produces an itching sensation, while *khimkhim* is a non-stinging nettle, *Forsskaolea tenacissima*. These plants are part of the Bedouin plant lexicon, which

"has carried these names without change for more than 1,100 years" (Mandaville, *Bedouin Ethnobotany*, 74, 92, 234, 262, 336).

221 That is, the Pleiades, a measure of the season since earliest times.

222 Soles: *n'āl*; as explained, Sājir healed his camel's bleeding soles by cutting a small amount of fat from the hump, melting it (*yaṣḥarih*) and placing the molten fat inside the hoof of the wounded sole pad. He used this original procedure instead of applying a *rug'ah*, a piece of cloth, to the sole.

223 Lit. "putting aside and bringing" (food). As Sowayan commented: "It is not just about serving food, but also advice that could promote or prevent aggressive action. It means that they are men of authority and sound opinions whose advice and leadership are sought after."

224 The owners have preserved the stallion's sperm. Therefore, they know for certain that the mount was fathered by a camel, not an ostrich, even though it runs like an ostrich.

225 The camel has the brand mark of Htēm, here a reference to a lower-status tribe, the Binī Rishīd (not to be confused with the dynasty of Ibn Rashīd).

226 That is, he does not seek out weaker opponents or booty alone, but goes after the high and mighty to prove his superiority to all and sundry.

227 As explained, the "mouse" (*fārah*) under the skin refers to movements of a sinew that seems to run back and forth above the hocks. The simile evokes the image of a well-trained, hardy camel.

228 These are places near Rafḥā, perhaps small black mountains. Al-Birrīt is a particularly deep well. An expert herdsman allows the camels to rest at the *mikhmār*, one day's easy march from the well.

229 He was approached by the guardians of Ibn Rashīd's reserve of protected grazing and brusquely ordered to clear out.

230 The names are those of Ibn Rashīd's guardians of the protected grazing area.

231 "Shithead": *yā-ṭag'atēn*, "you are (worth) two farts."

232 "Ḥawwās": explained as the name of *ṣlubī* who takes his seat behind the house or tent, as stated in the maxim "noblemen lining the majlis, the *ṣlubī* out of view at the backside" (*ashrāf bi-l-aṭrāf*,

aṣ-ṣlubi khalf al-bēt). He travels seated on the camel's rear, holding on to the rider in front; i.e., he is literally a hanger-on who scrounges from others.

233   The first words of the second hemistich are missing in the Arabic edition. In Ḥā'il, I was informed of the reading provided here.

234   'Adnān is the common ancestor of the northern Arabs; Idrīs, according to tradition, was the earliest prophet after Adam and Seth.

235   The reference is to the nine sons of 'Amīrah, the early ancestor of the Rmāl tribe, famous for its herds of pure white camels.

236   *'Algā*, a yellowish-green shrublet, "is an important grazing plant in some sandy regions"; *'ādhir* is a perennial bush, "wormwood [...] plant characteristic of the red sands of the Dahnā'" (Mandaville, *Bedouin Ethnobotany*, 97, 257–58).

237   "Evergreen oaks" (*sindiyān*) refers to a big tree like the Syrian cedar.

238   Hot weeds (*ḥamāṭ*) refer to "a many-branched shrublet [....] Children use it to play 'itching jokes' on one another," because when rubbed between the hands and applied to the face it produces an itching sensation (Mandaville, *Bedouin Ethnobotany*, 154, 268–69).

239   "Those fanatics": *hal ar-rī'*, lit. "the people of the narrow mountain pass"; i.e., the mountainous approaches from Najd to the Hijaz in the area of al-Ṭā'if, usually with reference to Ḥarb, a tribe notorious for shaking down pilgrim caravans on their way to Mecca. Here it has turned into a general reference to men from outside the Shammar tribal lands who were recruited by Ibn Saud to discipline wayward elements of the Shammar tribe.

240   The hems of the shirt stink, in contrast to the Ikhwān's harangues about purity, ritual washings, and the cleanliness of the faith. The poet makes the point that in reality their mindset is dirty: such a person is *'afin*, a revolting boor and good-for-nothing.

241   As explained, he is stuck between two countries, his Shammar kinsmen and the Ikhwān who renounced their tribal allegiance.

242   "Double ancestry," lit. "between two grandfathers." The verse expresses revulsion and amazement at the fact that someone with exemplary ancestry turned out such a bad apple.

243 The panther-sized cat is fearsome because he is backed by Saudi state power.

244 The Ikhwān shaved their mustaches in line with a tenet of the Ḥanbalī school of Islamic Law. They held the notion that "those Bedouins who wore the *ʿiqāl* instead of the newly fashioned *ʿimāma* (a thin white turban) were not real Muslims and could be fought" (al-Fahad, "The *ʿImama* vs. the *ʿIqal*," 35).

245 The full story is told in Sowayan, *Ayyām al-ʿarab*, 335–36.

246 In 1837, Khurshid Pasha, the chief of the Egyptian force in Medina, accepted ʿAbdallah ibn Rashīd as the ruler in Ḥāʾil in lieu of the Āl ʿAlī dynasty in exchange for plentiful supplies of pack camels. In consequence, ʿAbdallah and his cavalry attacked ʿAnazah at Ghnēm Mountain southeast of Tayma and despoiled the tribe of hundreds of camels (al-Suwaydāʾ, *Manṭiqat Ḥāʾil*, 355, 395; the story and a version of seven verses are found in al-Rashīd, *Nubdhah taʾrīkhiyyah ʿan Najd*, 72–73). This minor clash can hardly be considered proof in a dispute many decades later between other tribal chiefs over areas of influence in Mesopotamia. But such nitpicking does not take away from the story's broad sweep.

247 Ibn Burmān is a figure from a folktale. One day, the only prey his falcon could find was a coiled-up snake. Released from the air, the viper struck out at Ibn Burmān, who died instantly (a slightly different version is given in al-Suwaydāʾ, *Amthāl*, 266–67). The expression means "rewarding evil for good," though the tale itself does not presume evil intent on the part of the falcon.

248 An anachronism: Saudi Arabia as a country had not yet come into existence and there were no guarded border crossings.

249 The poet soft-pedals his sympathy for the House of Ibn Rashīd and clarifies that he makes a distinction between the rulers of the House of Saud and the hardline Ikhwān.

250 The governor assures the poet that the youngsters are better off under the guardianship of ʿAbd al-ʿAzīz ibn Saʿūd's than they were with their biological fathers. They were kept under close surveillance for the time being in Riyadh. For decades, members of the Ibn Rashīd family were not allowed to return to Ḥāʾil, as I was often told.

Glossary

'Abaklī (pronounced 'Abaćlī) ibn Fālih   a shaykh of the Shilgān.

Aba l-Gūr   a place near 'Ar'ar, on today's border with Jordan.

Abbas I   (r. 1848–54) grandson of Muḥammad 'Alī, the founder of the nineteenth-century dynasty of Egyptian rulers; he was keenly interested in Arabian horses.

'Abdah   the principal division of the Shammar confederation. It may have migrated from Yemen about seven centuries ago. The ruling families in Ḥā'il during the nineteenth century, Āl 'Alī and Ibn Rashīd, are both from the J'afar section of the 'Abdah.

'Abd al-Karīm al-Jarbā   (r. 1835–71) powerful leader of the Shammar tribe in Iraq. He was executed by the Ottoman government and buried in Mosul. His father, Ṣfūg al-Jarbā, was killed by the Ottoman Turks when 'Abd al-Karīm was not yet ten years old.

'Abd al-Karīm Qāsim   the military dictator who brought down the rule of the Iraqi royal family in 1958. He and 'Abd al-Karīm al-Jarbā were known as *al-kharābtān*, "the two scourges, (bringers of) ruin."

'Abdallah ibn Rashīd   ruler of the Ja'far clan of the 'Abdah division of the Shammar tribal confederation who founded the Ibn Rashīd dynasty in 1835, with its capital in Ḥā'il, after ousting the last ruler of the Ibn 'Alī family, Ṣāliḥ. On his death in 1847, he was succeeded by his son Ṭalāl. Included in the list of forty poets in 'Adwān al-Hirbīd's al-Shēkhah poem.

Abū Ṭāyih   the warlike chief of the Ḥuwayṭāṭ tribe (1874–1924), made famous by his portrayal in *Seven Pillars of Wisdom* by T. E. Lawrence ("Lawrence of Arabia").

Abū Zayd   nickname of the poet Muḥammad al-Aḥmad al-Sudayrī. Included in the list of forty poets in ʿAdwān al-Hirbīd's al-Shēkhah poem.

Abū Zayd al-Hilālī   hero-poet who led the Banū Hilāl on their western migration (*taghrībah*) from Arabia to Tunis.

ʿAjlān ibn Rakhīṣ   a shaykh of Abū Zwayyid's tribal section, appointed Ibn Rashīd's governor in Riyadh. He was killed together with numerous members of the garrison during the Saudi reconquest in 1902. That attack was launched by ʿAbd al-ʿAzīz ibn Saʿūd and his cousin ʿAbdallah ibn Jluwī, then the second-most powerful leader of the Saud dynasty and a relative of ʿAbd al-ʿAzīz al-Musāʿid.

Āl ʿAlī   a family of the Jaʿfar section of the Ribīʿiyyah branch of the ʿAbdah, who were appointed as governors in Ḥāʾil by the House of Saud. After the destruction of the Saudi capital al-Dirʿiyyah, they acted as vassals of the Turkish-Egyptian overlords. A sedentary family, their writ did not extend to the Bedouin. In 1835, ʿAbdallah ibn Rashīd was appointed governor by Fayṣal ibn Turkī, whom he had befriended on the Saudi military campaigns.

al-ʿAmārāt   a major tribe of the Bishr division of the ʿAnazah confederation, centered in the area around Hīt and Karbala in Iraq. In the eighteenth century, the tribe wandered in the northeastern part of central Arabia, joined the Wahhabi troops, and ventured farther north. The tribe's shaykhs are the Ibn Hadhdhāl family.

ʿAnazah   one of the oldest and largest Arabian tribal confederations, supposedly named after an eponymous ancestor, ʿAnnāz. About three centuries ago, they moved from their base around Khaybar in the Hijaz north toward Syria and Iraq. Genealogically, they are reckoned among the northern Arabs, Rabīʿah, whereas their hereditary rivals, Shammar, trace their origins to the southern Arabs. Around 1800, a second northward migration of the tribes of ʿAnazah and Shammar occurred, this time caused by Wahhabi pressure. The division of

Bishr (Fid'ān, Sba'ah, 'Amārāt) pastured along the Euphrates; Ḍanā Muslim (Ḥsanah, Wild 'Alī, Jlās/Rwalah) pastured more to the west, in Syria. Wars among these divisions were frequent. The only tribe to remain entirely in Arabia is Wild Slēmān. It was not originally part of 'Anazah and probably joined for political reasons.

'Antar 'Antarah ibn Shaddād, one of the most famous pre-Islamic poets and composer of one of the seven *al-Mu'allaqāt* poems. He is also the hero of a cycle of stories in the Middle East.

al-'Arfajī Muḥammad 'Arfaj of Āl Abū 'Layyān ('Ulayyān), headman of the town of Buraydah in al-Qaṣīm Province.

al-Ashmal nickname of Bnayyah ibn Fāris al-Jarbā. Included in the list of forty poets in 'Adwān al-Hirbīd's al-Shēkhah poem.

al-'Askarī 'Am'ūm al-'Askarī al-Dughmānī of the Rwalah tribe of 'Anazah. Included in the list of forty poets in 'Adwān al-Hirbīd's al-Shēkhah poem.

Banū Hilāl Arabian tribes that in 1050 set out from Egypt to invade North Africa, the so-called westward journey (*taghrībat Banī Hilāl*) described by the historian Ibn Khaldūn (732–808/1332–1406), who was the first to give examples of *hilālī*-style "Bedouin" poetry that later became known as Nabaṭī poetry. In more recent times, Banū Hilāl grew into a popular saga, featuring Abū Zayd and other heroes.

Banū Ṣakhr (also al-Ṣukhūr) originally from the northern Hejaz, these nomads and seminomads are the dominant tribe in the hinterland of northern Jordan. By causing trouble for pilgrim caravans, they leveraged their influence with the Ottoman Turks. At the outbreak of the First World War, the only tribe that still paid tribute to the Banū Ṣakhr were the Shararāt. After the war, they supported Emir 'Abdallah of Transjordan against raids of the Saudi Ikhwān in 1922 and 1924.

Barjas Barjas ibn 'Irdān of the Salmān of the Sinjārah division of Shammar. Included in the list of forty poets in 'Adwān al-Hirbīd's al-Shēkhah poem.

Battle of al-'Āmiriyyah the exact date of this tribal battle is unknown, but according to oral sources it probably occurred in the period 1906–11.

Tribesmen of al-Rwalah, led by Nawwāf and Mamdūḥ ibn Shaʿlān, and of al-Ḥuwaytāt, led by Abū Tāyih, raided Bedouin of the Zmēl of Shammar, led by Qāsim (Gāsim) ibn Rakhīṣ, at the wells of al-Ḥuzūl. Al-ʿĀmiriyyah is a valley in that area.

Battle of al-Jawf   battle fought in 1920 that pitted Nawwāf ibn Nūrī ibn Shaʿlān and ʿAwdah Abū Tāyih of the Ḥuwaytāt tribe against Sʿūd, who emerged victorious, one year before the final demise of the Ibn Rashīd rule.

Battle of al-Jmēmā (al-Jumaymāʾ)   battle fought in al-Jawf Province in 1910 between the troops of Ibn Rashīd and the ʿAnazah tribes of the Rwalah and the ʿAmārat. At that time, Sʿūd ibn ʿAbd al-ʿAzīz was about twelve years old and his maternal uncles of the Āl Sibhān family ruled as regents on his behalf.

al-Bāyiḥ   a shaykh of the Gîtāmīs tribe.

ʿBēd   ʿUbayd ibn Rashīd, brother of ʿAbdallah ibn Rashīd and the general of the armed forces.

Brēk   Brēk al-Asʿadī al-ʿUtaybī, headman of the town of Bagʿa to the east of Ḥāʾil, known for his poetic correspondence with Fēṣal al-Ṣwēṭ, the shaykh of the Ẓafīr tribe.

daḥḥah   a dance "whereby a girl facing a half circle of men moves a few steps back while playing with a sword. A man in the middle sings while to his right and left others answer each strophe. At the end of the song, the entire line claps its hands, while moving the upper body sideways" (HA). The *laʿb al-daḥḥah* is peculiar to the Bedouin of the Syrian desert and northern Arabia, in particular the ʿAnazah confederation. It served to lift the spirits of tribesmen before a fight or to celebrate victory and recount their feats. Nowadays it is danced at wedding parties and on feast days.

al-Dghērāt   a section of the ʿAbdah division of Shammar established on the southwestern side of Ajā Mountain.

al-Dhēmī   situated in the area of Sakaka and ʿArʿar in Wadi al-Khirr.

al-Dhirfān   one of the sections of the the Zmēl branch of the Sinjārah division of Shammar.

al-Dighmān   one of the five subtribes of the Rwalah.

Fahd ibn ʿAbd al-Muḥsin al-Hadhdhāl   (1840–1924) shaykh of the ʿAmārāt tribe of ʿAnazah, who camped on both sides of the middle Euphrates, nominally "shaykh of shaykhs" of the entire ʿAnazah confederation (*shaykh mashāyikh ʿAnazah*). He was given the Ottoman title of bey (Arabic: *bēk*). In 1922, he was elected a member of Iraq's Constituent Assembly.

Fahdah   daughter of al-ʿĀṣī ibn Shrēm, the mother of Mishʿal. Subsequently, she married King ʿAbd al-ʿAzīz, and their son Fahd was king of Saudi Arabia from 1982 to 2005.

Fajḥān al-Farāwī   (1817–97) warrior and poet of the Mṭēr (Muṭayr) tribe, who was rewarded with three horses for his eulogy of ʿAbd al-Karīm al-Jarbā.

al-Fawāʿirah   a relatively new tribal grouping established by Ḥasan al-Fāʿūr, who originated from the Faḍl tribe.

Fayṣal ibn Turkī   (1785–1865) ruled the second Saudi state in tumultuous times. His first term as a ruler (1834–38) ended with a forced exile in Cairo. On his return in 1843, he ruled until 1865, in alliance with his friend ʿAbdallah ibn Rashīd, whom he had appointed as prince of Ḥāʾil in 1835.

Fhēd   Fhēd ibn Mʿabhal ibn Shaʿlān of the Rwalah tribe of ʿAnazah. Included in the list of forty poets in ʿAdwān al-Hirbīd's al-Shēkhah poem.

al-Fidʿān   a tribe of the ʿAnazah confederation that migrated to Syria and Mesopotamia, where it fought with the migrated Shammar tribes over pasture grounds; see *Ibn Mhēd*. After the First World War, Turkī's son Mijḥim sided with the French occupation of Syria, and his nephew Ḥākim supported the Hashemite king Fayṣal and later the Turkish nationalists.

al-Fighm   Khalaf al-Fighm of the Mṭēr (Muṭayr) tribe. Included in the list of forty poets in ʿAdwān al-Hirbīd's al-Shēkhah poem.

ʿGāb ibn ʿIjil   the chief of the Snān section of the ʿAbdah division of Shammar and the Rashīdī prince's father-in-law. In 1920, he recaptured the Jawf oasis for Ibn Rashīd.

ʿGēl   see *ʿUqayl*.

al-Gfēʿi   the grandfather of Ṭalāl ibn Rmāl.

Ghaḍbān   a raid leader of the Rmāl who made his peace with Ibn Saud upon his return from his spell of self-exile in Iraq. He soon joined Ibn Musā'id on his military campaigns in Jordan, making no secret of his dislike of the Ikhwān.

al-Ghūṭah   an area to the west of Ajā Mountain; its principal settlement, Mōgag, is the base of al-Hirbīd's tribal group of the Swēd of the Zmēl, and a collection point for tax payments to Ibn Rashīd.

Gnēṭir ibn Rakhīṣ   a famous desert knight and raid leader who specialized in robbing camels of the Ḥwēṭāt and Sharārāt tribes. He was killed by a warrior of the Sharārāt.

'Gūb ibn Swēṭ ('Uqūb ibn Suwayṭ)   (d. 1911) a shaykh of the Ẓafīr tribe.

Ḥā'il (Ḥāyil)   the capital of northern Najd, the province of central Arabia, situated at almost equal distance from Mecca, Damascus, and Riyadh, halfway between the Red Sea and the Gulf. It is the center of Jabal Shammar, formerly Jabal Ṭayyi', an area of mixed nomadic and sedentary modes of life. Economically, it was primarily orientated toward the Mesopotamian riverine areas of Iraq and caravans plied up and down the old pilgrim road, *darb Zubaydah*, that skirted the southern edge of the Nafūd Desert. Historically, Ḥā'il has been in close interaction, often also adversarial and in competition, with the oases and trade hubs of al-Qaṣīm Province and its major towns of 'Unayzah and Buraydah, a few hundred miles to the south.

Ḥarb   a tribe of mostly seminomads and small cultivators, strategically located in the Hejaz where it straddles the pilgrim road between Medina and Mecca. To ensure the safety of pilgrim caravans from Egypt and Syria, their shaykhs received subventions from the Ottoman and Egyptian authorities. Nevertheless, disagreements were common, and tribesmen were notorious for ambushing and plundering the devout travelers at the mountain passes controlled by Ḥarb.

Ḥātim [al-Ṭā'ī]   a symbol of prodigious hospitality, the pre-Islamic Bedouin poet Ḥātim al-Ṭā'ī is one of the most widely known ancient figures in Saudi Arabia today. He is especially associated with the region of Ḥā'il, whose inhabitants claim him as one of their own. The tribe may have gone, but the mountain ranges are still called Jabal Ṭayyi'.

Ḥaṭṭāb   Ḥaṭṭāb ibn Sarrāḥ al-Shammarī, a prominent leader in al-Jawf
Province who corresponded in poetry with ʿUbayd ibn Rashīd. He
and his son Ghālib were imprisoned by ʿUbayd in 1842 when the
province was brought under direct Rashīdī rule.

al-Ḥamāṭiyyah   a well at the eastern border of the Nafūd Desert.

Ḥawwās al-Tbēnānī   poet specialized in invective poetry and innuendo,
especially known for targeting the poet al-Ẓalmāwi of the Shilgān
branch of Shammar.

al-Ḥazl   (pl. al-Ḥuzūl) wells of the Nabhān and Ibn Rakhīṣ, including
Lōgah, in the Ḥjarah region to the northeast of the Dahnāʾ sands,
on the way from Ḥāʾil and Jubbah to Karbala, Iraq. They mark the
eastern border of the Sinjārah division of Shammar, running from
al-Ghūṭah and Mōgag in the west across the Nafūd. This geogra-
phy almost destined the Sinjārah to excel at long-distance camel
raiding.

Hazzāʿ   the seventh and last son of Nāyif ibn Shaʿlān, and therefore an
uncle of Saṭṭām, and the father of the later leader of the tribe, al-Nūrī
ibn Hazzāʿ ibn Nāyif, born in 1847.

Hdēb   Hdēb ibn Ṣibīḥ al-Hirbīd of the Harābdah of the Swēd of Shammar.
Included in the list of forty poets in ʿAdwān al-Hirbīd's al-Shēkhah
poem.

al-Hijhūj   ibn Ṭalāl ibn Jārid, a daring raid leader (*ʿagīd*) of the Rmāl tribe
of Shammar.

al-Ḥirah   the capital of the Lakhmid dynasty near present-day Najaf
in Iraq. It attracted famous pre-Islamic poets like Ṭarafah, ʿAbīd,
al-Nābighah, and ʿAdī ibn Zayd.

Ḥīt   a town in the al-Anbar Province of Iraq, built on both sides of the
Euphrates River.

Ḥmūd ibn Rashīd   an inseparable companion of Muḥammad ibn Rashīd.
He acted as a general in the House of Ibn Rashīd.

Al-Ḥrērah   a section of the Ṣubḥī branch of the Ṣayiḥ division of Shammar
in Iraq.

Ḥsēn   Ḥsēn al-Dhnēb of the Swēd of Shammar. Included in the list of forty
poets in ʿAdwān al-Hirbīd's al-Shēkhah poem.

Htēm (Hutaym)   supposedly *aṣīl*, "pure," tribes would classify the Htēm among tribal groups without "purebred" ancestors. Accordingly, in their usage the word *Htēmī* was an insult, along with the word for an even lower rank, *ṣlubī*, a member of the "pariah tribe" of the Ṣalab. A typical classification would include the Sharārāt, ʿAwāzim, Banū Rashīd (not to be confused with Ibn Rashīd), Ḥuwaytāt, and Banū ʿAṭiyyah, but not the Ṣalab, who are held in even lower esteem in such classifications. Ironically, the camels of these Htēm, the Banū Rashīd and, especially, the Sharārāt, were rated as first-class purebreds and much coveted by the "noble" tribes for long and fast desert journeys and raiding.

Ibn ʿAngā   the poet Radhān ibn ʿAngā of the Ghfēlah branch of the Sinjārah division of Shammar was a contemporary of Shaykh ʿAbd al-Karīm al-Jarbā.

Ibn Baggār   shaykhs of Shammar who traced their lineage to the ancient tribe of Ṭayy and belonged to the Aslam division of Shammar. In the sixteenth century, they seem to have been on good terms with the sharifs of Mecca. Otherwise, little is known about them.

Ibn Dʿējā   Khalaf ibn Dʿējā, a shaykh of the Sharārāt tribe. A legendary figure in the Najdī genre of "martyrs of love." He comes to the rescue of someone who is prevented from marrying his beloved, but too late to save the life of the disconsolate lover.

Ibn Farwān   a family of raid leaders of the Ḥabkān clan of the Jirdhān, the biggest section of Āl Bēṭin of the Ghfēlah branch of the Sinjārah division of Shammar.

Ibn Hadhdhāl   one of the most respected families of Bedouin shaykhs, already known as such in the sixteenth century. Fahd ibn ʿAbd al-Muḥsin ibn Ḥmēdī, Fahd Bey, was made *qāimmaqām* of al-Razzāzah, near Kerbela in southern Iraq. He was known as a clever and thoughtful leader. After the First World War, he was on good terms with the British in Mandatory Iraq. He died in 1927.

Ibn Ḥithlēn   Rākān ibn Hithlēn, shaykh of al-ʿIjmān, who was imprisoned in Istanbul by the Ottoman Turks. The German scholar Julius Euting saw him when he visited Muḥammad ibn Rashīd in Ḥāʾil.

Ibn Jibrīn   the shaykh of the Mfaḍḍal branch of the ‘Abdah division of Shammar.

Ibn M‘abhal   family of shaykhs of the M‘abhal section of the Mir‘iḍ, a subdivision of the Rwalah, headed by the tribe's leading family, Ibn Sha‘lān.

Ibn Mashhūr   one of the two clans of the Ibn Sha‘lān shaykhs of the Rwalah tribe of the ‘Anazah confederation. In the early nineteenth century, Ibn Mashhūr was outmaneuvered by the other clan, ‘Abdallah. Bad feeling between both branches has continued ever since. For these reasons, many of the Mashhūr joined the Ikhwān in 1925 and followed the extremist rebels in their rebellion of 1929.

Ibn Mhēd (Muhayd)   around the middle of the nineteenth century, the house of the paramount shaykh of the Fid‘ān of ‘Anazah, Ibn Ghbēn (Ghubayn), was unseated by Ibn Mhēd. Jad‘ān ibn Mhēd carried out a daring attack on Turkish-Ottoman troops in 1857, but in the 1870s the Ottoman sultan appointed him as *qāimmaqām* of the Aleppo Bedouin with the title of bey. After his death in the early 1880s, he was succeeded by his son Turkī. Around 1887, Turkī was slain in close combat against the poet Khalaf al-Idhn of the Sha‘lān (who features in the ‘Ajlān ibn Rmāl chapter). As a result, the war between the Fid‘ān and the Rwalah intensified until mediators, among them Fahd ibn Hadhdhāl (who features in the ‘Ajlān and Abū Zwayyid chapters), restored the peace. Ibn Mhēd was legendary for his hospitality and generally known as "he who calls all and sundry to supper."

Ibn Mirdās   the nickname of Shāyi‘ al-Amsaḥ, the ancestor of the Shammar tribe of the Rmāl.

Ibn Musā‘id   ibn Jluwī ibn Turkī ibn ‘Abd Allāh Āl Saud, ‘Abd al-‘Azīz (1884/5–1977), from the Jluwī branch of the House of Saud. He entered Ḥā'il on October 30, 1921, as the first Saudi governor to rule the northern capital after the collapse of the Ibn Rashīd dynasty, which he did with an iron hand. He married seven wives, among whom were two from the former ruling families, Ibn Rashīd and Ibn Sibhān of Ḥā'il. He remained governor of Ḥā'il until the end of his life, even after he had retired and gone to live in Riyadh in 1970.

Ibn Rakhīṣ   the shaykhs of the Nabhān section of the Zmēl branch of the Sinjārah division of Shammar. In 1837, they sheltered the fugitive ʿAbdallah ibn Rashīd in their stronghold deep inside the Nafūd Desert when the Ibn ʿAlī clan for a short time regained power in Ḥāʾil. As trusted allies of Ibn Rashīd, they became influential and declared their independence from the shaykh of the Zmēl branch, Ibn Thnayyān. In 1877, Muḥammad ibn Rakhīṣ appointed Fahhād ibn Rakhīṣ as his governor in Riyadh. Ṣāliḥ ibn Rakhīṣ, a companion of Ibn Rashīd, features in European travel accounts.

Ibn Rashīd   the ruling house in Ḥāʾil and Jabal Shammar from 1834 to 1921. The name Ibn Rashīd is a shorthand designation for the house, its members, and the ruling emir.

Ibn Rashīd, ʿAbdallah ibn ʿAlī   (r. 1834–36, 1837–46) poet, warrior, and statesman who founded the House of Ibn Rashīd. He fled from Ḥāʾil when ʿĪsa ibn ʿAlī was reinstated by Turkish-Egyptian soldiers, and went into hiding. This flight and eventual victory became a founding legend of his rule. He was married to daughters of the previous rulers of Jabal Shammar, Ibn ʿAlī, and of Fayṣal ibn Saʿūd. To survive politically, he maintained a balancing act between the House of Saud in Riyadh, the Turkish-Egyptian commander in the Hejaz, and the Ottoman sultan.

Ibn Rashīd, ʿAbd al-ʿAzīz ibn Mitʿib   (r. 1897–1906) inherited the unenviable task of safeguarding the far-flung dominions conquered by his brilliant predecessor, Muḥammad ibn Rashīd. During his rule, the influence of the House of Ibn Rashīd waned, while the fortunes of the House of Saud saw a resurgence, starting with the Saudi reconquest of Riyadh in 1902. He was killed in 1906 during a campaign against the seditious al-Qaṣīm Province.

Ibn Rashīd, Bandar ibn Ṭalāl ibn ʿAbdallah   (r. 1869–73) started the internecine struggles that expedited the demise of the House of Ibn Rashīd. His father, Ṭalāl, had designated his younger brother Mitʿib as his successor, against the will of his sons. Unable to stomach being sidelined, they shot Mitʿib. Their uncle Muḥammad fled to Riyadh, and on his return killed Bandar and the other progeny of Ṭalāl.

Ibn Rashīd, Ḥmūd ibn ʿUbayd   (d. 1908) continued the role of his father, ʿUbayd, as the dynasty's field commander and right-hand man of Muḥammad ibn ʿAbdallah ibn Rashīd. Like his father, he was a prolific poet. He lived to witness the Rashīdī decline and the reckless part played in it by his sons, which made him seek refuge in Medina.

Ibn Rashīd, Muḥammad ibn ʿAbdallah   (r. 1873–97) the ruthless and powerful emir of Ḥāʾil and the surrounding area, called the Mountain of Shammar (Jabal Shammar) after the dominant tribe to which the House of Rashīd also belonged. He figures prominently in many descriptions by European travelers and was a vivid presence in popular imagination. His court was frequented by many poets, especially from the northern areas and the northern part of central Arabia. Though not a poet himself, this edition evidences his acute understanding of the art and its importance in his dominions' culture.

Ibn Rashīd, Saʿūd ibn ʿAbd al-ʿAzīz Abū Khashm   (r. 1908–20) ascended to the throne at the age of twelve as the only remaining prince of the lineage of ʿAbdallah, the founder of the House of Ibn Rashīd. He was nicknamed Abū Khashm, "Father of the Nose," because of its size. The regency of his in-laws, al-Sibhān, lasted until 1914, but matters of state remained largely in the hands of his maternal grandmother, Fāṭimah, the daughter of Zāmil al-Sibhān. Abū Khashm was killed by his relative ʿAbdallah ibn Ṭalāl ibn Nāyif ibn Ṭalāl ibn ʿAbdallah al-Rashīd in 1920, at the age of twenty-two.

Ibn Rashīd, Ṭalāl   (r. 1848–66) remained loyal to the House of Saud in Riyadh and took an active part in some of the Saudi campaigns, while staying on good terms with the Ottoman-Turkish authorities. Under his benign, tolerant, and largely peaceful rule, trade and commerce flourished: he invited traders from Basra and Wāsiṭ in Iraq to Yemen to set up shop in Ḥāʾil. Command of the armed forces was left in the hands of his uncle ʿUbayd ibn Rashīd. He committed suicide at the age of forty-five.

Ibn Rashīd, ʿUbayd ibn ʿAlī   (d. 1869) cofounder of the Rashīdī Emirate and the strong arm of his brother ʿAbdallah, he was instrumental in putting the fledgling state on a firm footing. He was known for strict adherence to the religious tenets of the brothers' Saudi overlords. His exploits are echoed in his poetry, which has been preserved in many manuscripts and remains popular today.

Ibn ʿRēʿir (ʿUrayʿir)   the popular name for the Āl Ḥumayd dynasty of the Banū Khālid tribe, which ruled the eastern al-Aḥsāʾ Province from 1669 to 1793, when their independence was ended by the Saudi rulers. A later episode of semi-independence ended in 1830, when the Ibn ʿRēʿir were defeated by Turkī ibn Saʿūd and surrendered on honorable terms.

Ibn Saud   also Ibn Saʿūd or Ibn Sʿūd family, the principal rulers of Najd and the political leaders of the religious reform movement known as Wahhabism.

Ibn Shaʿlān   considered one of the most important families of shaykhs in the period preceding the Saudi conquest of Ḥāʾil and al-Jawf. The early ancestor Shaʿlān started out as a poor herdsman. His successors cemented the family's position as shaykhs of the Rwalah tribe, notably Fayṣal, Saṭṭām, and al-Nūrī. Ibn Shaʿlān belongs to the ʿAbdallah division that eclipsed the other division of the Rwalah, the Mashhūr, to claim the leadership. Saṭṭām (d. 1901), a clever desert politician, received the title of pasha from the Ottoman sultan ʿAbd al-Ḥamīd. As in the case of Ibn Rashīd, his succession gave rise to much internecine murder.

Ibn Shrēm (Ibn Shuraym)   the shaykh of the Fḍēl branch of the ʿAbdah division of Shammar.

Ibn Smēr (Ibn Sumayr)   the paramount shaykh of the Wild ʿAlī tribe. The other leading family, al-Ṭayyār, took command in war and raiding. As guardians of the pilgrim caravan to Mecca, they enjoyed privileged relations with the Ottoman pasha of Damascus, especially during the fifty years of leadership by Shaykh Muḥammad ibn Dūkhī (d. 1895). His sons lost influence and became affiliated with their major rival, al-Nūrī ibn Shaʿlān.

Ibn Ṭwālah   the family of the paramount shaykhs of the Aslam, the southernmost division of Shammar at Jabal Salmā. Often somewhat reserved toward Ibn Rashīd and on good terms with Ibn Saud, they joined Ibn Rashīd on the expedition to reconquer al-Jawf.

al-Jarbā   of the Khriṣah division of Shammar, they are the first-known Bedouin shaykhs of Shammar. They led the Shammar tribes that in the late eighteenth century moved from Najd to Iraq after their defeat by the first Saudi state. With Ottoman permission, the Jarbā crossed the Euphrates, entered al-Jazīrah Province, and in 1802 or 1803 reached Sinjār Mountain in the north of Iraq. The area south of Sinjār and the Khābūr River's confluence with the Euphrates is considered Shammar Jarbā area. They were often troublesome for the Ottoman Turks: Shaykh Ṣfūg was killed in 1847 and his son ʿAbd al-Karīm met the same fate in 1871. ʿAjīl al-Yāwar (Turkish for "adjutant, aide-de-camp," 1882–1940, in this edition ʿAgīl al-Jāwar) represented Mosul in the first Iraqi parliament in 1924. His grandson Ghāzī al-Yāwar was the first president of Iraq after Saddam Hussein.

Jārid   Jārid ibn Zabin, shaykh of the Rmal of Shammar. Included in the list of forty poets in ʿAdwān al-Hirbīd's al-Shēkhah poem.

al-Jawf   also known as al-Jūbah, a large agricultural area and a town in a depressed plain bordering on its south the northwestern side of the Nafūd Desert and on its north opening to Wādī Sirḥān. Al-Jawf has been a trading town of Shammar, the Rwalah, and the Sharārāt.

Jdēʿ   Jdēʿ ibn Qublān ibn Milḥim, shaykh of the Manāhibah tribe of the Ḍanā Muslim branch of ʿAnazah. Included in the list of forty poets in ʿAdwān al-Hirbīd's al-Shēkhah poem.

Jifrān al-Maʿaklī   member of the Ṭurēf of the Maʿākilah clan of the Jirdhān, known as expert desert pilots; one of them, Khazʿal, was the pilot of Ibn Rashīd's war banner. A daughter of the leading al-Māyig family of the Jirdhān married Ḥmūd ibn Rashīd, and her sons Mājid and Sālim and daughter Mūḍi were to play a role in the later fortunes of the Ibn Rashīd dynasty. Emboldened by this connection, the Jirdhān, supported by most of the Zmēl and abetted by Ibn Rashīd, rebelled against the Ibn Rmāl shaykhs of the Ghfēlah.

Jimal   Jimal ibn Sʿēd ibn Libdah of the Ghaṭān (Qaḥṭān) tribe. Included in the list of forty poets in ʿAdwān al-Hirbīd's al-Shēkhah poem.

Jrēs Jres ibn Jilbān al-'Ajmī, also called Jrēs al-Yamānī, of the Ḥubaysh of the 'Ijmān tribe, which traces its roots to the Yām tribe in the south of the Arabian peninsula. He is a legendary figure, famous for his hospitality and forbearance in all circumstances. He lived at the time of the eastern Arabian ruler Mājid ibn 'Uray'ir (d. 1829/1830).

Jubbah a village and small oasis at the southern edge of the Nafūd Desert, mentioned in a verse by the *mukhaḍram* poet Namr ibn Tawlab al-'Uklī. Poets present it as a place teeming with wildlife, in particular oryx. Early Arabic sources praise its excellent pastures and remoteness from human habitation. For European travelers coming from al-Jawf, the miniature oasis offered the first vista of green on their way to Ḥā'il, fifty-six miles (ninety kilometers) south of Jubbah. The town was known for the manufacture of wooden camel saddles. Nineteenth-century Bedouin poetry and stories describe Jubbah and the sands of the Nafūd as a natural paradise for camels and Bedouin.

al-Kawāćbah (al-Kawakibah) one of the subtribes of the Rwalah. Unlike the other sections, it traces its origin to the southern Arabs, Qaḥṭān. On their wanderings, they met the Rwalah and their chief married his daughter to the Rwēlī shaykh Fahd ibn M'abhal.

Khḍēr al-Ṣ'ēlić the chief of the Manāṣir section of the Āl Ṭwālah, the lineage of the chiefs of the Aslam division of Shammar.

al-Kwēkibī (pronounced al-Kwēćbī) his full name is unknown; the tribal *nisbah* indicates that he belongs to the Kawākibah section of the Rwalah tribe of 'Anazah.

al-'Layyān (al-'Ulayyān) a tribal group of the Khriṣah of the 'Abdah division that left Najd for Mesopotamia.

Khālid son of Saṭṭām ibn al-Sha'lān; his mother was Turkiyyah, daughter of Ibn Mhēd, the shaykh of the Fid'ān division of 'Anazah.

Lōgah an important well of the Sinjārah of Shammar on the way to Iraq.

al-Ma'ākilah a section of the Āl Biṭēn group of the Ghfēlah branch of the Sinjārah division of Shammar.

'Mēr 'Mēr ibn Rāshid Āl Ḍēgham. Included in the list of forty poets in 'Adwān al-Hirbīd's al-Shēkhah poem.

Mghīr ibn Ghāzī Mghīr ibn Ghāzī ibn S'ēd of the 'Layyān clan of the Dghērāt of the 'Abdah division of Shammar. Included in the list of forty poets in 'Adwān al-Hirbīd's al-Shēkhah poem.

al-Mhādī al-Faḍlī, Muḥammad a legendary member of the Ghaṭān (Qaḥṭān) tribe or al-Fuḍūl of Banū Lām, remembered for his forbearance toward guests living under his protection. The few verses he left are no more than an adjunct to his legendary chivalry, especially his patience with misconduct of his protected neighbor.

Miḍḥi al-Wḥēr a poet of the Dghērāt of the 'Abdah division of Shammar.

Mish'al (1913–31) eldest son of S'ūd Abū Khashm and his wife Fahdah, daughter of 'Āṣī ibn Shrēm.

Mish'ān Mish'ān ibn Mghēlith ibn Hadhdhāl, shaykh of the 'Amārāt of 'Anazah. Included in the list of forty poets in 'Adwān al-Hirbīd's al-Shēkhah poem.

Miṭlag Miṭlag ibn Muḥammad al-Jarbā, the desert knight killed in the battle of al-'Udwah against Ibn Saud in 1791.

Mrēzīg' a raid leader and enforcer of Ibn Rashīd (probably a slave).

Mṣīkh Mṣīkh ibn Farḥān of the Rmāl tribe of Shammar. Included in the list of forty poets in 'Adwān al-Hirbīd's al-Shēkhah poem.

Mtāli', Mtāli'iyyāt the remnants of a mountain range running almost parallel with Ajā Mountain. A settlement of the Swēd clan stood there before civil strife destroyed it.

Mūḍī the daughter of Sibhān al-Salāmah al-Sibhān, the mother of S'ūd ibn Rashīd.

Muḥammad ibn Ṣāliḥ ibn Rakhīṣ al-Dimānī known as *rā' al-Ḥzul*, owner of the Ḥuzūl wells, nicknamed al-Dimānī on account of his short stature, and compared to cattle droppings (*dimnah*). Al-Dimānī's father was Ṣāliḥ ibn Rakhīṣ, a close friend of Abū Zwayyid. In protest, the poet absented himself from the court; in time, al-Dimānī was invited back. Ibn Rashīd told Ibn Jibrīn and Ibn Swēṭ that the well of al-Lōgah should be al-Dimānī's.

al-Mu'allaqāt "the suspended poems," a pre-Islamic collection of poems that in the early centuries of Islam were among the most

admired long poems of the qasida type. They are so called because
the poems, written on cloth in letters of gold, were said to have been
hung on the walls of the Meccan Kaaba, but other explanations are
also given.

al-Nabhān   the tribal group headed by the Ibn Rakhīṣ clan to which Abū
Zwayyid belongs. It has a somewhat anomalous position in Shammar
genealogy: it originated from the south Arabian Ṭayy, early owners
of what is now Jabal Shammar, some of whom joined Shammar and
others ʿAnazah.

Nafūd Desert   the Great Nafūd, or al-Nafūd, is the second-largest body
of sand of the Arabian Peninsula, though it is less than a tenth the
size of the Empty Quarter. These two sand bodies are connected by
the sand belt of al-Dahnāʿ, which runs more than 870 miles (1,400
kilometers) from the southeastern al-Nafūd to the northern edge of
the Empty Quarter. The Nafūd sands, with their rich vegetation after
rainfall and plentiful firewood, are considered a Bedouin paradise. At
the time of the events described in this volume, al-Nafūd appealed
to the imagination of Western visitors and the Bedouin of northern
Arabia alike.

Najd   generally understood as the central part of the Arabian Pen-
insula—the plateau area roughly situated to the east of the moun-
tain ranges of the Hijāz, south of the Nafūd Desert and west of the
al-Dahnāʾ sands, and including Wādī al-Dawāsir in the south. This
large region is subdivided into areas that differ greatly in character.
Historically and environmentally, its society has been characterized
by contrast between sedentary and Bedouin groups. Nabaṭī poetry is
essentially a Najdī phenomenon with roots in classical Arabian cul-
ture, a pedigree shared by many of the sedentary and Bedouin tribes
in Najd.

Nāyif   the headman of Jubbah and Ibn ʿBēkah (ʿUbaykah, pronounced
ʿBēćah) of the village Gnā, on the way between Ḥāʾil and Jubbah.

Nawwāf   Nawwāf ibn Nūrī al-Shaʿlān (d. 1921).

Nāzil   a famous leader of raids, and Musil's guide on his 1915 journey.

Nidā ibn Nhayyir   a member of the ʿAbdah division of Shammar, who founded the religious colony of al-Ajfar and was the raid leader of the Ikhwān in the area.

Nimr (ibn ʿAdwān)   (1745–1823) a famous romantic poet from al-Balqā' district in Jordan. He was admired for his touching dirges after the death of his beloved wife, Waḍḥā.

Nōmān   Nōmān al-Ḥsēnī al-Faḍlī of the Ẓafīr tribe. Included in the list of forty poets in ʿAdwān al-Hirbīd's al-Shēkhah poem.

ʿRār   ʿRār ibn Shahwān Āl Ḍēgham. Included in the list of forty poets in ʿAdwān al-Hirbīd's al-Shēkhah poem.

Rashīd ibn Nāṣir al-Laylā   the longtime agent of the Ibn Rashīds at the Ottoman court in Istanbul. At the outbreak of the First World War, he organized a shipment of arms to Ḥā'il to prop up Ibn Rashīd against Ibn Saʿūd, who enjoyed British support.

Rabdā   a well at the eastern border of the Nafūd Desert.

al-Rmāl   the shaykhs of the Rmāl section and the chief of the Ghfēlah branch of the Sinjārah of Shammar. Based in the small oasis of Jubbah, the Rmāl are the nomads of the Nafūd sands par excellence.

Rmēzān (Rumayzān)   Rmēzān ibn Ghashshām, a seventeenth-century poet of the ruling family of al-Rawḍah in Sudayr Province who was in frequent poetic correspondence with Jabr ibn Sayyār, the kinsman and predecessor of Ḥmēdān al-Shwēʿir.

Rshēd   Rshēd ibn Ṭōʿān of the Swēd of Shammar. Included in the list of forty poets in ʿAdwān al-Hirbīd's al-Shēkhah poem.

al-Rwalah   having left their basis in Khaybar some centuries ago, the Rwalah moved along the north side of al-Nafūd Desert from Taymā in the west, across al-Jawf, and as far as the well of Līnah in the east. Their pasture grounds included Wadī al-Sirhān and the southern part of the Syrian Desert. Rivalry between the Ibn Shaʿlān and Ibn Rashīd defined prickly relations with Shammar. After 1922, some sections of the Rwalah that had embraced Wahhabism no longer crossed into Syria. Together with three allied tribes, the *maḥlaf*, the Rwalah form a group known as the Jlās. A single person of the tribe is called a Rwēlī, and the tribe's war cry is "I am the rider of al-ʿAlyā from the

Rwalah," al-'Alyā being the first mother of the tribe's herds of white camels.

Ṣa'ab Ṣa'ab al-Ṣdēd of Shammar in Iraq. Included in the list of forty poets in 'Adwān al-Hirbīd's al-Shēkhah poem.

Sājir Sājir al-Rifdī, a desert knight and the shaykh of the Salgā section of the 'Amārāt of 'Anazah. Included in the list of forty poets in 'Adwān al-Hirbīd's al-Shēkhah poem.

Ṣalab singular *ṣlubī*, a member of the pariah tribe of handicraftsmen who used to accompany the Bedouin tribes on their migrations. Renowned as skilled hunters, they dressed in the hides of the game they killed and rode donkeys, not camels. They shod the Bedouin's horses, repaired their metalwork, and performed other manual jobs, but otherwise lived a life completely separate from them.

Ṣāliḥ ibn Rakhīṣ "the old warhorse"; together with Ḥmūd ibn Rashīd, he was an inseparable companion of Muḥammad ibn Rashīd. The shaykhs of Ibn Rakhīṣ had given refuge to the founder of the dynasty, 'Abdallah ibn Rashīd.

Āl Sarrāḥ of Shammar a branch of the Jarbā lineage belonging to Āl Muḥammad; it settled in al-Jawf, in the northwestern part of Saudi Arabia.

Saṭṭām ibn Ḥamad ibn Nāyif ibn 'Abdallah al-Sha'lān (d. 1904) shaykh of the Rwalah, one of the most powerful chiefs of the far-flung 'Anazah confederation. The Ibn Sha'lān shaykhs were often considered near peers of Ibn Rashīd and were referred to as princes by European travelers.

Sa'ūd the House of Saud, the ruling house of Saudi Arabia. One of the early poets of note was the imam Turkī (the First) ibn 'Abd Allāh ibn Muḥammad Āl Sa'ūd.

al-Sba'ah a tribe of the Bishr division of 'Anazah, less powerful than the Fid'ān. Known for their camels and horses, their market town is Ḥamāh in Syria. In fall, they pastured their animals in the Syrian steppe and desert.

al-Ṣēhad Ṭār al-Ṣēhad is a steep scarp that encloses on the north the flood plain of Wādī al-Khirr; *ṣēhad* means "sandy vastness."

Shammar   the tribal confederation after which the area around Ḥā'il is called Jabal Shammar (it is also called the Two Mountains, i.e., Ajā and Salmā). As early as the seventeenth century, Shammar families began wandering toward Mesopotamia, while the thrust of 'Anazah was toward Syria, as far as Aleppo. The area between the Euphrates and Tigris rivers is the northern heartland of Shammar. Genealogically, Shammar belongs to the southern Arabs, Qaḥṭān, of Ṭayy, while 'Anazah is north Arabian, 'Adnān.

al-Sharārāt   a tribe in northern Arabia that in Bedouin opinion belonged to the lower-status tribal group of Htēm (Hutaym) because its members paid protection money to other tribes and to the Ibn Rashīd princes in Ḥā'il. They enjoyed renown as hunters and were skilled breeders of excellent riding camels. After the establishment of Saudi rule, their status improved and many of them attained positions of privilege at the Saudi court in al-Jawf and elsewhere.

Sharīf   the family of the Great Sharifs of Mecca.

Shaṭṭ al-'Arab   the confluence of the Euphrates and Tigris rivers before they exit into the Gulf.

Shāyi' al-Amsaḥ   a legendary ancestor of the Rmāl tribe of Shammar whose lore in poetry and narratives has been transmitted in oral tradition. His poetry shows the influence of Banū Hilāl epic poetry and probably dates from the seventeenth century. His chivalry and hospitality made him an avatar of the legendary Ḥātim al-Ṭā'ī, who lived in the same area and is celebrated by Shammar and other inhabitants as the epitome of their land's excellence.

al-Shēkhah   a name given to poems considered a "shaykh" among the other poems (it is female because of the gender of the word for poem, *giṣīdah*, CA *qaṣīdah*). 'Adwān al-Hirbīd's al-Shēkhah names forty poets. Several other poems are called al-Shēkhah because of their importance to a tribe, e.g., poems by Mighim al-Ṣagrī, Mish'ān al-Hadhdhāl (mentioned in al-Hirbīd's al-Shēkhah), and Muḥammad al-Dasm for 'Anazah.

al-Shilgān   a tribe of the Zmēl branch of the Sinjārah division of Shammar.

al-Sibhān   from humble roots, the family married into the House of Ibn
Rashīd and rose to become regents for minor princes, and the power
behind the throne, in the final decade of its existence.

Sinjārah   one of the four divisions of Najdī Shammar. Its territory and
wells stretch from al-Ghūṭah district in the west through the Nafūd
sands to the wells of the water-rich area of al-Ḥuzūl in the east. This
edition's three poets belong to three different branches of Sinjārah:
Abū Zwayyid is from the Nabhān of the Zmēl branch, headed by Ibn
Rakhīṣ; al-Hirbīd is from the Swēd of Āl Thābit branch; and ʿAjlān of
the Rmāl, headed by Ibn Rmāl, of the Ghfēlah branch. Though Sin-
jārah were the most "Bedouin" of Shammar, many of them owned per-
manent water holes and palm groves. They were known as indepen-
dent-minded raiders with a particularly rich tribal and Bedouin lore.

al-Sirḥān   probably named after Wādī Sirḥān. They are neighbors of Banū
Ṣakhr in the southern reaches of Ḥawrān in southwestern Syria.
In 1925, they lost most of their camel herds to attacks by the Saudi
Ikhwān.

Sʿūd Abū Khashm   Abū Mishʿal. Included in the list of forty poets in
ʿAdwān al-Hirbīd's al-Shēkhah poem.

al-Ṭayyār   Kanʿān al-Ṭayyār, shaykh of the Wild ʿAlī tribe of ʿAnazah.
Included in the list of forty poets in ʿAdwān al-Hirbīd's al-Shēkhah
poem.

al-Tbēnānī   the poet Mbērić al-Tbēnāwī; the family of Tbēnāwī (pl.
Tibānā) belongs to the Shrēḥā branch of the Dghērāt of ʿAbdah.

Al-Thāyah   a place to the north of Sakaka.

Thmēl   a place near ʿArʿar, today on the border with Jordan.

al-Tīh   the herds of the Ḥwēṭāt (Ḥuwayṭāt) tribe in northwestern Arabia.

Ṭrād   Saṭṭām ibn Shaʿlān's son by Mahā, sister of Ḍbēʿān ibn Khashmān of
the Sirḥān tribe; a number of poems noted by Musil were recited to
him by Ṭrād, who learned them from his mother.

Turkiyyah, daughter of Ibn Mhēd   a remarkable and strong character, she
had married Saṭṭām ibn Shaʿlān from love. She intervened forcefully
after Saṭṭām's death to stop al-Nurī ibn Shaʿlān from capturing the
litter with the tribal emblem. In 1910, she was present at the battle

of al-Jmēmā, the subject of a poem by Abū Zwayyid. Her sons were often called "the children of Turkiyyah."

Ṭwayyah   a well near Mōgag.

'Ubayd ('Bēd) ibn Rashīd   brother of 'Abdallah ibn Rashīd, the first ruler of the dynasty. He died in 1869.

'Uqayl   also 'Uqaylāt ('Gēl, 'Gēlāt), camel traders mostly from al-Qaṣīm who bought up camels and, in much smaller numbers, horses all over Arabia. They drove the animals through Syria to sell them in the markets of Egypt and Iraq. They were intermediaries or agents who received the money to buy the camels from a wholesale dealer. The chief of the camp where the trader put up tents was also his host, insofar as he protected him as his guest but did not board him. The Bedouins as a rule sold their camels for cash. The purchased animal was marked with the 'Gēlī mark. To protect themselves against raiders, the 'Gēl paid to have a "brother" in every large clan: the brother was obliged to restore every camel stolen by another member of his clan.

Wādī al-Khirr   a riverbed that terminates at the Euphrates and upcountry comes close to al-Ḥazl (also al-Ḥuzūl), the wells of the Sinjārah division of Shammar.

Wahhabi   used in reference to the doctrines and practices preached by Muḥammad ibn 'Abd al-Wahhāb, and later established as the foundational principles of the Kingdom of Saudi Arabia, it is perceived as a pejorative term in its native country. In Saudi Arabia, the movement is called Salafī: a return to the religious practices of the *salaf*, the early generations of Muslims. With respect to doctrine, its adherents call themselves "those who profess the unicity of God" (*al-muwaḥḥidūn*).

Bibliography

ʿAbdallāh ibn Sbayyil. *See* Kurpershoek.

Blunt, Lady Anne. *A Pilgrimage to Nejd*. 2 vols. London: Frank Cass, 1968. First published 1881.

Burckhardt, John Lewis. *Notes on the Bedouins and Wahabys*. London: H. Colburn and R. Bentley, 1830. Reprint, Cambridge: Cambridge University Press, 2010.

Dhū l-Rummah, *Dīwān Dhī l-Rummah*. Edited by ʿAbd al-Qudūs Abū Ṣāliḥ. Beirut: Muʿassasat al-Īmān, 1982.

Doughty, Charles M. *Travels in Arabia Deserta*. 2 vols. London: Jonathan Cape, 1936. Reprint of the third edition, New York: Dover, 1979.

Euting, Julius. *Tagbuch einer Reise in Inner-Arabien*. 2 vols. Leiden, Netherlands: E. J. Brill, 1896–1914.

Al-Fahad, Abdulaziz H. "The *ʿImama* vs. the *ʿIqal*: Hadari-Bedouin Conflict and the Formation of the Saudi State." In *Counter-Narratives: History, Contemporary Society, and Politics in Saudi Arabia and Yemen*, edited by Madawi Al-Rasheed and Robert Vitalis, 35–76. New York: Palgrave Macmillan, 2004.

Goldziher, Ignác. *Abhandlungen zur Arabischen Philologie*. 2 vols. Leiden, Netherlands: E. J. Brill, 1896–99.

Hess, J. J. The Hess Archive (referred to in the text as HA). Unpublished. Archive of the Institute of Asian and Oriental Studies, University of Zurich. A dictionary of handwritten cards with lexical notes on nineteenth-century Bedouin language, primarily from the ʿUtaybah and Qaḥṭān tribes in Central Arabia, kept at the Institute of Asian and Oriental Studies of Zurich University.

Ḥmēdān al-Shwēʿir. *See* Kurpershoek.

Ibn Manẓūr. *Lisān al-ʿarab*. Cairo: Dār al-Maʿārif, n.d.

Al-Iṣfahānī, Abū l-Faraj. *Kitāb al-Aghānī*. 24 vols. Cairo: Maṭbaʿat Dār al-Kutub al-Miṣriyyah, 1927–94.

Jacob, Georg. *Altarabisches Beduinenleben*. 1897. Reprint of 2nd ed. Hildesheim, Germany: Georg Olms Verlag, 1967.

Kurpershoek, Marcel. *Oral Poetry and Narratives from Central Arabia*. 5 vols. Leiden, Netherlands: E.J. Brill, 1994–2005.

Kurpershoek, Marcel, ed. and tr. *Arabian Satire: Poetry from 18th Century Najd; Ḥmēdān al-Shwēʿir*. New York: New York University Press, 2017.

———. *Arabian Romantic: Poems on Bedouin Life and Love; ʿAbdallāh ibn Sbayyil*. New York: New York University Press, 2018.

———. *Love, Death, Fame: Poetry and Lore from the Emirati Oral Tradition; Al-Māyidī ibn Ẓāhir*. New York: New York University Press, 2022.

Lane, Edward William. *Manners and Customs of the Modern Egyptians*. London: Everyman's Library, 1966. First published 1836.

Mandaville, James. *Bedouin Ethnobotany*. Tucson: University of Arizona Press, 2011.

Al-Māyidī ibn Ẓāhir. *See* Kurpershoek.

Montgomery, J.E., ed. and tr. *War Songs: ʿAntarah ibn Shaddād*. New York: New York University Press, 2018.

Al-Mufaḍḍal, Abū ʿAbbās ibn Muḥammad aḍ-Ḍabbī. *Dīwān al-Mufaḍḍaliyyāt*. Edited by Charles James Lyall: vol. 1, *Arabic Text* (1921); vol. 2, *Translation and Notes*. Oxford: Clarendon Press, 1918–21.

Al-Musallam, Ibrāhīm. *Al-ʿUqayliyyāt*. Cairo: al-Dār al-Thaqāfiyyah, 2006.

Musil, Alois. *The Manners and Customs of the Rwala Bedouins*. Oriental Explorations and Studies 6. New York: American Geographical Society, 1928.

———. *Northern Neğd*. Oriental Explorations and Studies 5. New York: American Geographical Society, 1928.

Nolde, Eduard. *Reise nach Innerarabien, Kurdistan und Armenien, 1892*. Braunschweig, Germany: Vieweg, 1895.

Palgrave, William Gifford. *Narrative of a Year's Journey through Central and Eastern Arabia*. London: Macmillan, 1865.

Al-Rasheed, Madawi. *Politics in an Arabian Oasis: The Rashidi Tribal Dynasty*. London: I. B. Tauris, 1991.

Al-Rashīd, Ḍārī ibn Fuhayd. *Nubdhah ta'rīkhiyyah 'an Najd*. Edited by Wadī' al-Bustānī. Riyadh: Dār al-Yamāmah, 1966.

Al-Sa'dūnī, Musā'id ibn Fahd. *Wusūm al-ibl fī al-Jazīrat al-'Arabiyyah (bādiyah wa-ḥāḍirah)*. 2nd edition.'Unayzah: self-published, 2012.

Sowayan, Saad Abdullah. *Nabaṭī Poetry: The Oral Poetry of Arabia*. Berkeley, CA: University of California Press, 1985.

———. *The Arabian Oral Historical Narrative: An Ethnographic and Linguistic Analysis*. Wiesbaden, Germany: Otto Harrassowitz, 1992.

———. *Al-Shi'r al-nabaṭī: Dhā'iqat al-sha'b wa-sulṭat al-naṣṣ*. Beirut: Dār al-Sāqī, 2000.

———. *Fihrist al-shi'r al-nabaṭī*. Riyadh: self-published, 2001.

———. *Al-Ṣaḥrā' al-'arabiyyah, thaqāfatuhā wa-shi'ruhā 'abra al-'uṣūr, qirā'ah anthrūbūlūjiyyah*. Beirut: Arab Network for Research and Publishing, 2010.

———. *Ayyām al-'arab al-awākhir: Asāṭīr wa-marwiyyāt shafahiyyah fī l-tārīkh wa-l-adab min shamāl al-jazīrah al-'arabiyyah ma'a shadharāt mukhtārah min qabīlat Āl Murrah wa-Subay'*. Beirut: Arab Network for Research and Publishing, 2010.

———. "Tonight My Gun Is Loaded: Poetic Dueling in Arabia," *Oral Tradition* 4, nos.1–2 (1989): 151–73.

———. "A Poem and Its Narrative by Riḍa ibn Ṭārif al-Shammarī." *Zeitschrift für arabische Linguistik* 7 (1982): 48–73.

———. "Customary Law in Arabia: An Ethnohistorical Perspective." http://www.saadsowayan.info/Publications/pub_E_13.pdf.

———. "Studying Nabaṭi Poetry." http://66.39.147.165/articles/Studying_Nabati_Poetry.pdf.

Steinberg, Guido. "Ecology, Knowledge, and Trade in Central Arabia (Najd) during the Nineteenth and Early Twentieth Centuries." In *Counter-Narratives: History, Contemporary Society, and Politics in Saudi*

Arabia and Yemen, edited by Madawi Al-Rasheed and Robert Vitalis, 77–102. New York: Palgrave Macmillan, 2004.

Stewart, Frank Henderson. *Texts in Sinai Bedouin Law*. 2 vols. Wiesbaden, Germany: Harrassowitz, 1988.

Al-Suwaydāʾ, ʿAbd al-Raḥmān ibn Zayd. *Al-Amthāl al-shaʿbiyyah al-sāʾirah fī manṭiqat Ḥāʾil*. Riyadh: Dār al-Suwaydāʾ, 2007.

———. *Faṣīḥ al-ʿammī fī shamāl Najd*. 2 vols. Riyadh: Dār al-Suwaydāʾ, 1987.

———. *Manṭiqat Ḥāʾil ʿabra al-taʾrīkh*. Riyadh: Dār al-Suwaydāʾ, 2009.

———. *Min shuʿarāʾ al-jabal al-ʿāmiyyīn*. 3 vols. Riyadh: Dār al-Suwaydāʾ, 1988.

———. *Al-Nakhlah al-ʿarabiyyah adabiyyan wa-ʿilmiyyan wa-iqtiṣādiyyan*. Riyadh: Dār al-Suwaydāʾ, 1993.

———. *Shuʿarāʾ al-jabal al-shaʿbiyyūn*. 5 vols. Riyadh: Dār al-Suwaydāʾ, 2013.

Al-ʿUbūdī, Muḥammad ibn Nāṣir. *Muʿjam al-tijārah wa-l-māl wa-l-faqr wa-l-ghinā*. Riyadh: Dār al-Thalūthiyyah, 2012.

———. *Muʿjam al-uṣūl al-faṣīḥah li-l-alfāẓ al-dārijah*. 13 vols. Riyadh: n.p., 2008.

Von Oppenheim, Max Freiherr, *Die Beduinen*. 5 vols. Wiesbaden, Germany: Harrassowitz, 1939–.

Watts, David, and Abdulatif H. Al-Nafie. *Vegetation and Biogeography of the Sand Seas of Saudi Arabia*. London: Kegan Paul, 2003.

Al-Ẓafīrī, Muḥammad Muhāwish. *Dīwān al-shāʿir Abū Zuwayyid, ḥakīm Shammar wa-shāʿiruhā*. Dammām, Saudi Arabia: Dār al-Adab al-ʿArabī, 2015.

Further Reading

'Aqīl, Abū 'Abd al-Raḥmān ibn, al-Ẓāhirī. *Dīwān al-shi'r al-'āmmī bi-lahjat ahl Najd.* 5 vols. Riyadh: Dār al-'Ulūm, 1982–86.

Ashkenazi, Touvia. "The 'Anazah Tribes." *Southwestern Journal of Anthropology* 4, no. 2 (1948): 222–39.

Geiger, Bernhard. "Die Mu'allaqa des Ṭarafa." *Wiener Zeitschrift für die Kunde des Morgenlandes* 19 (1905): 323–70.

Habib, John S. *Ibn Sa'ud's Warriors of Islam: The Ikhwan of Najd and Their Role in the Creation of the Sa'udi Kingdom, 1910–1930.* Leiden, Netherlands: E. J. Brill, 1978.

Al-Ḥaqīl, 'Abd al-Karīm ibn Ḥamad ibn Ibrāhīm. *Alfāẓ dārijah wa-madlūlātuhā fī al-Jazīrah al-'Arabiyyah.* Riyadh: Maṭābi' al-Farazdaq, 1989.

Hess, J. J. *Von den Beduinen des innern Arabiens.* Zurich: Max Niehaus Verlag, 1938.

Hinds, Martin, and El-Said Badawi. *A Dictionary of Egyptian Arabic: Arabic-English.* Beirut: Librairie du Liban, 1986.

Holes, Clive. "The Language of Nabaṭi Poetry." In *Encyclopaedia of Arabic Language and Linguistics On-Line Edition*, edited by R. De Jong and L. Edzard. Leiden, Netherlands: E. J. Brill, 2012.

Huber, Charles. "Voyage dans l'Arabie Centrale, 1878–1882." *Bulletin de la Société de Géographie* 7, no. 5 (1884): 304–63, 468–530.

———. *Journal d'un voyage en Arabie (1883–1884).* Paris: Société Asiatique et la Société de Géographie, 1891.

Ibn Khamīs, ʿAbd Allāh ibn Muḥammad. *Al-Adab al-shaʿbī fī al-jazīrat al-ʿarabiyyah*. 2nd ed. Riyadh: Maṭābiʿ al-Farazdaq, 1982.

Ibn Mandīl, Mandīl ibn Muḥammad, Āl Fuhayd. *Min ādābinā al-shaʿbiyyah fī l-jazīra al-ʿarabiyyah, qiṣaṣ wa-ashʿār*. 4 vols. Riyadh: Maṭābiʿ al-Farazdaq, 1981–84.

Ibrāhīm, ʿAbd al-ʿAzīz ʿAbd al-Ghani. *Najdiyyūn warāʾa al-ḥudūd: Al-ʿUqayliyyāt wa-dawruhum fī ʿilāqat Najd al-ʿaskariyyah wa-l-iqtiṣādiyyah bi-l-ʿIrāq wa-l-Shām wa-Miṣr (1750–1950)*. 2nd ed. Beirut: Dār al-Sāqī, 2014.

Imruʾ al-Qays. *Dīwān*. Beirut: Dār Bayrūt, 1986.

Ingham, Bruce. *Bedouin of Northern Arabia: Traditions of the Āl Ḍhafīr*. London: KPI, 1986.

Al-Jāsir, Ḥamad. *Al-Muʿjam al-jughrāfī li-l-bilād al-ʿArabiyyah al-Saʿūdiyyah, Shamāl al-Mamlakah: Imārāt Ḥayil wa-l-Jawf wa-Tabūk wa-ʿArʿar wa-l-Qurayyāt*. 3 vols. Riyadh: Dār al-Yamāmah, 1977.

Al-Juhaymān, ʿAbd al-Karīm. *Al-Amthāl al-shaʿbiyyah fī qalb al-jazīrah al-ʿarabiyyah*. 10 vols. Riyadh: Dār al-Ashbāl al-ʿArab, 1982.

Ingham, Bruce. "The Pool of Oaths—A Comparative Study of a Bedouin Historical Poem." In *A Miscellany of Middle Eastern Articles: In Memoriam Thomas Muir Johnstone*, edited by A. K. Irvine et al., 40–54. Harlow, UK: Longman, 1988.

Kurpershoek, P. Marcel. "Two Manuscripts of Bedouin Poetry in Strasbourg National and University Library and the Travels of Charles Huber in Arabia." *La Revue de la BNU* (Bibliothèque Nationale Universitaire de Strasbourg) 17 (2018): 92–103.

Lane, Edward William. *An Arabic-English Lexicon*. Beirut: Librairie du Liban, 1980. First published 1863.

March, Jenny. *The Penguin Book of Classical Myths*. London: Penguin, 2008.

Al-Mutanabbī, Abū l-Ṭayyib. *Dīwān Abī l-Ṭayyib al-Mutanabbī bi-sharḥ Abī l-Baqāʾ al-ʿUkbarī*. 4 vols. 2nd ed. Cairo: Maṭbaʿat Muṣṭafā al-Bābī al-Ḥalabī, 1956.

Philby, H. St. John. *Saʿudi Arabia*. Beirut: Librairie du Liban, 1968. First published 1955.

Reynolds, Dwight Fletcher. *Heroic Poets, Poetic Heroes: The Ethnography of Performance in an Arabic Oral Epic Tradition.* Ithaca, NY: Cornell University Press, 1995.

Sowayan, Saad Abdullah, ed. *Al-Thaqāfah al-taqlīdiyyah fī al-mamlakah al-ʿarabiyyah al-suʿūdiyyah.* Riyadh: The Circle for Publishing and Documentation, 1999.

Al-Tibrīzī, Abū Zakariyā Yaḥyā ibn ʿAlī. *Kitāb Sharḥ al-qaṣāʾid al-ʿashr.* Edited by Charles J. Lyall. Calcutta: Asiatic Society of Bengal, 1894. Reprint, Farnborough, UK: Gregg Press, 1965.

Al-ʿUbūdī, Muḥammad ibn Nāṣir. *Al-Amthāl al-ʿāmmiyyah fī Najd.* 5 vols. Riyadh: n.p., 1979.

———. *Muʿjam al-anwāʾ wa-l-fuṣūl.* Riyadh: n.p., 2011.

———. *Muʿjam al-azwāj fī al-turāth.* Riyadh: Dār al-Thalūthiyyah, 2017.

———. *Muʿjam al-ḥayawān ʿind al-ʿāmmah.* 2 vols. Riyadh: Maktabat al-Malik Fahd al-Waṭaniyyah, 2011.

———. *Muʿjam al-kalimāt al-dakhīlah fī lughatinā al-dārijah,* 2 vols. Riyadh: Maktabat al-Malik ʿAbd Al-ʿAzīz al-ʿĀmmah, 2005.

———. *Muʿjam al-malābis fī al-maʾthūr al-shaʿbī fī al-manṭiqat al-wusṭāʾ min al-Mamlakah al-ʿArabiyyah al-Suʿūdiyyah.* Riyadh: Dār al-Thalūthiyyah, 2013.

———. *Muʿjam alfāẓ al-maraḍ wa-l-ṣiḥḥah.* Riyadh: Dār al-Thalūthiyyah, 2015.

———. *Muʿjam wajh al-arḍ.* Riyadh: Dār al-Thalūthiyyah, 2014.

Wallin, Georg August. *Travels in Arabia.* Cambridge, UK: The Oleander Press, 1979.

Al-Wuhaybī, ʿAbd al-Laṭīf ibn Ṣāliḥ ibn Muḥammad. *Al-ʿUqaylāt, maʾāthir al-ābāʾ wa-l-ajdād ʿalā ẓuhūr al-ibl wa-l-ajyād.* Riyadh: Obeikan, 2017.

Al-Zawzanī, Abū ʿAbd Allāh al-Ḥusayn ibn Aḥmad ibn al-Ḥusayn. *Sharḥ al-muʿallaqāt al-sabʿ.* Beirut: Dār Bayrūt, 1982.

Index

coins, §6.8

cold: cold-hearted, §5.5; freezing, §37.2, §37.3, §50.1, §52.3; frost, §52.2; frostbitten, §31.10; icy, §52.5; severest, §50.5; snow and ice, §50.1, §52.3; wintery, §5.5, §31.10, §40.13

color, 227n102

combat, §17.5, §26.1. *See also* battle

commander, 228n116, 233n157

conversation, xliii, xliv, l, lxiv n49, lxiv n54, §6.1, §7.1, §12.1, §18.4, §18.7, §31.5, §33.2, §49.4, §§49.10–11, §50.1, §53.5, §53.12, 222n53, 235–236n189

cooking. *See* fire; food

cotton, §25.2

counsel. *See* advice/counsel

courage, §49.7

court, §2.3, §48.2, §53.2

cowardice/cowardliness: accused of, xxv; and avarice, 228–229n118; chickenhearted, §27.5; cowardly babblers, §49.16; cowardly sons of owls, 231n141; cowards, §25.10; lazy cowards, §14.4; poets as cowards, §§49.16–18; provides no escape, §25.3; sissies, §24.2; wimps, §27.5

cows, §49.9, §49.19

cranes, 223n68

cravenness, §2.5

Creation, xxvii, §40.2, §§43.1–2, §52.6

Creator, xxxix, §5.5, §25.2, §25.5, §27.5, §29.1

crows, §50.2

curse, xlvii, li, §6.4, §6.5, §6.8, §10.3, §14.2, §30.7, §33.3, §40.6

customary law, xxx, xxxiii, lxi n26, §9.2, §9.3, §11.1, §17.1, 217n7. *See also* tribal law

customs, §21.1, §53.3, 231n135

Ḍabbī ibn Fāliḥ, §§16.1–4, §16.6, §16.7

Ḍāfī ibn Ḍabʿān, §54.1

daggers, §45.3, §50.5

daḥḥah, §27.5

Damascus, xxii, §5.5

Ḍanā Slēmān (tribe), §49.12

dance, §27.5, §40.3, §41.1, §49.11

Ḍārī ibn Ṭwālah, §27.5

dates, §31.5, §32.1, §32.2, §33.4, §34.2, §35.1, §35.3, §§36.1–4, §37.2, §40.3, §42.3, §48.5, §§49.2–3, §49.19, §50.4, §51.3. *See also* palms

al-Ḍaww branch, §9.2

al-Ḍayāghim, §10.4, 219n25

death: birds of, §30.5; of camels, §§16.1–2; clouds of, §12.1; dates, lix n10, §1.3, 217n2, 218n13, 227n101; death-defying, §3.1, §39.3; demise, xxviii, §22.1; and destruction, §12.1; and doom, §29.1; expressions, 235n178; grave's stone slabs, §31.6; life and, §25.2; life or, lii, §50.4; market of, §3.2; perdition, §22.1; pools of, §12.1, §16.7, §27.5; red-hot, §17.5; ruin, §31.10; scared to, §52.7; seeking, §40.3; shafts of, §17.6; slaughter on the occasion of, §10.3; by snakes, 241n247

debts, lxii n32, §6.5, §§27.1–3, §27.4, §27.5, 234n169

decadence, §12.1

decay, §12.1

al-Fāliḥ (brother of Falāḥ ibn Fāliḥ),
§19.6
fall (autumn), §16.1, §16.2, §40.3,
§40.6, §49.8, §49.9, §49.10, §52.6,
234n172
falling out, §49.1, §49.17
falsehood, §25.2, §28.1, §31.8, §52.7
fame, §19.1, §27.5, §33.7
al-Farazdaq, xlvi
Fāris al-Jarbā, §53.9
Fāris al-Siṭam, §52.6
Far' Ṣwāb, §10.4
fasting, §34.2, §40.8
fat (food), §17.6, §25.5, §31.3, §31.6,
§31.10, §31.13, §42.2
Fate/fate, xxxvii, lii, §5.5, §16.4,
§25.2, §25.3, §25.9, §27.2, §30.3,
§30.4, §33.2, §40.13, §43.2, §49.1,
§49.19, 220n32. *See also* destiny
Fāṭimah (daughter of Zāmil
al-Sabhān), xliii
favor, §16.7, §17.2, §18.6, §25.3, §25.8,
§31.4, §44.4, 226n89, 230n131
al-Fawā'irah (tribal grouping), §10.2
al-Fdēd, §52.7
Fgarā tribe, 220–221n42
Fhēd (poet), §49.19
al-Fhēdī, §52.7
al-Fid'ān of 'Anazah, xxix, §6.1
Fiḍīl Abū Hijhūj, §17.3
al-Fighm (poet), §49.19
fighters, §5.5, §25.2, §25.7, §27.5,
§40.10, §44.1, §46.1, §49.15,
§49.19, §51.1. *See also* warriors
fights: brawls, §27.5; discord, §9.3,
225n87; disputes, §11.1, §17.1, §53.7;
dustups, §49.1, §49.17; falling out,
§49.1, §49.17; with her shadow,
§50.4; melees, §50.5; over spoils,

§9.2; quarrels, §5.2, §5.4, §9.1,
§9.3, §49.17. *See also* battle
Fihrān ibn Hēshān, §27.5
fihrist, xxv
fire: blackened by, 235n179; burning,
§24.2; cooking, §6.3, §15.4, §17.6,
§30.4, §35.3, §40.5, §42.2, §52.3,
228n115; embers, §5.5, §25.5, §32.6,
§42.2, §49.15, §50.4; fireball,
§5.5, 221n50; flames, §28.1, §43.2;
furious, §25.5; Hell's, §27.5; jump
into, §7.3; lighting a, §32.10,
§53.14, 220n33; set on, §23.4,
§48.5, §52.10; Shammar's, §12.1;
smoldering, §45.1; sparks, §27.5,
§28.1; of war, §11.2; welcoming,
§50.4
firearms, xxii, §19.5, §27.4
Firsīn (Fāris al-Siṭam), §52.6
First World War, xxii
flames, §28.1, §43.2
food: for animals, §32.7, §43.1,
238n214; appetite, xlvi, §48.7;
beans, §35.3; bread, §6.3, §50.2;
breakfast, §15.4, §43.2, §52.3;
butter, li, §17.6, §25.5, §32.3,
§32.5, §48.2, §50.6, 225n86,
228n118, 229–230n125; crushed
wheat, §50.6; dinner, §2.5, §4.1,
§6.3, §6.7, §13.2, §19.3, §31.10,
§32.10; (dried) cheese, §17.6,
§25.5, §31.3; drinks, §24.2,
230n131; eating, §12.1, §31.1,
222n55; edible *kurrāth* grass,
§14.3; fat, §17.6, §25.5, §31.3, §31.6,
§31.10, §31.13, §42.2; feasts, §48.9,
§49.19; feeding guests, §12.1,
§29.1, §32.10, §36.4, §42.1, §48.2,
§49.2, §49.14, §50.5, 220n33;

love, xxvii; for camels, xxxiii; for
children, §31.3, §31.6; for clans,
§24.1; fallen in, §34.1; head over
heels, §18.5; loved ones, §30.4,
230n128; lovers, §33.6, §36.4;
love's embrace, §24.1; passion,
§21.1, §23.1, §40.2; plays with
us, §37.3; poetry, xxvii, xlii;
songs, §40.1, §41.1; stories, xliii;
unrequited, §17.5; for wives, §6.3;
for women, §18.8
loyalty, lxii n31
Lubdah (quarter in Ḥā'il), §27.4
luck: bad luck, §6.3, §14.5, §49.4,
228n110, 235n181; doom, §7.2,
§12.1, §29.1, §30.5, §52.1; fortune,
§5.5, §14.4, §25.4, §25.8, §25.9,
§49.8; gloom, xxvii, §25.8, §53.12;
good fortune, lii, lxiv n56, §15.3,
§16.7, §18.4, §25.3, §27.2, §30.5,
§53.9, 227n105, 233n159; good
luck (ḥaẓẓik), 218n8, 235n181;
ill-starred, §33.2, §44.1; lucky,
§5.5, §14.4, §25.3, §25.4, §32.8;
lucky raid leader (miḥrām), §33.6,
227n105; mentioned, xxix, §53.11;
of raiders, xliv, lxii n35, §16.3;
soothsayers, §30.5; spells, §18.8;
well of infirmity, §25.10
lunch, §9.3, §10.1, §16.4, §32.1, §50.2
lyricism, xxvii, xxxi, §24.2

maggots, §49.8
Maḥrūt ibn Hadhdhāl, §§53.1–5,
§53.11, §53.17
Mājid (nephew of Muḥammad Ibn
Rashīd), §28.1
Mamdūḥ ibn Shaʿlān, §6.1, §6.3, §6.7
Māniʿ, xxx

al-Marāmshah (tribe), §35.2
al-Marbūb, §32.11
mares, xlix, lxvi n74, §2.4, §3.1, §6.3,
§6.4, §6.5, §6.7, §7.3, §12.1, §18.8,
§25.2, §29.1, §34.2, §38.5, §40.2,
§50.2, §50.5, §53.14, 227n98
Maria Theresa dollars/thalers, §36.4,
222n56, 236n196
marksmen, §§40.9–10, §48.8, §48.9,
§51.2
al-Markūz, §50.5
Marrān ibn Hazīm, §§42.3–5
marriage: announcement, §23.4;
bride-price/dower, §6.3, §20.1;
brides, §23.3, §39.1; counseling,
xxx, xl; first-cousin marriage
(jīrah), 231n135; given in, §7.2,
§53.1; from love, xliii; marriage-
saving, xlix, l; nuptial bed, §6.6;
old enough for, §34.2; prospect,
xlii; remarrying, §31.1, §46.1; seal
the, §19.6; to a tribal woman,
221n47; unsuited for, §37.1;
unwillingness for, §40.12; wedding
tent, xxx, §18.9. See also husbands;
wives
Martini rifles, §51.2, §51.3
al-Mashwī, §40.5, 237n203
matchlocks, xxii, §31.5, §45.3, §48.2
Mbērīc al-Tbēnāwī, lxiii n37
meadows, xxv, §19.5, §23.4, §31.10,
§32.10, §33.7, §38.4, §40.2, §49.9,
§49.15, §51.2, 231n140
meals, §1.2, §31.6, 217n1
meat, §10.4, §31.6, §31.12, §49.9,
§49.11, §53.10
Mecca, xxxvii, xlii, xlv, 240n239
Medina, xxii, xxxvii, §48.4, §52.6,
241n246

protection, of poets (cont.)
224–225n78; of the princely
house, §27.5; protected grazing,
219n23, 239nn229–230; protective
veil, §29.1; from rain, §31.3; refuge,
xxii, xxxiv, §9.3, §11.2, §17.6, §25.3,
§27.5, §31.6, §43.2, §49.11, §52.9,
§53.12; against a stud, §15.1; against
those who pretend to be devout,
§54.4; from tribal groups, §10.1;
against the ubiquitous enemies,
§49.11; of waterskins, §23.1

Qabbās, §27.5
Qanā, xlii
al-Qasīm, xli, 219n28
quarrels, §5.2, §5.4, §9.1, §9.3, §49.17.
See also fights
Qurʾan, xliii, §48.2, 220n30

Rabdā, §8.1, §10.4
rabid, §4.1, §4.2, §37.3, §50.4, 219n21
raconteur, §18.7
Radhān ibn ʿAngā, §19.2,
229–230n125
Rāḍī ibn Fārān, §29.1
Rafḥā, 239n228
raids: by ʿAnazah and Shammar,
lxivn56; bloody, §30.3; capture,
lviii–lixn7, §32.10; champion
raiders, §33.6; death-defying
raiders, §39.3; expeditions, li,
§10.2, §14.1, §16.3, §17.6, §§32.4–5,
§32.8; by Ibn Rashīd, lxvn59;
leader (ʿagîd), lxiin31, §2.1,
217n7, 227n105; lucky raiders,
xliv, lxiin35, §16.3; lucky raid
leader (mihrām), §33.6, 227n105;
mounts for, §25.8; pilfering, §6.8;

plunder, xliv, xlv, lxvin74, §10.2,
§15.1, §16.4, §17.4, §32.3, §49.8;
raided and stripped bare, §33.4;
raiders, xxvii, xxxiv, xlvii, xlviii, l,
lviii–lixn7, §2.1, §2.3, §9.1, §10.2,
§13.2, §14.2, §16.5, §16.7, §17.1,
§17.5, §27.5, §49.11, 217n7, 232n144,
236n190; raiding, xxx, xliv, xlix,
lixn11, 229n123; raiding party,
l, §9.1, §13.1; raid leaders, §16.3,
§16.6, §23.1, §23.3, §50.1; robbers,
§32.11, §40.3, §40.7, §49.12, §49.15,
220n35, 220n40; for sport, §32.10;
taking part in, 227n106. *See also*
spoils
rail, §52.6
rain: of Arcturus, §30.5, §40.2,
§49.10; chances of, §49.12;
clouds, §29.1, §48.1, 238n213,
238n216; curtains of, §40.3; fall
(autumn), §49.8, §49.10, 234n172;
hail, §36.4; on Ḥayyah's eyes,
§48.2; heavy, §9.3, §35.3, §48.1;
Mikāʾīl (angel of rain), 238n213;
morning, §33.6; not a single drop
of, §53.10; Pleiades rains, §28.1;
plentiful, xxv, lxivn56, §13.2;
pools of, §§18.1–2, §49.19, §50.1;
pouring, §24.2, §40.3; protection
from, §31.3; raindrops, 238n212;
rain-fed grazing/pastures, §15.2,
§17.6, 229n124; rainwater, §28.1,
§30.4; refreshed by, §40.2; relief
by, lii; scattered, §17.5; showers,
§18.1, §40.10; soaked by, §31.3;
spring, xxxiv, lviiin4, §30.1, §40.2,
§49.10; sprinkles of, §18.1, §18.4,
§19.5, §34.2; steady drum of, §47.1;
torrents, §10.4, §27.5, §32.10,

About the NYU Abu Dhabi Research Institute

The Library of Arabic Literature is a research center affiliated with NYU Abu Dhabi and is supported by a grant from the NYU Abu Dhabi Research Institute.

The NYU Abu Dhabi Research Institute is a world-class center of cutting-edge and innovative research, scholarship, and cultural activity. It supports centers that address questions of global significance and local relevance and allows leading faculty members from across the disciplines to carry out creative scholarship and high-level research on a range of complex issues with depth, scale, and longevity that otherwise would not be possible.

From genomics and climate science to the humanities and Arabic literature, Research Institute centers make significant contributions to scholarship, scientific understanding, and artistic creativity. Centers strengthen cross-disciplinary engagement and innovation among the faculty, build critical mass in infrastructure and research talent at NYU Abu Dhabi, and have helped make the university a magnet for outstanding faculty, scholars, students, and international collaborations.

About the Translator

Marcel Kurpershoek is a senior research fellow at New York University Abu Dhabi and a specialist in the oral traditions and poetry of Arabia. He obtained his PhD in modern Arabic literature at the University of Leiden. He has written a number of books on historical, cultural, and contemporary topics in the Middle East, including the five-volume *Oral Poetry and Narratives from Central Arabia* (1994–2005), which draws on his recordings of Bedouin tribes. For the Library of Arabic Literature, he has edited and translated *Arabian Satire* by Ḥmēdān al-Shwēʿir (2017), *Arabian Romantic* by ʿAbdallāh ibn Sbayyil (2018), *Love, Death, Fame* by al-Māyidī ibn Ẓāhir (2022), *Bedouin Poets of the Nafūd Desert* by Khalaf Abū Zwayyid, ʿAdwān al-Hirbīd and ʿAjlān ibn Rmāl (2024), and *Arabian Hero* by Shāyiʿ al-Amsaḥ (2024). In 2016, Al Arabiya television broadcast an eight-part documentary series based on the travelogue of fieldwork he had undertaken in the Nafūd desert of northern Arabia for his book *Arabia of the Bedouins* (in Arabic translation *The Last Bedouin*). In 2018, Al Arabiya broadcast his five-part documentary on Najdī poetry. He spent his career as a diplomat for the Netherlands, having served as ambassador to Pakistan, Afghanistan, Turkey, Poland, and special envoy for Syria until 2015. From 1996 to 2002, he held a chair as professor of literature and politics in the Arab world at the University of Leiden.

The Library of Arabic Literature

For more details on individual titles, visit www.libraryofarabicliterature.org

Classical Arabic Literature: A Library of Arabic Literature Anthology
Selected and translated by Geert Jan van Gelder (2012)

A Treasury of Virtues: Sayings, Sermons, and Teachings of ʿAlī, by al-Qāḍī
al-Quḍāʿī, with the *One Hundred Proverbs* attributed to al-Jāḥiẓ
Edited and translated by Tahera Qutbuddin (2013)

The Epistle on Legal Theory, by al-Shāfiʿī
Edited and translated by Joseph E. Lowry (2013)

Leg over Leg, by Aḥmad Fāris al-Shidyāq
Edited and translated by Humphrey Davies (4 volumes; 2013–14)

Virtues of the Imām Aḥmad ibn Ḥanbal, by Ibn al-Jawzī
Edited and translated by Michael Cooperson (2 volumes; 2013–15)

The Epistle of Forgiveness, by Abū l-ʿAlāʾ al-Maʿarrī
Edited and translated by Geert Jan van Gelder and Gregor Schoeler
(2 volumes; 2013–14)

The Principles of Sufism, by ʿĀʾishah al-Bāʿūniyyah
Edited and translated by Th. Emil Homerin (2014)

The Expeditions: An Early Biography of Muḥammad, by Maʿmar ibn Rāshid
Edited and translated by Sean W. Anthony (2014)

Two Arabic Travel Books
  Accounts of China and India, by Abū Zayd al-Sīrāfī
    Edited and translated by Tim Mackintosh-Smith (2014)
  Mission to the Volga, by Aḥmad ibn Faḍlān
    Edited and translated by James Montgomery (2014)

Disagreements of the Jurists: A Manual of Islamic Legal Theory, by
  al-Qāḍī al-Nuʿmān
  Edited and translated by Devin J. Stewart (2015)

Consorts of the Caliphs: Women and the Court of Baghdad, by Ibn al-Sāʿī
  Edited by Shawkat M. Toorawa and translated by the Editors of the
  Library of Arabic Literature (2015)

What ʿĪsā ibn Hishām Told Us, by Muḥammad al-Muwayliḥī
  Edited and translated by Roger Allen (2 volumes; 2015)

The Life and Times of Abū Tammām, by Abū Bakr Muḥammad ibn
  Yaḥyā al-Ṣūlī
  Edited and translated by Beatrice Gruendler (2015)

The Sword of Ambition: Bureaucratic Rivalry in Medieval Egypt, by
  ʿUthmān ibn Ibrāhīm al-Nābulusī
  Edited and translated by Luke Yarbrough (2016)

Brains Confounded by the Ode of Abū Shādūf Expounded, by
  Yūsuf al-Shirbīnī
  Edited and translated by Humphrey Davies (2 volumes; 2016)

Light in the Heavens: Sayings of the Prophet Muḥammad, by
  al-Qāḍī al-Quḍāʿī
  Edited and translated by Tahera Qutbuddin (2016)

Risible Rhymes, by Muḥammad ibn Maḥfūẓ al-Sanhūrī
  Edited and translated by Humphrey Davies (2016)

A Hundred and One Nights
  Edited and translated by Bruce Fudge (2016)

The Excellence of the Arabs, by Ibn Qutaybah
>   Edited by James E. Montgomery and Peter Webb
>   Translated by Sarah Bowen Savant and Peter Webb (2017)

Scents and Flavors: A Syrian Cookbook
>   Edited and translated by Charles Perry (2017)

Arabian Satire: Poetry from 18th-Century Najd, by Ḥmēdān al-Shwēʿir
>   Edited and translated by Marcel Kurpershoek (2017)

In Darfur: An Account of the Sultanate and Its People, by Muḥammad
>   ibn ʿUmar al-Tūnisī
>   Edited and translated by Humphrey Davies (2 volumes; 2018)

War Songs, by ʿAntarah ibn Shaddād
>   Edited by James E. Montgomery
>   Translated by James E. Montgomery with Richard Sieburth (2018)

Arabian Romantic: Poems on Bedouin Life and Love, by ʿAbdallah
>   ibn Sbayyil
>   Edited and translated by Marcel Kurpershoek (2018)

Dīwān ʿAntarah ibn Shaddād: A Literary-Historical Study,
>   by James E. Montgomery (2018)

Stories of Piety and Prayer: Deliverance Follows Adversity, by al-Muḥassin
>   ibn ʿAlī al-Tanūkhī
>   Edited and translated by Julia Bray (2019)

*Tajrīd sayf al-himmah li-stikhrāj mā fī dhimmat al-dhimmah: A Scholarly
>   Edition of ʿUthmān ibn Ibrāhīm al-Nābulusī's Text*, by Luke Yarbrough
>   (2019)

*The Philosopher Responds: An Intellectual Correspondence from the Tenth
>   Century*, by Abū Ḥayyān al-Tawḥīdī and Abū ʿAlī Miskawayh
>   Edited by Bilal Orfali and Maurice A. Pomerantz
>   Translated by Sophia Vasalou and James E. Montgomery
>   (2 volumes; 2019)

The Discourses: Reflections on History, Sufism, Theology, and Literature—
   Volume One, by al-Ḥasan al-Yūsī
   Edited and translated by Justin Stearns (2020)

Impostures, by al-Ḥarīrī
   Translated by Michael Cooperson (2020)

Maqāmāt Abī Zayd al-Sarūjī, by al-Ḥarīrī
   Edited by Michael Cooperson (2020)

The Yoga Sutras of Patañjali, by Abū Rayḥān al-Bīrūnī
   Edited and translated by Mario Kozah (2020)

The Book of Charlatans, by Jamāl al-Dīn ʿAbd al-Raḥīm al-Jawbarī
   Edited by Manuela Dengler
   Translated by Humphrey Davies (2020)

*A Physician on the Nile: A Description of Egypt and Journal of the Famine
   Years*, by ʿAbd al-Laṭīf al-Baghdādī
   Edited and translated by Tim Mackintosh-Smith (2021)

The Book of Travels, by Ḥannā Diyāb
   Edited by Johannes Stephan
   Translated by Elias Muhanna (2 volumes; 2021)

Kalīlah and Dimnah: Fables of Virtue and Vice, by Ibn al-Muqaffaʿ
   Edited by Michael Fishbein
   Translated by Michael Fishbein and James E. Montgomery (2021)

Love, Death, Fame: Poetry and Lore from the Emirati Oral Tradition,
   by al-Māyidī ibn Ẓāhir
   Edited and translated by Marcel Kurpershoek (2022)

The Essence of Reality: A Defense of Philosophical Sufism, by ʿAyn al-Quḍāt
   Edited and translated by Mohammed Rustom (2022)

The Requirements of the Sufi Path: A Defense of the Mystical Tradition,
   by Ibn Khaldūn
   Edited and translated by Carolyn Baugh (2022)

The Doctors' Dinner Party, by Ibn Buṭlān
   Edited and translated by Philip F. Kennedy and Jeremy Farrell (2023)

Fate the Hunter: Early Arabic Hunting Poems
   Edited and translated by James E. Montgomery (2023)

The Book of Monasteries, by al-Shābushtī
   Edited and translated by Hilary Kilpatrick (2023)

In Deadly Embrace: Arabic Hunting Poems, by Ibn al-Muʿtazz
   Edited and translated by James E. Montgomery (2023)

The Divine Names, by ʿAfīf al-Dīn al-Tilimsānī
   Edited and translated by Yousef Casewit (2023)

Bedouin Poets of the Nafūd Desert, by Khalaf Abū Zwayyid, ʿAdwān al-Hir-
   bīd, and ʿAjlān ibn Rmāl
   Edited and translated by Marcel Kurpershoek (2024)

The Rules of Logic, by Najm al-Dīn al-Kātibī
   Edited and translated by Tony Street (2024)

*Najm al-dīn al-Kātibī's al-Risālah al-Shamsiyyah: An Edition and Transla-
   tion with Commentary*, by Tony Street (2024)

A Demon Spirit: Arabic Hunting Poems, by Abū Nuwās
   Edited and translated by James E. Montgomery (2024)

Arabian Hero: Oral Poetry and Narrative Lore from Northern Arabia, by
   Shāyiʿ al-Amsaḥ
   Edited and translated by Marcel Kurpershoek (2024)

The Genius of Invective: Ibn Zaydūn's Letter Explained, by Ibn Nubātah
   Edited and translated by Peter Webb (2025)

The Turks and the Caliphal Army, by al-Jāḥiẓ
   Edited and translated by Robert G. Hoyland (2025)

Leg over Leg, by Aḥmad Fāris al-Shidyāq (2 volumes; 2015)

The Expeditions: An Early Biography of Muḥammad, by
Maʿmar ibn Rāshid (2015)

The Epistle on Legal Theory: A Translation of al-Shāfiʿī's Risālah, by
al-Shāfiʿī (2015)

The Epistle of Forgiveness, by Abū l-ʿAlāʾ al-Maʿarrī (2016)

The Principles of Sufism, by ʿĀʾishah al-Bāʿūniyyah (2016)

A Treasury of Virtues: Sayings, Sermons, and Teachings of ʿAlī, by al-Qāḍī
al-Quḍāʿī with the *One Hundred Proverbs* attributed to al-Jāḥiẓ (2016)

The Life of Ibn Ḥanbal, by Ibn al-Jawzī (2016)

Mission to the Volga, by Ibn Faḍlān (2017)

Accounts of China and India, by Abū Zayd al-Sīrāfī (2017)

Consorts of the Caliphs: Women and the Court of Baghdad, by Ibn al-Sāʿī (2017)

A Hundred and One Nights (2017)

Disagreements of the Jurists: A Manual of Islamic Legal Theory, by
al-Qāḍī al-Nuʿmān (2017)

What ʿĪsā ibn Hishām Told Us, by Muḥammad al-Muwayliḥī (2018)

War Songs, by ʿAntarah ibn Shaddād (2018)

The Life and Times of Abū Tammām, by Abū Bakr Muḥammad ibn Yaḥyā
al-Ṣūlī (2018)

The Sword of Ambition, by ʿUthmān ibn Ibrāhīm al-Nābulusī (2019)

Brains Confounded by the Ode of Abū Shādūf Expounded: Volume One, by
Yūsuf al-Shirbīnī (2019)

Brains Confounded by the Ode of Abū Shādūf Expounded: Volume Two,
by Yūsuf al-Shirbīnī and *Risible Rhymes,* by Muḥammad ibn Maḥfūẓ
al-Sanhūrī (2019)

The Excellence of the Arabs, by Ibn Qutaybah (2019)

Light in the Heavens: Sayings of the Prophet Muḥammad, by al-Qāḍī al-Quḍāʿī (2019)

Scents and Flavors: A Syrian Cookbook (2020)

Arabian Satire: Poetry from 18th-Century Najd, by Ḥmēdān al-Shwēʿir (2020)

In Darfur: An Account of the Sultanate and Its People, by Muḥammad al-Tūnisī (2020)

Arabian Romantic: Poems on Bedouin Life and Love, by Ibn Sbayyil (2020)

The Philosopher Responds: An Intellectual Correspondence from the Tenth Century, by Abū Ḥayyān al-Tawḥīdī and Abū ʿAlī Miskawayh (2021)

Impostures, by al-Ḥarīrī (2021)

The Discourses: Reflections on History, Sufism, Theology, and Literature— Volume One, by al-Ḥasan al-Yūsī (2021)

The Yoga Sutras of Patañjali, by Abū Rayḥān al-Bīrūnī (2022)

The Book of Charlatans, by Jamāl al-Dīn ʿAbd al-Raḥīm al-Jawbarī (2022)

The Book of Travels, by Ḥannā Diyāb (2022)

A Physician on the Nile: A Description of Egypt and Journal of the Famine Years, by ʿAbd al-Laṭīf al-Baghdādī (2022)

Kalīlah and Dimnah: Fables of Virtue and Vice, by Ibn al-Muqaffaʿ (2023)

Love, Death, Fame: Poetry and Lore from the Emirati Oral Tradition, by al-Māyidī ibn Ẓāhir (2023)

The Essence of Reality: A Defense of Philosophical Sufism, by ʿAyn al-Quḍāt (2023)

The Doctors' Dinner Party, by Ibn Buṭlān (2024)

The Requirements of the Sufi Path: A Defense of the Mystical Tradition, by Ibn Khaldūn (2024)

Fate the Hunter: Early Arabic Hunting Poems (2024)

The Book of Monasteries, by al-Shābushtī (2025)

In Deadly Embrace: Arabic Hunting Poems, by Ibn al-Muʿtazz (2025)

The Divine Names: A Mystical Theology of the Names of God in the Qurʾan,
by ʿAfīf al-Dīn al-Tilimsānī (2025)

The Rules of Logic, by Najm al-Dīn al-Kātibī (2025)

Bedouin Poets of the Nafūd Desert, by Khalaf Abū Zwayyid, ʿAdwān
al-Hirbīd, and ʿAjlān ibn Rmāl (2025)